Battle of Britain
Memorial Flight
in Camera

Battle of Britain
Memorial Flight
in Camera

Keith Wilson

First published in July 2013

A catalogue record for this book is available from the British Library

ISBN 978 0 85733 303 2

Library of Congress control no. 2013932260

Published by Haynes Publishing, Sparkford, Yeovil, Somerset BA22 7JJ, UK
Tel: 01963 442030 Fax: 01963 440001
Int. tel: +44 1963 442030 Int. fax: +44 1963 440001
E-mail: sales@haynes.co.uk
Website: www.haynes.co.uk

Haynes North America Inc.
861 Lawrence Drive, Newbury Park,
California 91320, USA

Printed and bound in the USA by Odcombe Press LP,
1299 Bridgestone Parkway, La Vergne, TN 37086

Credits
Project Manager: Sophie Blackman
Copy editor: Jane Hutchings
Page design: Rod Teasdale
Proofreader: Dean Rockett
Index: Peter Nicholson

Contents

Foreword

In this book, Keith Wilson opens the window on evocative and iconic images of the Battle of Britain Memorial Flight. While the Flight exists primarily to pay tribute to that extraordinary generation who fought in the air during the Second World War, the many and varied photographs in this book tell the tale of the Flight itself, of its priceless aircraft and of the professionals who have flown and maintained the aircraft through the years.

I have had the fortune to fly great aircraft of the Royal Air Force, including the Harrier and the Typhoon, but I have had no greater privilege than to fly the Spitfires and Hurricanes of the Flight. Along with the Lancaster, the Dakota and the Chipmunks, each of these aircraft tells two stories: first, the story of the original airframe itself, and secondly, the story told by the paint scheme. These aircraft are the enduring stars of the Flight; the aircrew and groundcrew are merely the temporary custodians.

Crown Copyright/SAC Tim White

However, without the flying skills of pilots like Parky, or the craftsmanship of engineers like Paul Blackah, the aircraft would be condemned to remain earthbound exhibits in a museum. But they are not; they are flying tributes to 'The Few' of Fighter Command and to 'The Many' of Bomber Command. Keith Wilson allows the reader to see the Flight on show, flying over London landmarks and going behind the scenes, to see poppies loaded on to the Lancaster and the Hurricane stripped bare during maintenance.

The aircrew, groundcrew and support staff of the Flight share the same humour, dedication and skill as the forebears we honour and whose personal characteristics reflect the core values of our Air Force. Through their professionalism and passion, the Flight of today aspires to pay a fitting tribute to past generations and to inspire airmen and airwomen of the future.

As the years pass, the numbers of that remarkable generation honoured by the Flight reduce and the onus falls to this generation to tell their heroic story. Every time the Flight takes to the air we salute our forefathers and keep their memories alive, not simply to commemorate their extraordinary sacrifices but to act as a guard against Edmund Burke's warning that 'those who don't know history are destined to repeat it'. Therefore, the importance of this national institution and the heritage it preserves will only grow in time.

I am enormously grateful to the many supporters of the Flight, from the members of the Lincolnshire Lancaster Association to the spectators on the other side of the wire at RAF Coningsby. The Flight could not operate without their support. By bringing together so many vivid images, Keith Wilson provides an invaluable fresh perspective of both the public and private face of the Flight, and by doing so he plays his part in honouring those to whom we owe such a great debt of gratitude.

'Lest we forget.'

Air Vice-Marshal Stuart Atha DSO MA BSc RAF
Air Officer Commanding Number 1 Group
Royal Air Force

Acknowledgements

A project of this size requires the help and support of many people, who have contributed in different ways to make this book possible. The author would like to offer his sincere thanks to the following:

The team at the Royal Air Force Battle of Britain Memorial Flight, without whose help and support, the book would not have been possible. Special thanks go to OC BBMF, Sqn Ldr Duncan 'Dunc' Mason; Administration Officer and Adjutant, Flt Lt Anthony 'Parky' Parkinson MBE; Station Commander at Coningsby, Gp Capt Martin 'Sammy' Sampson; OC Operations at Coningsby, Wg Cdr Paul 'Godders' Godfrey; OC BBMF Designate, Sqn Ldr Paul 'Milli' Millikin; former OC BBMF, Sqn Ldr Ian 'Smithy' Smith; BBMF PRO, Yvonne Masters; Flt Lt David Hawkins; Jim Stewart (Flight Operations); Flt Lt Ernie Taylor (Bomber Leader 2012); Flt Lt Tim 'Twigs' Dunlop; Flt Lt Roger Nichols; Flt Lt Loz Rushmere; Sqn Ldr William 'Russ' Russell (Navigator Leader 2012); Sqn Ldr Tony 'Sluf' Beresford; Flt Lt Ady Hargreaves; Flt Lt James 'Big Jim' Furness; Loadmaster Flt Sgt Paul Simmons; and both SEngOs, WO Dave Marshall and WO Kevin Ball, the latter whose patience and tolerance I tested on many occasions. Also, to all the members of the enthusiastic BBMF Engineering Team at Coningsby who were always willing to help with my requests – what a great group of people you are!

The Photographic Section at RAF Coningsby: Sgt Pete Mobbs ABIPP, CertEd., Cpl Paul Robertshaw, Senior Aircraftsman Steve Buckley, Senior Aircraftsman Daniel Herrick LBIPP and Senior Aircraftsman Graham Taylor, who allowed me to access their archive, assisted with research and pointed me in the right direction at Coningsby on so many occasions.

Lee Barton and Sebastian Cox, for allowing me to access the excellent archives at the Air Historic Branch at RAF Northolt.

The publishers gratefully acknowledge the original research by Jarrod Cotter into the identity of the founder of the Battle of Britain Flight.

For providing access to the Aircraft Restoration Company at Duxford, as well as information on the restorations, I would like to thank Billy Fletcher and the team of engineers working on PZ865.

For providing access to Retro Track and Air Limited, and for guiding me around the facility, I would like to thank Rachel Watts, Peter Watts and Robert Gardner.

For providing a steady camerarship platform for the air-to-air photographic sessions, I would like to thank Bill Giles of Giles Aviation.

For providing media facilities at airshows and events, and getting me close to the action, I would like to thank: Dave Poile at the BBC Children in Need Airshow at Little Gransden; Emma Wilkinson and Tracey Drake at Airbourne Eastbourne; Lindsey Askin at Waddington Air Show; and Richard Arquati at the Royal International Air Tattoo.

For providing a selection of images to help with illustrating the book I would like to thank: Peter R. March, E.J. van Koningsveld, Stephanie Watters at Rolls-Royce and Oliver Wilson.

At Haynes Publishing, I would like to thank Jonathan Falconer, Jane Hutchings, Rod Teasdale and Sophie Blackman for keeping me on track whenever I wavered.

My very special thanks must go to Sqn Ldr Stuart Reid RAF Retired, a superb mentor throughout my time at the Flight and without whose considerable help and co-operation, this book would not have been completed. Thank you Stu!

Finally, sincere thanks to my wife Carol and sons Sam and Oliver. Thank you for your patience and support throughout the project. I couldn't have done it without you.

Introduction

After the end of the Second World War, the Battle of Britain Day parade over London on 15 September 1945 was led by a Spitfire, flown by the legendary Group Captain Douglas Bader CBE DSO DFC, at the head of numerous RAF fighters. Millions of people turned out in Trafalgar Square and along The Mall to Buckingham Palace to watch the flypast, most of whom recognised the debt of gratitude owed to the men in the aeroplanes passing overhead, as well as to their comrades who hadn't survived the conflict. The RAF was proud to commemorate the Battle of Britain with such a tribute to a highly successful achievement, and in the years immediately following the Second World War it became traditional for a Hurricane and Spitfire to lead the annual Battle of Britain Day flypast over London.

As the years went by, aircraft that had once been the mainstay of RAF fighter operations decreased in numbers, as they were replaced with modern jet aircraft. Spitfire PR Mk XIX, PS888, had the accolade of carrying out the last operational sortie flown by an RAF Spitfire on 1 April 1954 and by the mid-1950s, the only remaining airworthy Hurricane was operated by the Station Flight at Biggin Hill, under the control of Wg Cdr Peter Thompson.

Thompson and others recognised the importance of having a Spitfire and Hurricane at the head of the annual Battle of Britain Day fly-by and thought that a small flight of Battle of Britain aircraft should be formed so that the parade could continue well into the future, as a lasting memory to those whose lives were sacrificed during the Battle of Britain.

When the last three remaining Spitfire PR Mk XIXs were coming to the end of their service careers at the Temperature and Humidity Flight, Thompson sought permission to create the Memorial Flight and have all three Spitfires delivered to him at Biggin Hill. His initiative was accepted, but on very difficult terms – all flying and maintenance was to be carried out on a strictly volunteer basis as they were to have no income from the public purse. With help from a small but willing group of enthusiastic individuals, the Memorial Flight was created and operated.

Thank goodness Peter Thompson had the vision to create the Memorial Flight, and over the years it has grown to become what we all affectionately know as the Battle of Britain Memorial Flight. Some people refer to it as the 'BBMF', others simply as 'The Flight'. The correct title is the Royal Air Force Battle of Britain Memorial Flight. The name doesn't really matter; what is more important is what the BBMF represents – a permanent reminder of the 544 aircrew killed in the three months and three weeks of what we now refer to as the Battle of Britain. As well as those souls who sacrificed their lives, a further 422 aircrew were wounded and 1,547 Allied aircraft were lost. However, it was a major turning point in the war against Germany.

In addition there were the 55,573 who died while in the service of the RAF Bomber Command. They were finally recognised more than 60 years later when the Bomber Command Memorial was unveiled by Her Majesty the Queen in Green Park, London, on 28 June 2012.

The Flight has a worldwide reputation and encourages very large attendances at airshows across the UK and occasionally in Europe. Most audiences just stand quietly, watching and listening; admiring both the aircraft and the wonderful sound they produce. Is there a better sound in aviation than the unique tone and roar of the Rolls-Royce V-12 Merlin engine? What you cannot mistake is the spine-tingling thrill or the hairs standing up on the back of your neck when the sound of six Rolls-Royce Merlin engines can be heard heading in your direction.

During the making of this book, I have been privileged to watch the BBMF team at work in a variety of situations, from practice sessions through the Public Display Authority inspection, to displays at small, medium and very large events. On each and every occasion, the team give it their very best.

Once the BBMF three-ship formation makes its final formation flypast and leaves the display areas, many audiences break out into spontaneous applause – a purely emotional reaction to the aircraft and what they represent.

◄ After 11 years of painstaking restoration work at the BBMF, Spitfire LF XVIe TE311 made its first post-restoration flight on 19 October 2012, 57 years after its previous flight. The aircraft is painted in 74 Squadron markings as '4D-V'. It was photographed over Lincolnshire on 13 December 2012 with OC BBMF Sqn Ldr 'Dunc' Mason at the controls. *(Keith Wilson)*

Who can ever forget those very special Battle of Britain Memorial Flight flypasts over London in 2012? Even though it had been in doubt with the threat of bad weather, the BBMF led the Queen's Jubilee Flypast over Buckingham Palace on 5 June 2012, while the Queen and other senior royals watched from the balcony. Then, three weeks later, there was the amazingly moving and symbolic poppy drop onto the opening of the Bomber Command Memorial in London's Green Park on 28 June. One million poppies fell onto the park below.

Three Mk XVI Spitfires joined the Flight in August 1957, but sadly they didn't last long. SL574 made a flypast over London on 20 September 1959, but crashed onto the OXO Cricket Ground at Bromley shortly afterwards. TE330 was donated to the United States Air Force Academy during a ceremony at RAF Odiham on 2 July 1958, and TE476 was transferred to gate guard duties at RAF Neatishead in 1960.

In 2012, after many years of painstaking restoration, the BBMF team of volunteers led by Chief Technician Paul Blackah and Cpl Andy Bale watched as Spitfire Mk XVIe TE311 made its first flight at RAF Coningsby on 13 October. It has flown on a number of occasions since and will be displaying during the 2013 season in 74 Squadron colours as '4D-V'; it will be a most welcome addition to the Flight and the air display scene.

Also in 2012, a train was named after the Flight in a moving ceremony at York during the Railfest 2012 event. The train they chose to carry the nameplate 'Battle of Britain Memorial Flight', along with a spectacular colour scheme depicting the Lancaster, Spitfire and Hurricane aircraft, is the fastest train in the UK: 91110 currently holds the UK national speed record for electric trains, achieved when it ran at 162mph along Stoke Bank, north of Peterborough, on 17 September 1989. It operates on the East Coast Main Line from King's Cross to Scotland, running through Lincolnshire – appropriately named Bomber County due to the very large number of bomber bases located there during the Second World War – passing close to RAF Coningsby. If you live close to or travel on the East Coast Main Line, keep a look out for it.

Such is the demand for public visits to RAF Coningsby that the BBMF has its own Visitor Centre where people can, in exchange for a small fee, take part in an accompanied tour around the hangar with a knowledgeable guide and watch the aircraft being maintained at close quarters or prepared for a show. The Visitor Centre is operated in conjunction with Lincolnshire County Council and in addition to informative displays it offers a good selection of BBMF memorabilia and books and is well worth a visit.

Each and every member of the team that is the RAF BBMF is a volunteer – all proud to have been chosen. Next time you are at an airshow, make a point of chatting with them; not just with the pilots and aircrew, but also with the all-important members of the groundcrew.

△ Sqn Ldr 'Dunc' Mason at the controls of Spitfire PR Mk XIX PS915 during a photoshoot along the south-east coast on 11 August 2012. *(Keith Wilson)*

Without them, the wonderful old Lancaster, Dakota, Chipmunks, Spitfires and Hurricanes would not be in the air. They are proud of what they do for the Flight and are very happy to share it with you.

The Battle of Britain Memorial Flight is not just another display team; it is a living reminder of the debt of gratitude we all owe to those who gave their lives during the Second World War, in both the Battle of Britain as well as with Bomber Command. Its annual budget is around 20% of the cost of running the Red Arrows – who themselves offer UK plc good value for money. Put all that in perspective and the BBMF provides amazing value for money, while still being a wonderful ceremonial and commemorative asset of this country's great history.

We must ensure that the generations to come learn about our past and remember the debt of gratitude we all owe. Perhaps, the final word on the matter should go to Winston Churchill: 'A nation that forgets its past has no future.'

'Lest we forget.'

Keith Wilson
Ramsey, Cambridgeshire

▼ A rare colour image taken at Biggin Hill on 11 July 1957. The last three Spitfire PR XIXs of the Temperature and Humidity Flight (THUM) at RAF Woodvale, had flown from Duxford to Biggin Hill to join the newly formed Historic Aircraft Flight. For the flights from Duxford to Biggin Hill, the aircraft were flown by Gp Capt J.E. 'Johnnie' Johnson DSO DFC in PS853, Gp Capt James Rankin DSO in PM631 and Wg Cdr Peter Thompson in PS915. After landing at Biggin Hill, the Spitfires were joined by the last Hawker Hurricane, LF363, as well as Javelins of 46 Squadron and Hunters of 41 Squadron. *(Crown Copyright/Air Historical Branch image T-301)*

History of the
BBMF

damage in a flying incident at Martlesham and was sent away to 71 Maintenance Unit (MU) at Bicester for repair on 4 June, returning on 1 July. Then on 10 September, TE476 was damaged in a flying accident. Reports suggest that the pilot landed back at Martlesham Heath after his radio failed and forgot to lower his undercarriage. As a result, it was decreed that September 1959 would be the last time that the Battle of Britain Flight fighters, including the Hurricane, would participate in the flypast over London. That decision was perhaps vindicated when SL574 suffered a complete engine failure during that very sortie and the pilot, AVM Maguire, force-landed on the OXO cricket ground at Bromley.

In November 1961, the Flight was once again forced to move; this time it went to Horsham St Faith in Norfolk (now known as Norwich Airport). At the time, the Flight consisted of Hurricane LF363 and Spitfire Mk XIX PM631. It would remain like this until 1964.

Yet another setback was to befall the Flight when it was announced that Horsham St Faith was to close on 1 April 1963. The Flight upped sticks and moved to RAF Coltishall where things began to improve significantly.

In a letter dated 1 April 1969 it was announced that the Flight should be established on a formal basis at RAF Coltishall, with the necessary servicing personnel established on a full-time basis. It

was also announced that the 'Waddington Lancaster' PA474, would be kept in flying condition at RAF Waddington until the end of 1969, when its future would be reviewed.

Having popularly become known as the Battle of Britain Memorial Flight (BBMF), the unit officially took this name on 1 June 1969.

Less than two years later, it was announced that due to the planned introduction of the new Jaguar aircraft at the base, the BBMF was moving from Coltishall to Coningsby in Lincolnshire. On 1 March 1976, the Flight's aircraft began ferrying across to their new home, the Lancaster leading a formation that included a single Hurricane and three of the Flight's Spitfires. Spitfire AB910 and Hurricane LF363 followed a few days later – along with the remains of Spitfire Mk IX MK732, which had been used at Coltishall as a source of spare parts. Thankfully, the Flight has remained at Coningsby right up to the present day.

Forever in demand

Records show that for many years after its formation the Flight conducted relatively low-key operations, typically making 50–60 appearances per season, a situation that continued into the mid-1960s. By the early 1990s, the number of appearances had trebled and demand for participation by the Flight's aircraft was continuing to grow. In 1996 individual aircraft appearances exceeded 500 and

by 2003 tasking for over 700 individual aircraft appearances during each year's display season had become the norm, many of which are flypasts that are scheduled to take place en route to a display. The demand for appearances by the Flight's aircraft shows no sign of decline and indeed increases every year.

Flying hours are carefully restricted to ensure longevity on the Flight. The Lancaster can fly no more than 104 hours per display season, while the Dakota is permitted no more than 180 hours in any one year. The Spitfires are limited to 200 hours in total each season, and that is for all six airframes, not each. There is a total of 120 hours imposed on the Hurricanes, shared between the two aircraft.

Today, the Battle of Britain Memorial Flight is a household name and a national institution, but the modern BBMF was created from humble beginnings and though it paid the same mark of respect it did so under tight constraint. It has gone from being a loose collection of obsolete types tucked away in the corner of various hangars, to a dedicated unit with its own headquarters, entrusted with caring for priceless assets of British aviation heritage.

The Flight's aircraft now appear in front of an estimated total audience of seven million people per year – a fitting and permanent reminder of the absolute sacrifice given by so few for so many.

'Lest we forget.'

Another early colour image of the Battle of Britain Flight based at Martlesham Heath, Norfolk, in September 1960. The formation consists of Hurricane IIc, LF363, and a camouflaged Spitfire PR XIX, PM631. *(Crown Copyright/Air Historical Branch image T-2082)*

⋀ Avro Lancaster BI, PA474/M, in 1963 while in use with the Royal College of Aeronautics at Cranfield to test a laminar flow wing developed by Handley Page for use in connection with the proposed HP 117. While at Cranfield, the aircraft retained its earlier 82 Squadron crest and 'M' code. *(Crown Copyright/Air Historical Branch image AHB-Collier-PA474-01)*

⋘ A photograph taken shortly after the presentation of Supermarine Spitfire Mk Vb, AB910, to the Royal Air Force by the British Aircraft Corporation (Vickers-Armstrong) at RAF Coltishall, on 15 September 1965. Standing on the wing of AB910 is Battle of Britain ace Air Cdre Al Deere, with former Spitfire test pilot Jeffrey Quill in the cockpit of AB910; AM Sir Douglas Morris, Air Officer Commanding-in-Chief Fighter Command is to the right. *(Crown Copyright/Air Historical Branch image PRB-1-31534)*

⋗ In 1968, the Flight's aircraft were used for the filming of the following year's aviation classic *Battle of Britain.* The film used a large number of historic aircraft of various types and was to prove a turning point in the worldwide warbird movement. The Flight's aircraft were on filming duty from Monday to Friday, and then carried out their displays at the weekend. They were often seen wearing their film markings, giving many airshow visitors a chance to see and photograph them in unusual combat liveries. Once the film work was completed, the Flight secured another major coup when it was presented with Spitfire Mk IIa P7350. This was – and still is – the world's oldest airworthy example of its type and a genuine combat veteran of the Battle of Britain. Hurricanes and Spitfires – both real and replica – pictured at Henlow in 1968 for use in the film *Battle of Britain. (Crown Copyright/ Air Historical Branch image T-8365)*

Further expansion of the Flight occurred in March 1972, when Hurricane IIc PZ865 was presented to the BBMF after being refurbished by Hawker Siddeley, bringing the Flight's complement of airworthy Hurricanes to two. PZ865 had been completed at Hawker's Langley factory on 27 July 1944, the last of more than 14,000 Hurricanes to be built. The aircraft was named *The Last of the Many!* and the name was painted on the fuselage sides, just behind the cockpit. PZ865 was rolled out in the presence of Hawker's remaining Hart, G-ABMR, bedecked in banners. After its appearance in *Battle of Britain* in 1969, PZ865 was refurbished and subsequently returned to flying condition in 1971. On 30 March 1972, PZ865 was presented to the Flight at Coltishall. *(Crown Copyright/Air Historical Branch image CH-13671)*

The fighter aircraft of the BBMF based at Coltishall in 1969; Hurricane IIc, LF363/LE-D; Spitfire IIa, P7350/ZH-T; Spitfire Vb, AB910/SO-T; Spitfire PR XIXs, PS853 (uncoded) and PM6231/AD-C. *(Crown Copyright/Air Historical Branch image TN-1-2690)*

Avro Lancaster B.I, PA474/KM-B, during a flight from Waddington in September 1972. The aircraft was maintained and operated by 44 Squadron at this time, and flown on a number of ceremonial occasions. In 1965, the squadron had painted the aircraft as 'KM-B' to commemorate the aircraft in which Sqn Ldr John Nettleton won the Victoria Cross following a raid by 44 and 97 Squadrons on Augsburg in April 1942. *(Crown Copyright/Air Historical Branch image TN-1-6669-19)*

For a number of years, 207 Squadron at Northolt provided valuable assistance to the Flight, giving logistical support and escort facilities on occasions when the Flight was deployed away from its home base. This was particularly important when Flight aircraft had to transit Controlled Airspace (with very limited radio and avionics on board the fighters) or attend shows overseas. Here, XS779, a Basset CC1, was 'escorting' Spitfire PR XIX PM631/AD-C and Hurricane IIc LF363/LE-D along the south coast on 4 July 1973. *(Crown Copyright/Air Historical Branch image TN-1-6797-9)*

◀ The fighter aircraft of the BBMF at Coningsby, on 15 October 1973. From front to rear: Spitfire Vb, AB910/QJ-J; Spitfire IIa, P7350/ZH-T; Hurricane IIc, LF363/LE-D; Hurricane IIb PZ865/DT-A; Spitfire PR XIXs, PM631/AD-C along with the uncoded PS853. *(Crown Copyright/Air Historical Branch image TN-1-6846-32)*

▶ Aircraft of the BBMF outside their hangar at Coningsby in July 1983. From front to rear: Spitfire IIa, P7350/SH-D; Spitfire Vb, AB910/XT-M; Spitfire PR XIX, PM631/AD-C; and, to the left, Hurricane IIc, LF363/VY-X. *(Crown Copyright/Air Historical Branch image TN-1-9504-30)*

▶ For a number of years, 207 Squadron at Northolt provided Basset aircraft in the Logistical Support and Escort role to the BBMF. Later, its Devon C2/2 took over the role. In 1985, after the disbandment of 207 Squadron, VP981 was officially handed over to the BBMF where it provided useful twin-engine training capabilities in addition to its logistical and support roles. Shortly after arriving at Coningsby, it was repainted in this attractive silver and blue colour scheme with 'Battle of Britain Memorial Flight' titles added to the fuselage. It was photographed at the 1987 Mildenhall Air Fête when arriving with a number of the Flight's aircrew. *(Keith Wilson)*

A new type joined the Flight on 20 July 1993 when Douglas Dakota III ZA947 arrived at Coningsby after transfer from the Defence Research Agency. Before delivery to the Flight, the aircraft was overhauled by the Air Atlantique engineering division at Coventry. It was then flown to Marham for the aircraft to be repainted in the colours of 271 Squadron, to depict the individual aircraft flown by Flt Lt David Lord, who was posthumously awarded the Victoria Cross following the Arnhem operations in September 1944. *(Geoffrey Lee/ Planefocus GL951353)*

◁ In January 2001, the BBMF took delivery of a pair of Spitfire Mk XVIs – TB382 and TE311 – which had been placed on the Flight's strength following many years with the RAF's recruitment roadshow. They had been stored in one of Coningsby's hardened aircraft shelters since October 1999. Both aircraft were structurally examined: TB382's skin was in poor condition but TE311 was in remarkably good shape. As a result, TB382 was dismantled for spares and subsequently struck-off charge. TE311 was initially retained as part of a spares recovery programme, but work to restore the fuselage as a 'spare' began in October 2001. Unfortunately, it had to be carried out at no cost to the Ministry of Defence (MoD), which resulted in the two technicians principally responsible for the project – Chief Technician Paul Blackah and Cpl Andy Bale – carrying out the work in their spare time. The project received generous help from several companies and many other BBMF engineers. Subsequently, and because of the high standard of the restoration, permission was given to complete a full restoration to flying condition. It has been a long task, taking 11 years, and the aircraft made its first flight at Coningsby on 19 October 2012, adding the important Mk XVI to the Flight's inventory for the coming years. (Keith Wilson)

⋀ The BBMF in 1990. The Lancaster PA474/PM-M² leads an eight-ship formation consisting of Spitfire Mk Vb AB910/EB-J in 41 Squadron markings; Hurricane IIc PZ865/RF-U in 303 (Polish) Squadron markings; Hurricane IIb LF363/GN-A in 249 (Gold Coast) Squadron markings; Spitfire Mk IIa P7350/UO-T in 266 (Rhodesia) Squadron markings; Spitfire PR XIX PS853/C in 16 Squadron colours; Spitfire PR XIX PM631/N in South East Air Command colours; and the uncoded Spitfire Mk XIX PS915. (Geoffrey Lee/Planefocus GL-9007789)

The classic BBMF three-ship formation in August 2012 consisting of Hurricane IIb LF363/YB-W, Spitfire PR XIX PS915 *The Last!*, and Lancaster B1 PA474 painted as *Phantom of the Ruhr*; over the Kent countryside on 11 August 2012. *(Keith Wilson)*

▽ The *Phantom of the Ruhr* in flight along the south coast near Dover in August 2012. The aircraft is painted to represent Lancaster III, EE139, which operated with both 100 and 550 Squadrons. On the port side of the aircraft it carries the 100 Squadron code 'HW-R', with which it flew 30 operations. *(Keith Wilson)*

Aircraft of the Flight

Spitfire PR Mk XIX PM631

1945–57 Joined the RAF on 6 November 1945 and was placed in storage until 1949. Joined the THUM Flight in 1951.

1957–66 PM631 is the BBMF's longest-serving aircraft and has been in continuous service with the Flight since its formation on 11 July 1957. Shortly after joining the Flight it was painted in camouflage but without code letters. Inscription 'The last operational Spitfire still flying at RAF Biggin Hill' added.

1967–83 Painted in grey/green camouflage as 'AD-C' of 11 Squadron.

1984–9 To commemorate the 40th anniversary of D-Day, PM631 was painted as 'DL-E' of 91 Squadron to represent a Spitfire Mk XIV at the time.

1990–5 Painted as 'N' of 11 Squadron in South East Asia Command (SEAC) colours of 1945, with the name *Mary* added to the cowling.

1996–2001 Painted to represent another SEAC aircraft, this time a 681 Squadron example with the code 'S'.

2002–current Painted into 541 Squadron colours, to represent an aircraft flown by Flt Lt Ray Holmes.

◄ To commemorate the 40th anniversary of D-Day, PM631 was painted as 'DL-E' of 91 Squadron to represent a Spitfire Mk XIV at the time. It was photographed at Alconbury at an open day in 1988. *(Keith Wilson)*

Λ In 1967, PM631 was painted in the colours of 11 Squadron and the code 'AD-C' added. It remained in these colours until 1983. It was photographed on a flight from Coningsby on 15 October 1973. *(Crown Copyright/Air Historic Branch TN-1-6846)*

In 1996, PM631 was painted to represent a SEAC aircraft, a 681 Squadron example with the code 'S'. *(Geoffrey Lee/ Planefocus GL-983966-35)*

In 2002, PM631 was repainted in 541 Squadron colours, to represent an aircraft flown by Flt Lt Ray Holmes, one of the courageous pilots who conducted photographic reconnaissance missions over Europe in early 1945. PM631 carries no squadron code or identification letter. *(Keith Wilson)*

Spitfire PR Mk XIX PS915

1945–57	Joined the RAF in June 1945 and later joined the THUM Flight in 1951.
1957	Officially joined the Historic Aircraft Flight on 11 July 1957. Shortly after joining the Flight was inspected and found to be in poor condition.
1957–68	Painted in camouflage without code letters and allocated to gate-guard duties at West Malling, Leuchars and Brawdy. After being modified to take an ex-Shackleton Griffon 58 engine, the aircraft was refurbished to flying condition by British Aerospace and rejoined the Flight in 1987.
1987–91	Painted PR blue overall without any obvious squadron markings.
1992–7	Painted to represent the prototype Spitfire Mk XIV, JF319, with camouflage topsides and a Prototype 'P' in a yellow circle on the fuselage.
1998–2003	Painted into the colours of 'UM-G' of 152 Squadron, a SEAC Spitfire Mk XIV. It also carried the black panther motif on the side of its fuselage.
2004–current	Painted in a colour scheme to represent PS888, a Spitfire PR XIX of 81 Squadron based at Seletar, Singapore. PS888 had the accolade of carrying out the last operational sortie flown by an RAF Spitfire on 1 April 1954 and to mark the event, the groundcrew painted *'The Last!'* on the port engine cowling. PS915 carries the same inscription.

◁ **PS915 was one of the three founding Spitfire members of the Flight, when it arrived at Biggin Hill on 11 July 1957. It was in poor condition and was allocated for gate-guard duties at West Malling before going to Leuchars and Henlow for the film** Battle of Britain**. It then moved to Brawdy where it was seen in the hangar just before being moved to Samlesbury for the refurbishment programme.** *(Peter R. March)*

◁ **After being modified to take a Rolls-Royce Griffon 58 engine from the Shackleton, Spitfire PR XIX PS915 was refurbished by British Aerospace (Warton Division) and rejoined the BBMF on 7 April 1987, painted PR blue overall without any obvious squadron markings. It was photographed at the Boscombe Down Battle of Britain Day in June 1990.** *(Peter R. March)*

In 1998, PS915 carried the colours of a SEAC Spitfire Mk XIV with 152 Squadron and the code letters 'UM-G', as well as the black panther motif on the side of its fuselage. *(Geoffrey Lee/ Planefocus GL-983966-33)*

From 1992, PS915 was painted to represent the prototype Spitfire Mk XIV, JF319, with camouflage topsides and a Prototype 'P' in a yellow circle on the fuselage. It was photographed at the RIAT, Fairford, in 1993. *(Peter R. March)*

Following a major servicing at ARC Duxford over the winter of 2003/4, PS915 was repainted in a scheme to replicate PS888, a Spitfire PR XIX of 81 Squadron based at Seletar, Singapore. PS888 carried out the last operational sortie flown by an RAF Spitfire on 1 April 1954, and in recognition the groundcrew painted *'The Last!'* on the port engine cowling. PS915 carries the same inscription. It was photographed near the south-east coast in August 2012 where it demonstrated its excellent manoeuvrability at the hands of OC BBMF Dunc Mason.
(Keith Wilson)

Spitfire Mk Vb AB910

1941–65 Built at Castle Bromwich in 1941 and served on front-line duties for four years. After the end of the war was sold to Gp Capt Alan Wheeler and registered G-AISU. After landing accident, returned to Vickers-Armstrong.

1965–8 Presented to the Flight by Vickers-Armstrong in September 1965 and delivered in camouflage as 'QJ-J' of 92 Squadron, the first aircraft of the Flight to wear unit markings.

1969–72 Painted as 'SO-T' of 145 Squadron. Erroneously, it had been painted as 'PB-T' but was soon changed.

1973–8 Painted as 'QJ-J' of 92 Squadron once again, albeit in slightly larger form than previously.

1981–5 Painted as 'XT-M' of 603 Squadron.

1986–9 Following a major service at the College of Aeronautics, Cranfield, in 1986, it was repainted as 'BP-O' of 457 Squadron, representing one of five aircraft presented to the nation by the American Research Foundation. It also carried the words 'In Memory of R.J. Mitchell'.

1990 Repainted as 'EB-J' of 41 Squadron and inscribed 'The Guinea Pig Club', representing the aircraft flown by Sqn Ldr George Bennions DFC who was shot down on 1 October 1950, suffering horrific injuries and being subsequently treated at East Grinstead with the pioneering plastic surgery techniques of Sir Archibald McIndoe.

1991–3 Repainted as 'MD-E' of 133 (Eagle) Squadron. AB910 operated with this squadron at RAF Biggin Hill from June 1942 until the Squadron upgraded with Spitfire Mk IXs in September 1942. During this time AB910 flew 29 operational sorties.

1994–8 Repainted as 'AE-H' of 402 Squadron and carried D-Day invasion stripes as would have appeared on aircraft taking part in operations in this theatre in June 1944. In January 1944, AB910 was

˄ After the Second World War, AB910 was purchased by Gp Capt Alan Wheeler for air racing and was placed on the civil aircraft register as G-AISU. Following a heavy landing during the King's Cup Air Race in 1953, the aircraft was returned to Vickers-Armstrong where it was refurbished and subsequently flown by Jeffrey Quill until being donated to the Flight in 1965. It was photographed at Exeter in 1958. *(Peter R. March)*

˄ A flight of Spitfire Mk Vbs of 92 Squadron with their engines running at Biggin Hill, Kent, on 14 June 1941. The nearest aircraft, R7161/QJ-J, is a converted Mk I. *(Crown Copyright/ Air Historic Branch CH-3549)*

˄ When Spitfire Mk Vb AB910 was presented to the Flight by Vickers-Armstrong in September 1965, it carried the code letters 'QJ-J' of 92 Squadron. It was the first aircraft of the Flight to wear unit markings. Since then it has become the norm to paint aircraft into representative colours, especially when they undergo their major servicing. The photograph was taken during a flight from Coltishall in 1968. *(Crown Copyright/Air Historic Branch T-8105)*

transferred to 402 (Winnipeg Bear) Squadron. In June 1944, it became the personal aircraft of Canadian Flg Off George Lawson who flew a number of sorties on beachhead cover patrol on D-Day, 6 June 1944. In 1997, the aircraft was briefly painted as 'XR-A' of 71 (Eagle) Squadron and carried an Eagle Squadron badge on its forward fuselage for its appearance at Nellis AFB, Nevada, in April, in celebration of the 50th anniversary of the formation of the United States Air Force.

1999–2002 Repainted as 'ZD-C' of 222 (Natal) Squadron with the wording 'President Roosevelt – Warner Bros.' on its fuselage sides, just below the cockpit.

2003–6 Repainted in desert camouflage as 'IR-G' of 244 Wing, to represent Spitfire Mk Vb AB502, the personal aircraft of Wg Cdr Ian Richard Gleed DSO DFC when he became Wing Leader of 244 Wing at Goubrine South, Tunisia, in 1943. His aircraft carried his initials in place of the regular squadron codes and had a 'Figaro the Cat' cartoon image below the cockpit on the starboard side.

2007–10 Repainted to represent the personal Spitfire Mk Vb, EN951/'RF-D', of Sqn Ldr Jan Zumbach when he flew with 303 (Kosciuszko) Squadron in 1942. Having already fought in France, Sqn Ldr Zumbach was a founder member of 303 Squadron and became an ace during the Battle of Britain, scoring eight aircraft destroyed and one probably during that period alone while he was flying Hurricane Is.

2011–current Repainted as 'MD-E' of 133 (Eagle) Squadron, colours it wore serving with the squadron in 1942.

In 1973, the markings of 92 Squadron were once again applied to AB910, with the code letters 'QJ-J' appearing again, albeit in slightly larger form than previously. During a flight out of Coningsby on 15 October 1973, AB910 is seen in formation with Spitfire IIa, P7350/ZH-T; Hurricane IIcs, LF363/LE-D and PZ865/DT-A; and Spitfire PR XIXs PM631/AD-C and PS853. *(Crown Copyright/Air Historic Branch TN-1-6846-21)*

After a major service at the College of Aeronautics, Cranfield, in 1986, AB910 appeared in 457 Squadron colours with the code 'BP-O'. It was inscribed with the words 'In Memory of R.J. Mitchell', a fitting tribute to the genius whose creation this beautiful aircraft was. It is seen at Middle Wallop in July 1986. *(Keith Wilson)*

In 1991, the colours chosen for AB910 were of 133 (Eagle) Squadron with the code 'MD-E'. *(Peter R. March)*

From 1994 to 1998, AB910 flew as 'AE-H' of 402 Squadron and carried D-Day invasion stripes as would have appeared on aircraft taking part in these operations in June 1944. It was the personal aircraft of Canadian Flg Off George Lawson who flew a number of sorties on D-Day, 6 June 1944. *(Crown Copyright/Air Historic Branch AHN-MIS-AB910)*

AB910 holds the record as the aircraft to have displayed the furthest distance from base when it performed at Nellis AFB, Nevada, in April 1997, in celebration of the 50th anniversary of the formation of the United States Air Force. AB910 was dismantled and airlifted from Brize Norton. It also was specially painted as 'XR-A' of 71 (Eagle) Squadron and carried an Eagle Squadron badge on its forward fuselage. *(Peter R. March)*

➤ From 1999 to 2002, AB910 flew as 'ZD-C' of 222 (Natal) Squadron with the wording 'President Roosevelt – Warner Bros.' below the cockpit. (Geoffrey Lee/Planefocus GL-983966-32)

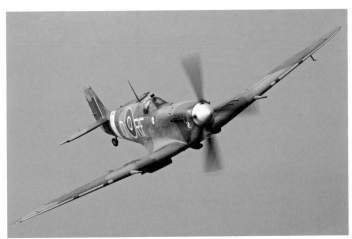

Λ In 2007, AB910 acquired a new paint scheme, this time to represent the personal Spitfire Mk Vb, EN951/'RF-D' of Sqn Ldr Jan Zumbach when he flew with 303 (Kosciuszko) Squadron in 1942. (Crown Copyright/RAF Coningsby Photographic Section)

Λ In 2011, AB910 once again took on the colours of 133 (Eagle) Squadron with the code 'MD-E', colours it wore when serving with the squadron in 1942. It was photographed at the RIAT, Fairford, in July 2012, with Flt Lt Anthony 'Parky' Parkinson in the cockpit. (Keith Wilson)

Λ Probably one of the more 'unusual' colour schemes applied to the Flight's Spitfires was to AB910 when it carried the desert camouflage scheme of Spitfire Mk Vb AB502, the personal aircraft of Wg Cdr Ian Richard Gleed DSO DFC, Wing Leader of 244 Wing at Goubrine South, Tunisia, in 1943. His initials replaced the squadron codes and a 'Figaro the Cat' cartoon image appeared below the cockpit on the starboard side. This image was taken on 15 May 2004. (Crown Copyright/Air Historic Branch BBMF-119)

Λ Wg Cdr Gleed learned to fly at Hatfield before he joined the RAF in March 1936 on a short-service commission. Gleed's small stature earned him the nickname 'The Widge'. By the end of 1940, flying the Hurricane, he had destroyed nine German aircraft, probably destroyed three others and had been awarded half shares in two other victories. He is seen here with a Hurricane carrying his 'Figaro the Cat' cartoon. (Crown Copyright/Air Historic Branch CH-1639)

Spitfire Mk IIa P7350

1940–68 Built at Castle Bromwich and delivered to RAF in August 1940. Served on front-line duties until April 1942. Sold as scrap in 1948 but then donated to RAF Museum at Colerne. Restored to flying condition for film *Battle of Britain*.

1968 Presented to the Flight on 8 November 1968.

1969–71 Painted as 'ZH-T' of 266 Squadron. In September 1940, P7350 had been delivered to 266 (Rhodesia) Squadron at Wittering and fought during the Battle of Britain.

1972–6 Repainted as 'UO-T', the original 266 Squadron code that it wore in September 1940.

1977–81 Repainted as 'QV-B' of 19 Squadron to represent a Spitfire Mk IIa, which were operated from September 1940 to October 1941.

1982–4 Repainted as 'SH-D' of 64 Squadron, which operated the type from February to November 1941.

1985–8 To celebrate the 60th anniversary of the Royal Observer Corps, P7350 was painted to represent Spitfire P7666, which was handed over to 41 Squadron in November 1940 and flew with the words 'Observer Corps' on the fuselage.

1989–90 Repainted as 'UO-T' of 266 Squadron.

1991–3 Repainted as 'YT-F' of 65 (East India) Squadron. It had the words 'East India Squadron' on the fuselage sides, just below the cockpit.

1994–6 Repainted as 'RN-S' of 72 (Basutoland) Squadron to represent Spitfire P7832. Named *Enniskillen*, it also carries 'Belfast Telegraph Spitfire Fund' wording in recognition of the fund run by the *Belfast Telegraph* to raise the money to buy this aircraft, which was presented to the Squadron in January 1941.

1997–8 Repainted as 'BA-Y' of 277 Squadron and named *The Old Lady*. The aircraft was financed in May 1941 by the Bank of England, hence The Old Lady (of Threadneedle Street).

1999–2006 Repainted as 'XT-D' of 603 Squadron to represent Spitfire Mk Ia, L1067, which was flown by Sqn Ldr George 'Uncle' Denholm, CO of 603 Squadron from June 1940 to April 1941.

2007–9 Repainted as 'XT-L' of 603 Squadron, the aircraft flown by Plt Off 'Stapme' Stapleton during the Battle of Britain.

2010–11 Repainted as 'QJ-K' of 616 Squadron.

2012–current Repainted as 'EB-G' of 41 Squadron to represent a Spitfire Mk Ia N3162, the aircraft flown by Battle of Britain ace, Plt Off Eric Lock on 5 September 1940, when he achieved four confirmed kills and one probable in a single day.

◁ Having survived the war, P7350 was then sold for scrap to Messrs John Dale Ltd in 1948 for £25. Thankfully, the historical significance of the aircraft was recognised and it was presented to the RAF Colerne station museum collection. After appearing in the film *Battle of Britain*, P7350 was presented to the Flight and flew to Coltishall on 8 November 1968. Its first identity with the Flight was as a 266 (Rhodesia) Squadron Spitfire, coded 'ZH-T', with which it had fought during the Battle of Britain. It was later transferred to 603 (City of Edinburgh) Squadron. This image of P7350 was taken during a flight from Coltishall, Norfolk, on 31 July 1972. *(Crown Copyright/Air Historic Branch TN-1-6620-25)*

At the Biggin Hill Air Fair in May 1972, P7350 displayed with Hurricane IIb LF363/DT-A. *(Keith Wilson)*

Later in 1972, P7350 was painted as 'UO-T', the original 266 Squadron code that it wore in September 1940. It was photographed at Coningsby on 11 September 1977. *(Crown Copyright/Air Historic Branch TN-1-7748-13)*

From 1982 to 1984, P7350 was painted as 'SH-D' of 64 Squadron, which flew the type in 1941. It was photographed at a Families' Day at RAF Wyton in July 1984. *(Keith Wilson)*

To mark the 60th anniversary of the Royal Observer Corps, P7350 was painted to represent Spitfire P7666, which served with 41 Squadron from November 1940 and carried the words 'Observer Corps' on the fuselage. It wore these colours from 1985 to 1988 and was photographed at the Great Warbirds Air Display at West Malling. *(Keith Wilson)*

For the 1991 display season P7350 changed its colours to 'YT-F' of 65 (East India) Squadron, with the words 'East India Squadron' inscribed below the cockpit. It wore this colour scheme through to the 1993 season. *(Geoffrey Lee/Planefocus GL-9104385)*

P7350 took on the colours of another presentation aircraft from 1997 to 1998. This time it appeared as a 277 Squadron example coded 'BA-Y' and named *The Old Lady* in recognition of Bank of England funding in 1941. It was photographed at North Weald in 1998. *(Peter R. March)*

In 1999 the colours on P7350 were changed to represent a 603 Squadron Spitfire Mk Ia, L1067, with the code 'XT-D'. L1067 was flown by Sqn Ldr George 'Uncle' Denholm, CO of 603 Squadron from June 1940 to April 1941. This image was taken on 27 September 2003 on a flight from Coningsby. *(Crown Copyright/Sgt Mick Scraggs via Air Historic Branch)*

In 2007, P7350 was repainted in the colours of a 603 Squadron Spitfire with the code letters 'XT-L', the aircraft flown by Plt Off 'Stapme' Stapleton during the Battle of Britain. It was photographed at Duxford in May 2007. *(Peter R. March)*

The next colour scheme for P7350 was as 'QJ-K' of 616 Squadron. To celebrate the 70th anniversary of the Battle of Britain, the Tucano Display Team for 2010 was painted in a Second World War-style camouflage and flew a special air-to-air photographic session in May 2010. *(Geoffrey Lee/ Planefocus GLD-105596)*

The current colour scheme for P7350 was applied for the 2012 season and features P7350 representing a Spitfire Mk Ia N3162, of 41 Squadron, coded 'EB-G', the aircraft flown by Battle of Britain ace, Plt Off Eric Lock on 5 September 1940, when he achieved four confirmed kills and one probable in a single day. P7350 was photographed at Coningsby in April 2012 with the then OC BBMF Sqn Ldr Ian 'Smithy' Smith at the controls. *(Keith Wilson)*

V-S Spitfire Mk LFIXe MK356

1944–67	Built at Castle Bromwich in early 1944. It was allocated to B Flight of 443 (Fighter) Squadron of the Royal Canadian Air Force. After the war it was allocated as an instructional airframe at RAF Halton, followed by a variety of gate-guard duties.
1968–9	Ground role in the film *Battle of Britain*.
1970–96	Placed on display at St Athan. In 1980s, selected as a potential Spitfire restoration.
1997–2007	After being restored to flying condition by technicians at St Athan, the fighter made its first flight since 1944 on 7 November 1997. It arrived at Coningsby on 14 November 1944 painted in the only operational colours in which it flew, as '2I-V' of 443 (Fighter) Squadron, Royal Canadian Air Force.
2008-current	Repainted as 'UF-Q' of 601 (County of London) Squadron in an unusual silver paint used during late 1944 when 601 Squadron carried out fighter-bomber missions over the Balkans from bases in southern Italy. It is painted to represent MJ250, the aircraft of Flt Lt Desmond 'Ibby' Ibbotson DFC*.

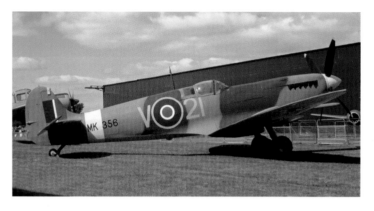

Spitfire LFIXe MK356 while with the RAF Museum Reserve Collection at St Athan in September 1996. *(Peter R. March)*

After being restored to flying condition by technicians at St Athan, MK356 was painted as '2I-V' of 443 (Fighter) Squadron, Royal Canadian Air Force. It made its first flight since 1945 on 7 November 1997 at the hands of the then OC BBMF, Sqn Ldr Paul 'Major' Day OBE AFC. MK356 arrived at Coningsby on 7 November 1997. It was photographed on a sortie during the Lincolnshire Lancaster Association Members' Day on 26 September 2006. *(Crown Copyright/SAC Scott Lewis)*

In 2008, MK356 was repainted in this unusual silver paint used during late 1944 when 601 (County of London) Squadron carried out fighter-bomber missions over the Balkans from bases in southern Italy. It is painted to represent MJ250, the aircraft of Flt Lt Desmond 'Ibby' Ibbotson DFC*. It was photographed during the PDA at Coningsby in April 2012 with Grp Cpt 'Sammy' Sampson at the controls. *(Keith Wilson)*

V-S Spitfire Mk XVIe TE311

1944–98 Built at Castle Bromwich in 1945 and allocated to the Empire Central Flying School Handling Squadron at Hullavington on 5 October 1945, followed by a variety of RAF tasks until 1955 and then gate-guard duties.

1968–9 Ground role in film *Battle of Britain*.

1970–98 RAF Exhibition Flight followed by storage.

1999–2001 Arrived at Coningsby and stored in a hardened aircraft shelter.

2001–current Arrived with the Flight in January 2001 and was retained as a spares recovery programme. Permission was gained to restore the fuselage as a 'spare', and later a decision was taken to complete a full restoration to flying condition. It made its first post-restoration flight on 19 October 2012, painted as '4D-V' of 74 Squadron, with Sqn Ldr Ian 'Smithy' Smith at the controls.

△ Spitfire Mk LFXVIe TE311 at Henlow in 1968 having been modified (but not yet painted) with a 'high-back' rear fuselage and rounded wing tips, fin and rudder to resemble an early mark of Spitfire for taxiing scenes in the film *Battle of Britain*. It later reverted to its more 'normal' LFXVIe guise and was displayed on the gate at RAF Benson for a number of years. *(Peter R. March)*

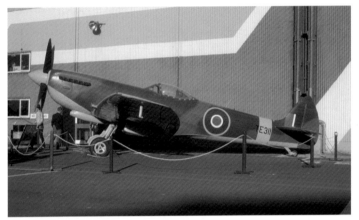

△ TE311 was later used by the RAF Exhibition Flight as a travelling exhibit and was displayed at the Southampton Hall of Aviation in 1986, during the 50th anniversary of the first flight of the Spitfire K5054 at Eastleigh on 10 March 1936. *(Keith Wilson)*

➤ TE311 arrived with the Flight in January 2001 and permission was granted to restore the fuselage as a 'spare'. Such was the quality of the work, carried out by Chief Technician Paul Blackah and Cpl Andy Bale, with assistance from other members of the BBMF, that it was later decided to complete a full restoration to flying condition. By September 2012, work on TE311 was progressing well and the aircraft was close to making its first flight, which took place on 19 October 2012, with Sqn Ldr Ian 'Smithy' Smith at the controls. *(Keith Wilson)*

TE311 was flown for a special photoshoot over Lincolnshire on 13 December 2012 with OC BBMF Sqn Ldr 'Dunc' Mason at the controls. TE311 will be a very welcome addition to the Flight in 2013. *(Keith Wilson)*

Hurricane IIb LF363

1944–57	First flew and is believed to be the very last Hurricane to join the RAF.
1957–68	Officially joined the Historic Aircraft Flight on 11 July 1957. Shortly after joining the Flight it was painted in camouflage but without code letters.
1968–9	Took part in the filming of *Battle of Britain*.
1969–72	Painted as 'LE-D' of 242 Squadron to represent the Hurricane flown by Sqn Ldr Douglas Bader, using thin-style fuselage code letters.
1973–8	Remained as 'LE-D' of 242 Squadron continuing to represent the Hurricane flown by Sqn Ldr Douglas Bader, but the letters 'LE-D' were thicker in size.
1979–82	Painted as 'GN-F' to represent a Hurricane of 249 (Gold Coast) Squadron, which was actively engaged in the Battle of Britain, operating from North Weald.
1983–6	Painted as 'VY-X' of 85 Squadron code in an all-over black night-fighter scheme applied to 85 Squadron aircraft while at Debden during the Battle of Britain.
1987–9	Painted as 'NV-L' of 79 Squadron which was active during the Battle of Britain, based at Biggin Hill and Hawkinge.
1990–1	In readiness for the 50th anniversary of the Battle of Britain in 1990, LF363 was painted as 'GN-A' to represent 242 Squadron Hurricane I, P3576, flown by Flt Lt James Nicolson, Fighter Command's only Victoria Cross winner. Aircraft crashed at Wittering on 11 September 1991 and was seriously damaged.
1991–4	Stored at Coningsby.
1995–6	Restoration with Historic Flying Ltd at Audley End. First post-restoration flight made on 29 September 1998.
1998–2005	Painted as 'US-C' of 56 Squadron, which at the time was operating Tornado F3 aircraft from Coningsby.
2006–current	Painted as 'YB-W' of 17 Squadron representing a Hurricane I P3878 flown by Flg Off Harold 'Birdy' Bird-Wilson, who was awarded a Distinguished Flying Cross for his exploits after shooting down six enemy aircraft and sharing in the destruction of others.

∧ **An early colour air-to-air image of LF363 in formation with Spitfire PR XIX PM631, taken when the Flight was based at Martlesham Heath in September 1960.** *(Crown Copyright/Air Historic Branch T-2082)*

➤ **Aside from its various colour schemes used during the making of the film** Battle of Britain**, the first representative identity given to LF363 was in 1969 when the 242 Squadron code LE-D was applied, to represent the Hurricane flown by Sqn Ldr Douglas Bader. The aircraft is seen along the south-east coast in August 1969, with all five of the Flight's fighter aircraft together in the air, while based at RAF Coltishall. The name 'Battle of Britain Memorial Flight' was officially adopted on 1 June 1969.** *(Crown Copyright/Air Historic Branch TN-1-2690)*

LF363's next scheme was 'GN-F', representing a Hurricane of 249 (Gold Coast) Squadron, which took part in the Battle of Britain, operating from North Weald. Photographed here in September 1981. *(Peter R. March)*

LF363 was painted in an all-over black scheme with the 85 Squadron code 'VY-X' applied. This was a night-fighter scheme for 85 Squadron aircraft while at Debden during the Battle of Britain. It wore these colours for the 1983–6 seasons and was photographed at Duxford in 1984. *(Keith Wilson)*

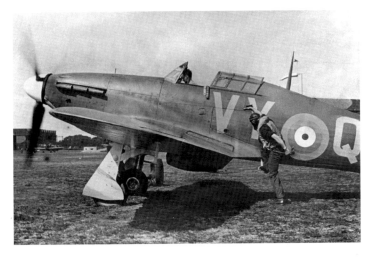

A wartime image of 85 Squadron Hurricane at RAF Debden in the all-black night-fighter colour scheme, this one coded VY-Q. *(Crown Copyright/Air Historic Branch image)*

In 1987, the 79 Squadron code 'NV-L' was applied. No 79 Squadron was active during the Battle of Britain, based at both Biggin Hill and Hawkinge. Photographed at Duxford in July 1988. *(Keith Wilson)*

In readiness for the 50th anniversary of the Battle of Britain in 1990, LF363 was painted as GN-A to represent 242 Squadron Hurricane I, P3576, flown by Flt Lt James Nicolson, Fighter Command's only Victoria Cross winner. Photographed in June 1990. *(Peter R. March)*

LF363 suffered a broken camshaft and subsequently forced-landed at Wittering on 11 September 1991, while en route from Wittering to Jersey. It was seriously damaged in the ensuing fire. The aircraft was moved by road to Coningsby on 13 September and placed into storage for almost three years while its future was decided. *(Peter R. March)*

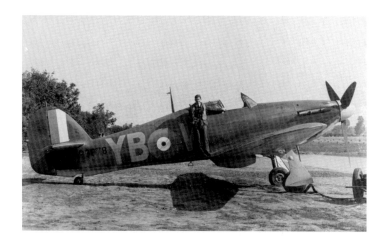

◁ Wartime image of Pilot Officer Denis Heathcote Wissler pictured with the 17 Squadron Hurricane, P3878/YB-W, at Debden in September 1940. This aircraft was lost on 24 September 1940 when, with Flying Officer Harold 'Birdy' Bird-Wilson at the controls, it crashed into the sea following an attack by a Me109. It later emerged that Bird-Wilson was Adolf Galland's 40th victim and fortunately, Bird-Wilson managed to bail out and was later rescued by a Royal Navy Motor Torpedo Boat (MTB). *(Crown Copyright/Air Historic Branch image reference H-1979)*

▷ In October 2005, LF363 went to ARC at Duxford for a repaint and an equalised maintenance programme. It emerged in March 2006 wearing the 17 Squadron code 'YB-W' representing a Hurricane 1 P3878 flown by Flying Officer Harold 'Birdy' Bird-Wilson who was awarded a DFC for his exploits after shooting down six enemy aircraft and sharing in the destruction of others. LF363 was photographed during a special air-to-air photoshoot close to the south-east coast in August 2012 while being flown by OC BBMF Sqn Ldr Ian 'Smithy' Smith. *(Keith Wilson)*

Hawker Hurricane Mk IIc PZ865

1944–68 Last Hurricane built at Langley in 1944 and retained by Hawkers. Registered G-AMAU in 1950.

1968–9 Took part in the filming of *Battle of Britain*.

1972–7 Presented to the BBMF at RAF Coltishall on 30 March 1972. Initially operated without a code, but was repainted as 'DT-A' of 257 (Burma) Squadron to represent a Hurricane I V6864 – the personal aircraft of Sqn Ldr R.R. 'Bob' Stanford Tuck from June 1940 to February 1941.

1978–81 Repainted as 'JU-Q' of 111 Squadron representing a Hurricane I aircraft from the period September 1939 to May 1941.

1982–8 Reverted to its post-war camouflage colour scheme without squadron codes, but had the title *The Last of the Many* repainted onto both sides of its fuselage.

1989–92 Repainted to represent an aircraft of No 303 (Polish) Squadron flown by Czech pilot Sgt Josef Frantsiek. The squadron was based at Northolt and Frantsiek was the highest scoring fighter pilot during the Battle of Britain with a total of 17 kills.

1993–7 Repainted in desert camouflage as 'J' of 261 Squadron to represent a Hurricane I P3731 which was one of the first 12 Hurricanes to be delivered to Malta by the aircraft carrier HMS *Argus* in Operation Hurry in September 1940.

1997–8 Major service.

1998–2004 Repainted as 'Q', a representative aircraft of 5 Squadron, SEAC.

2004–5 Major service at ARC.

2005–10 Repainted as 'JX-E' of 1(F) Squadron to represent Hurricane IIc BE581 *Night Reaper* as flown by the Czech fighter ace Flt Lt Karel Kuttelwascher during night intruder operations from Tangmere in 1942.

2010–13 From October 2010 to March 2013, PZ865 underwent a major maintenance at ARC, Duxford.

2013–current Repainted as 'EG-S' of 34 Squadron in a SEAC camouflage.

⋀ PZ865 rolled off the production line at Langley, Buckinghamshire, in 1944. It is the last Hurricane ever built and carried the inscription *The Last of the Many*. *(Courtesy of Peter R. March)*

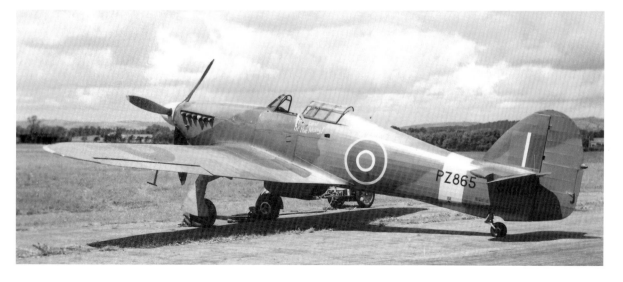

◁ In the 1960s, returned to wartime camouflage, PZ865 was used by Hawkers as a communications aircraft and a chase plane in the early P1127 trials. It also made a number of airshow appearances under the control of fighter pilot and test pilot Bill Bedford. PZ865 was presented to the BBMF at Coltishall in March 1972. It was photographed at Exeter in 1958. *(Peter R. March)*

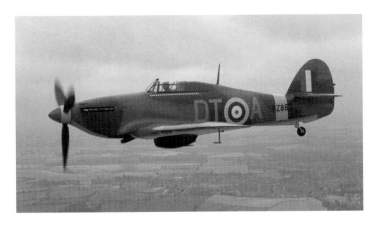

⋀ Initially, PZ865 operated with the Flight uncoded, retaining the
inscription *The Last of the Many*. In 1972 it was painted with the code
'DT-A' to represent a 257 Squadron Hurricane I V6864 from the period June
1940 to February 1941 – the personal aircraft of Sqn Ldr R.R. 'Bob' Stanford
Tuck. It was photographed during a flight from Coltishall on 31 July 1972.
(Crown Copyright/Air Historic Branch TN-1-6620-18)

⋀ Following a major servicing, PZ865 emerged in the colours of 'Q', a
representative aircraft of 5 Squadron, SEAC. No 5 Squadron is currently
resident with Typhoon aircraft at Coningsby where this photograph was
taken on 16 April 2003. *(Crown Copyright/RAF Coningsby Photographic Section)*

⋀ In 1978, the code letters on PZ865 were changed to 'JU-Q', to represent
a 111 Squadron Hurricane I aircraft from the period September 1939 to
May 1941. PZ865 was photographed at an Open Day at Hatfield aerodrome
in 1979. *(Keith Wilson)*

⋀ Following a major winter servicing in 2005, PZ865 emerged in a new
colour scheme representing Hurricane IIc BE581 *Night Reaper* as flown
by the Czech fighter ace Flt Lt Karel Kuttelwascher during night intruder
operations from Tangmere in 1942 with number 1(F) Squadron. The aircraft
was photographed during a sortie on 6 June 2007. *(Geoffrey Lee/Planefocus
GLD-072383)*

⋀ From 1982 to 1988, PZ865 reverted to its post-war colours, with *The Last
of the Many* inscribed on both sides of its fuselage. It was photographed
at Alconbury in 1984. *(Keith Wilson)*

⋀ At the end of the 2010 display season, PZ865 was due another major
maintenance and was flown to ARC at Duxford in November 2010. Initially,
it was hoped that the aircraft would be completed by the end of 2011 but
engineering issues caused delays and the aircraft made its first post-
restoration flight at Duxford on 27 March 2013, at the hands of Sqn Ldr
'Dunc' Mason, in South East Air Command colours to represent Hurricane
IIc HW840 of 34 Squadron, which wore the code 'EG-S'. *(Keith Wilson)*

Avro Lancaster B1 PA474

On 7 March 1954, PA474/M was transferred to the College of Aeronautics at Cranfield, where it was to be used for trials with several experimental aerofoil sections, including the Handley Page Laminar Flow Wing. In doing so, it effectively saved an airworthy Lancaster for the nation. It was photographed during a flight in 1963 with a Handley Page wing section above the fuselage. *(Crown Copyright/Air Historic Branch)*

In 1964, PA474's work at Cranfield was completed, the test aircraft being replaced with an Avro Lincoln. It was ferried to Wroughton and repainted in wartime camouflage colours. The aircraft was adopted by the Air Historical Branch with the intention of exhibiting it in the proposed RAF Museum. On 25 September 1964, the aircraft was flown to Henlow and entered storage for the new museum. It wasn't long before the CO of 44 (Rhodesia) Squadron, the first unit to be equipped with Lancasters, asked permission for PA474 to be transferred into its care. It was ferried to Waddington and repainted as 'KM-B', the markings of Sqn Ldr John Nettleton VC who carried out the low-level daylight raid on the MAN factory at Augsburg on 17 April 1942. PA474 was pictured during a flight from Waddington in September 1972. *(Crown Copyright/Air Historic Branch TN-1-6669-19)*

1944–65

Built by Vickers-Armstrong at Hawarden Airfield, Chester, on 31 May 1945, just after the war in Europe came to an end. PA474 was prepared for use against the Japanese as part of the Tiger Force. However, the war in the Far East ended before it was deployed and it did not take part in any hostilities. After a period in storage, PA474 was converted for photo-reconnaissance work; modifications for these duties included being stripped back to the bare metal. PA474 was loaned to Flight Refuelling Ltd at Tarrant Rushton to be used as a pilotless drone, an uncertain future. However, before the conversion started, the Air Ministry decided to use a Lincoln for the drone programme and PA474 was reprieved. It was transferred to the Royal College of Aeronautics at Cranfield where it was used as a trial platform for the testing of various experimental aerofoil sections between 1954 and 1964.

1965

After storage at Henlow, PA474 was moved into the care of 44 (Rhodesia) Squadron at Waddington, the first unit to be equipped with Lancasters. It was ferried to Waddington on 18 August. Shortly afterwards, it was decided to paint the aircraft as 'KM-B', the markings of Sqn Ldr John Nettleton who was awarded the Victoria Cross while carrying out the low-level daylight raid on the MAN factory at Augsburg on 17 April 1942.

1973–9

Joined the BBMF in November 1973 with 'City of Lincoln' titles and coat of arms applied to the front fuselage.

1980–3

At the end of the 1979 display season, PA474 was flown to Lyneham where it was repainted with the famous 'AJ-G' code of 617 Squadron's ED932. This was the Lancaster flown by Wg Cdr Guy Gibson VC DSO* DFC* during the Dam Busters raid of 16/17 May 1943.

1984–7

Having undergone a major servicing at St Athan over the winter of 1983/84, PA474 was repainted as 'SR-D' to represent an aircraft of 101 Squadron.

1988–92

PA474's next major service was contracted out to West Country Air Services at Exeter. When the aircraft returned to Coningsby in March 1988, it was wearing the 'PM-M²' code to represent ED888 while it was with 103 Squadron. During its service life with 103 and 576 Squadrons, ED888 completed 140 missions.

1994–9 Repainted after servicing at St Athan over the winter of 1993/4 as 'WS-J' of 9 Squadron to represent W4964, with the distinctive Johnnie Walker nose art and *Still Going Strong* wording – another centurion as W4964 also completed more than 100 operations.

2000–6 Following a scheduled maintenance at St Athan over the winter of 1999/2000, PA474 returned to Coningsby after being repainted as 'QR-M' of 61 Squadron, representing Lancaster III EE176, *Mickey the Moocher*. EE176 is thought to have flown between 115 and 128 operations. The Disney cartoon Mickey Mouse was painted onto the port forward fuselage of the aircraft.

2007–12 During the winter of 2006/7, PA474 underwent a major maintenance with Air Atlantique at Coventry. It emerged as the *Phantom of the Ruhr*. The aircraft was painted to represent Lancaster III, EE139, which operated with both 100 and 550 Squadrons, and flew a total of 121 operations. On the port side of the aircraft it carried the 100 Squadron code 'HW-R', with which the aircraft flew 30 operations, while on the starboard side it carried the 550 Squadron code 'BQ-B'. The Phantom artwork is not applied to the starboard side, instead it retains its 'City of Lincoln' wording and coat of arms.

2012–current In September 2012, PA474 was repainted at Eastern Airways, Humberside, to represent a Lancaster B1 DV385 of the famous 617 Squadron, with the code 'KC-A' applied. DV385 was delivered

△ **A rarely seen air-to-air shot looking down onto the upper flying surfaces of PA474/'KM-B' during the same sortie on 12 April 1975.** *(Crown Copyright/Air Historic Branch TN-1-7237-48)*

to 617 Squadron at Coningsby in November 1943. The nose art of PA474 is now *Thumper Mk III* (replacing *Phantom of the Ruhr* on the port side) and features a cartoon rabbit from the 1942 Walt Disney film *Bambi*, holding a foaming pint of beer, and is similar to that carried on DV385 during its time with 617 Squadron.

◁ **At the end of the 1979 display season PA474 was given the 'AJ-G' code of 617 Squadron's ED932, the Lancaster flown by Wg Cdr Guy Gibson during the Dam Busters raid of 16/17 May 1943. It was photographed in its new guise at Mildenhall in May 1980.** *(Keith Wilson)*

A After a major servicing at St Athan over the winter of 1983/84, PA474 was given the code 'SR-D' to represent an aircraft of 101 Squadron. It was photographed at Alconbury in 1984. *(Keith Wilson)*

A Flg Off A.E. Manning and his crew gather by their aircraft, Lancaster I, W4964/WS-J, of 9 Squadron shortly after their return to Bardney, Lincolnshire, in the early hours of 6 January 1944, after raiding Stettin, Germany. W4964 went on to complete 106 missions; its 100th saw it drop a giant Tallboy bomb on the German battleship *Tirpitz* on 15 September 1944. *(Crown Copyright/Air Historic Branch CH-11972)*

V In 2000, after another scheduled maintenance at St Athan, PA474 came back to Coningsby painted as *Mickey the Moocher*, representing a 61 Squadron Lancaster III EE176 with the code letters 'QR-M'. This image was taken during a BBMF photoshoot in May 2006. *(Geoffrey Lee/Planefocus GLD-061032)*

A PA474 on 16 March 1988, wearing the 'PM-M²' code to represent ED888 while it was with 103 Squadron. *(Crown Copyright/Air Historic Branch TN-2-275-2)*

A Repainted after servicing at St Athan over the winter of 1993/4, PA474 was to fly as 9 Squadron's W4964 with the code 'WS-J' and the distinctive Johnnie Walker nose art and *Still Going Strong* wording. It was representing another Lancaster centurion as W4964 also completed more than 100 operations. *(Peter R. March)*

◁ During the winter of 2006/7, PA474 underwent another major service, this time with Air Atlantique at Coventry where it was photographed in December 2006. The aircraft was to emerge from its service painted as *Phantom of the Ruhr*. (Peter R. March)

△ In September 2012, PA474 was repainted at Eastern Airways, Humberside, as a Lancaster B1 DV385 of 617 Squadron, with the code 'KC-A' applied. DV385 was delivered to 617 Squadron at Coningsby in November 1943. It was later fitted with bulged bomb-bay doors to accommodate the 12,000lb Tallboy bomb. It dropped a total of 15 Tallboys as well as five 12,000lb HC blast bombs. (Keith Wilson)

▷ The nose art of PA474 is now *Thumper Mk III* and features a cartoon rabbit from the 1942 Walt Disney cartoon *Bambi*, holding a foaming pint of beer. (Keith Wilson)

The *Phantom of the Ruhr* in flight along the south coast in August 2012. The starboard side of PA474 carries the 550 Squadron code 'BQ-B' and retains its 'City of Lincoln' wording and coat of arms. After being transferred from 100 to 550 Squadron, EE139 flew a further 91 operations. The port side of the aircraft carries the 100 Squadron code 'HW-R', with which it flew 30 operations. *(Keith Wilson)*

Douglas Dakota III ZA947

1943–69 Built as a C-47A Skytrain, 42-24338, at Long Beach, California, and delivered to the USAAF on 7 September 1943. Transferred to the Royal Canadian Air Force (RCAF) as '661'.

1970–92 Acquired by RAF with serial 'KG661'. Subsequently allocated ZA947. Operated with RAE at West Freugh and Farnborough (later, Defence Research Establishment).

1993–7 ZA947 was adopted by Strike Command and allocated to the BBMF in March 1993. After engineering and structural work by Air Atlantique at Coventry, the aircraft was flown to Marham for painting in the colours of Flt Lt David Lord's 271 Squadron aircraft 'YS-DM', KG374, in which he was awarded the Victoria Cross for his heroism and bravery during a supply drop to troops at Arnhem on 19 September 1944 that ultimately cost him his own life.

1998–2002 Following a minor service with Air Atlantique at Coventry during the winter of 1997/8, ZA947 was painted as a 77 Squadron Dakota 'YS-H' that participated in the Berlin Airlift, to celebrate the 50th anniversary of that event.

2003–8 Repainted in the livery of 267 'Pegasus' Squadron, which flew in the transport, trooping and resupply roles in the Middle East and the Mediterranean theatres during 1943/4. The squadron employed various colour schemes on its aircraft, but always displayed its 'Pegasus' emblem prominently on the aircraft's nose.

2011–12 Painted to represent Dakota FZ692 of 233 Squadron, around the D-Day period in 1944. This aircraft, named Kwicherbichen, was involved in para-dropping operations on the eve of D-Day and subsequently in resupply and casualty evacuation missions into and out of forward airfields in the combat areas.

◄ While operating with the Royal Aircraft Establishment, ZA947 was painted in the RAE's traditional red, white and blue 'raspberry ripple' colours. It was a welcome exhibit at the RIAT at Fairford in July 1985, carrying special stickers to its fuselage, wings and tail in celebration of the Dakota's 50 years in service. *(Keith Wilson)*

◄ The aircraft was adopted by Strike Command and allocated to the BBMF in March 1993. At Marham, ZA947 was painted in the colours of Flt Lt David Lord's 271 Squadron aircraft 'YS-DM', KG374, in which he was awarded the Victoria Cross for his heroic supply drop to troops at Arnhem on 19 September 1944. *(Geoffrey Lee/ Planefocus GL-951353)*

ʌ ZA947 is now painted to represent Dakota FZ692 of 233 Squadron, around D-Day in 1944. Named 'Kwicherbichen' by her crews, the aircraft carried out para-dropping operations on the eve of D-Day and casualty evacuation missions. The nurses who escorted the casualties on these flights become known as 'The Flying Nightingales'. *(Keith Wilson)*

ʌ During the winter of 1997/8, ZA947 was painted as a 77 Squadron Dakota 'YS-H' to mark the 50th anniversary of the Berlin Airlift. It appeared in the new colours at the RIAT in July 1998. *(Peter R. March)*

➢ In January 2003, ZA947 was repainted in the livery of 267 'Pegasus' Squadron, which flew in the transport, trooping and resupply roles in the Middle East and the Mediterranean theatres during 1943/4. The 'Pegasus' emblem is displayed on the aircraft's nose. *(Geoff Lee/Planefocus GLD-054545)*

De Havilland Canada DHC1 Chipmunk T10 WK518

1952–83	Built at Chester in January 1952 and delivered to the Royal Air Force College at Cranwell. Subsequently operated with a variety of RAF units.
1983	Arrived with the Flight in April 1983 in the standard RAF red and white training colours.
1994–9	Repainted in Royal Air Force College Cranwell silver and blue colour scheme.
2000–12	Repainted in the RAF's standard all-over black training colour scheme with white bars on wings and rear fuselage and identification letter 'K' added to the tail.
2012–current	Repainted in its former Hull University Air Squadron silver and orange Day-Glo colours with the identification letter 'C' on the tail.

Chipmunk T10 WK518/C resplendent in its Hull University Air Squadron colours over Lincolnshire on 13 December 2012, with Flt Lt Anthony 'Parky' Parkinson at the controls. *(Keith Wilson)*

De Havilland Canada DHC1 Chipmunk T10 WG486

1952–83	Built at Chester in January 1952 and delivered to 5 Basic Flying Training School. Subsequently operated with a variety of RAF units.
1995–99	Arrived with the Flight in 1995, in its all-over grey operational paint scheme from its time at the Gatow Station Flight.
2000–current	Repainted in the RAF's standard all-over black training colour scheme with white bars on wings and rear fuselage and identification letter 'G' added to the tail.

The two Chipmunks operated by the BBMF are the last of the type in RAF service; they are also the least-seen of the Flight's aircraft. They are used all year round primarily for the conversion and continuation training of BBMF pilots on tail-wheel aircraft. Chipmunk T10 WK518/C has been painted in Hull University Air Squadron colours while WG486 was repainted in the all-over black with white fuselage band and wing strips as utilised with RAF training aircraft. The code letter 'G' was also added. They were captured maintaining perfect formation over Lincolnshire on 13 December 2012, with Flt Lt Anthony 'Parky' Parkinson and Wg Cdr Paul 'Godders' Godfrey at the controls respectively. *(Keith Wilson)*

In 2000 WK518 was repainted in the RAF all-over black training colour scheme with the code 'K' added to the tail and was photographed in formation with the Flight's other Chipmunk, WG486/G, on 24 May 2006. *(Crown Copyright/SAC Barbara Robinson)*

In June 1995, the Flight gained a second Chipmunk. Having previously served in an 'operational' role at Gatow, Berlin, during the Cold War, WG486 was delivered to the Flight in a rather plain colour scheme. It was photographed in June 1996. *(Peter R. March)*

Chipmunk T10 WG486/G during a photoshoot over Lincolnshire on 13 December 2012, with Wg Cdr Paul 'Godders' Godfrey at the controls. *(Keith Wilson)*

The BBMF Team gathered together at the end of the Lincolnshire Lancaster Association Members' Day at Coningsby on 30 September 2012. The photograph was taken shortly after OC BBMF Sqn Ldr Ian 'Smithy' Smith had made his last display flight in Spitfire PR XIX PM631. The event also marked a farewell to the Flight's SEngO, WO Dave Marshall and to the Station Commander, Gp Capt 'Sammy' Sampson DSO. *(Keith Wilson)*

the People

The People

When the Historic Aircraft Flight was officially formed at Biggin Hill on 11 July 1957 it had no commanding officer, no maintenance staff and no public funding for either fuel or maintenance costs. All manpower for the Flight would have to be provided on a purely volunteer basis. A rather inauspicious start for what has grown to become one of the world's foremost airworthy historic aircraft collections and a household name in the UK.

At the very outset, the main driving force behind the idea of forming what he thought of as the 'Battle of Britain Flight' was Wg Cdr Peter Thompson DFC. At the time he was Station Commander at Biggin Hill and had a single Hurricane of the Station Flight's strength.

➤ **OC BBMF 2009–2012, Sqn Ldr Ian 'Smithy' Smith, at the controls of Hurricane IIb LF363/YT-W, along the south-east coast near Manston on 11 August 2012.** *(Keith Wilson)*

When Thompson needed help to get the fledgling Flight off the ground he called upon Sqn Ldr E.H. Sowden, who was then OC Engineering at Biggin Hill. It was Sqn Ldr Sowden, working with a small volunteer engineering team that got the first Spitfire aircraft of the Flight into an airworthy condition. In February 1958, Thompson was promoted to Group Captain and posted to America, well away from Biggin Hill and his treasured Flight. As a consequence, he lost direct contact with the Flight and was kept up to date with news on the grapevine.

In September 1998, Thompson accepted an invitation to visit the BBMF at Coningsby and received a very warm welcome. His final RAF appointment was as Air Attaché at the British Embassy in

Lima, Peru. After retirement, he settled with his family in Menorca. Thompson died on 2 March 2003, aged 82.

After Thompson left Biggin Hill in 1958, a steady stream of volunteer and full-time individuals have worked at various RAF stations across the country, with a variety of aircraft, to keep his dream a reality. In 2013, thanks to the work and dedication of so many, that reality is a household name – the RAF Battle of Britain Memorial Flight.

While the aircraft may be the stars of the BBMF, it is the people that ensure they are seen by so many throughout the year; and it is not just the fighter and bomber pilots that make things happen, the BBMF Engineering Team have a massive part to play in keeping the aircraft in the air.

Officer Commanding BBMF

On 30 September 2012, at around 15:30hrs, Sqn Ldr Ian 'Smithy' Smith landed back at Coningsby in Spitfire PR XIX PM631 and taxied to the BBMF ramp after his display during the Lincolnshire Lancaster Association Members' Day at Coningsby. It was a poignant moment as it represented Smithy's last flight as Officer Commanding BBMF, a role he had served for three years after almost seven years in total with the Flight.

Smith has flown the BBMF fighters since 2006 and completed four seasons as a volunteer fighter pilot, pre-selected to take over as OC BBMF, before actually taking command of the Flight in November 2009.

The new OC BBMF, who assumed command of the Flight at the beginning of October 2012, Sqn Ldr 'Dunc' Mason. He is seen at the controls of Spitfire PR XIX, along the south-east coast near Manston on 11 August 2012, ahead of his display at Eastbourne. *(Keith Wilson)*

Sqn Ldr 'Dunc' Mason, OC BBMF. *(Crown Copyright/SAC Graham Taylor)*

As Officer Commanding the BBMF, he was responsible for overseeing all the operations, administration and engineering functions, and for the overall planning and management of the display programme undertaken by the Flight each year. He was also responsible for training the BBMF fighter pilots and for conducting air tests on all the BBMF fighter aircraft.

Soon after completing that memorable flight on 30 September 2012, a short ceremony was held where the reins were handed over to the then OC BBMF designate, Sqn Ldr Duncan 'Dunc' Mason.

Mason joined the Royal Air Force in 1991 and after flying training completed tours on No 3(F) Squadron at Laarbruch on the Harrier GR7 and 19(F) Squadron at RAF Valley as a Flying and Weapons Instructor on the Hawk T1. Mason was selected to join the Red Arrows where he flew as Red 3 (2003), Red 5 (2004) and Red 9 (2005). He was then posted back to the Harrier as a Flight Commander on No 1(F) Squadron and later to 800 Naval Air Squadron, both based at Cottesmore. Mason undertook operations in the Balkans and Afghanistan with the Harrier GR9.

Why did Dunc choose the BBMF?

'*I joined the RAF because of the people who had flown the Spitfires and Hurricanes. When I was an Air Cadet at 13 years old, I read all the books I could find on the Spitfire, Hurricane, Lancaster and Mosquito. As a teenager, I got my glider pilot licence with the Royal Navy FAA Officer Association. Then I joined the Air Force and the first aircraft I flew was a Chipmunk at RAF Abingdon. It was a childhood dream to fly the Spitfire and Hurricane and I'm sure it was in my blood all along.*'

Which is Mason's favourite aircraft on the Flight?

'*They all have their own characteristics but Spitfire AB910 has a special place in my heart as it was the first Spitfire that I flew.*'

BBMF's Administration Officer/Adjutant from June 2012, Flt Lt Anthony 'Parky' Parkinson MBE, in the cockpit of Spitfire AB910/MD-E waiting for engine start ahead of the Flight's display slot at the RIAT on Sunday 8 July 2012. *(Keith Wilson)*

The BBMF's new OC-designate, Sqn Ldr Andy 'Milli' Millikin, in Spitfire IIa P7350/EB-G shortly after Milli had completed his first flight in the aircraft at Coningsby on 4 September 2012. *(Keith Wilson)*

First flights in the BBMF fighter aircraft are usually celebrated with a bottle of vintage Champagne! On 8 September 2011 Station Commander Gp Capt 'Sammy' Sampson DSO (centre) made his first flight in Hurricane LF363/YT-W at Coningsby under the watchful eye of Sqn Ldr Ian 'Smithy' Smith, the Flight's OC (left) and Flt Lt Anthony 'Parky' Parkinson MBE (right). *(Crown Copyright/SAC Insley)*

This system of succession for the post of OC BBMF, which will now continue into the future, ensures that each new 'Boss' gains the necessary experience before taking command of the Flight for a three-year tour.

Sqn Ldr Andy 'Milli' Millikin was OC Requirements Capture at the Typhoon Missions Support Centre at RAF Coningsby when he saw the Transfer Signal for the post of OC BBMF Designate being advertised. Millikin was 38 years old at the time and having reached pensionable age was preparing to retire from the Air Force. In order

to apply for the post, he requested, and achieved, an extension to his service period so he could attend the interviews and undertake the flight tests. He was subsequently offered the job. 'It was a bit like doing X-Factor,' Millikin recalled. Initially, the post is a four-year volunteer posting with the Flight as a secondary RAF duty, followed by the three-year tenure that the post offers.

His current post at Coningsby is non-flying but he continues to fly the Typhoon across the Coningsby squadrons as both front-line squadrons as well as the OCU are relatively short of people. He

◁ **Another Champagne moment! Sqn Ldr Andy 'Milli' Millikin made his first flight in Hurricane LF363/YT-W at Coningsby on 2 April 2012. His 'welcoming committee' consisted of, left to right: Flt Lt Anthony 'Parky' Parkinson MBE, Sqn Ldr Ian 'Smithy' Smith, Sqn Ldr 'Dunc' Mason and Wg Cdr Paul 'Godders' Godfrey.** *(Crown Copyright/SAC Graham Taylor)*

▷ **Three of the bomber pilots for 2013 in front of Lancaster PA474** *Thumper Mk III***, on 30 September 2012. Left to right: Flt Lt Roger Nichols, Flt Lt Tim Dunlop and Flt Lt Loz Rushmere.** *(Crown Copyright/Sgt Pete Mobbs)*

volunteers for and is a regular participant in QRAs (Quick Readiness Alerts) when two Typhoon jets are on constant stand-by to deal with the possible problem of a renegade airliner or a threat from the East.

Milli's grandfather, father and brother have all served as pilots in the RAF. His father, Paul Millikin, is remembered as the Vulcan Display Pilot.

Having starting flying at the age of 16 at the Marham Gliding Club, Milli flew fixed-wing aircraft at RAF Newton with the Combined Cadet Force (CCF) on the venerable Chipmunk and was awarded a Flying Scholarship at Cambridge Airport, which he completed on Cessna 152 aircraft. He went to Southampton University and joined the University Air Squadron (UAS) where he flew Bulldog aircraft.

After leaving university, he joined the Royal Air Force and was posted to the Elementary Flying Training Squadron at Barkstone Heath, flying Slingsby Firefly aircraft. Next stop was training on the Tucano at RAF Linton-on-Ouse before a short holding period at 100 Squadron. Following some refresher flying on the Tucano at Linton-on-Ouse, he moved to RAF Valley and the Hawk T1 to complete his flying training.

A spell at RAF Lossiemouth on the Jaguar OCU was followed by his first operational tour, with No 6 Squadron at Coltishall. Here he flew on operations over Iraq to protect the Kurds from attack by Saddam Hussein. Next stop was the Qualified Weapons Instructor course at 16 Squadron, which he completed in 2003 before joining 54 Squadron as a Qualified Instructor (QI). In total, Millikin accrued over 1,200 hours on the Jaguar.

In 2005, Millikin crossed over to the Typhoon on 17 Squadron and was involved in the operational development of the aircraft, specialising in its capability as a strike platform. He was promoted to a Qualified Pilot Instructor and posted to 29 (R) Squadron – the Tornado OCU – teaching both RAF and Saudi pilots to fly the Typhoon. He also

ran the first Typhoon Qualified Weapons Instructor course. Because of his strike experience, he was detached to 11 Squadron in the summer of 2011 flying the Typhoon on operations over Libya.

What has been the highlight of his career so far? 'I intercepted a couple of Russian Bears on a QRA in April 2011 and did three months in Italy operating over Libya. It has only been the last six months of my career that has seen any real action!'

Which is Millikin's favourite aircraft on the Flight? 'I'm not sure I've really had time to decide, but it's either the Spitfire IIa or the Mark Vb – only time will tell!'

Why did Millikin apply to join the BBMF?

'For me, the Flight has four major themes – Display, Ceremonial, Commemorative and Historic, but the most important is Commemorative. We owe so many people a debt of gratitude. The next generation may not understand the relevance of the Flight and so we must continue to ensure that people who have lost their lives continue to be recognised and commemorated.'

In addition to Smithy, Dunc and Milli, the fighter pilots on the Flight's strength in 2012 also included the Coningsby Station Commander, Gp Capt Martin 'Sammy' Sampson DSO, and the OC Operations Wing at Coningsby, Wg Cdr Paul 'Godders' Godfrey – both roles having the secondary duty of flying the fighters with the BBMF. The final member of the team is Flt Lt Anthony 'Parky' Parkinson MBE, who joined the Flight as a volunteer fighter pilot in 2008 and in May 2012 was appointed to the BBMF on a full-time basis as the Flight's Operations Officer and Adjutant (more later).

Flt Lt Tim 'Twigs' Dunlop at the controls of Lancaster PA474 *Phantom of the Ruhr*, just ahead of the display at Eastbourne on 11 August 2012. The year 2012 was Twigs's fourth season as a Dakota captain and his first as a Lancaster captain. (*Keith Wilson*)

Five of the BBMF's Navigators at Coningsby on 24 April 2012, shortly after the award of the Flight's Public Display Authority (PDA). Left to right: Sqn Ldr Tony 'Sluf' Beresford, Flt Lt Alun Pepper, Flt Lt James 'Big Jim' Furness, Sqn Ldr William 'Russ' Russell (Navigator Leader) and Flt Lt Ady Hargreaves. (*Keith Wilson*)

◁ Three of the BBMF's Dakota Loadmasters at Coningsby shortly after the award of the PDA on 20 April 2012. Left to right: Flt Sgt Ian Handford, Flt Sgt Paul Simmons and MACR Andy Whelan. (Keith Wilson)

∧ The 2013 team of Flight Engineers at Coningsby on 30 September 2012. Left to right: MACR Archie Moffat, MACR Gav Ovendon, Flt Sgt Jon Crisp, Flt Sgt Martin Blythe (Air Engineer Leader 2013) and Flt Sgt Mark Fellowes. (Crown Copyright)

◄ The 2013 BBMF Engineering Team at Coningsby on 30 September, with the SEngO, WO Kevin Ball, at the front. *(Crown Copyright/Sgt Pete Mobbs)*

➤ The Dakota crew after a display sortie at Coningsby on 30 September 2012. Left to right: Sqn Ldr Tony 'Sluf' Beresford (Navigator), Flt Lt Rich Gibby, Flt Lt Loz Rushmere (Captain) and Flt Sgt Ian Handford. *(Keith Wilson)*

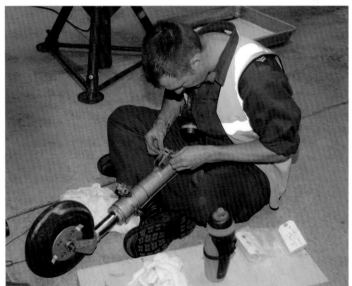

◄ One of the key members of the Flight is Chief Technician Paul Blackah MBE, the BBMF's Airframe Specialist and Engineering Controller. Paul joined the Flight's Engineering Team in 1993 and 2013 will be his 19th season with the Flight. In addition to his duties with the BBMF, Paul has co-authored the *Lancaster*, *Spitfire*, *Bf109*, *Hurricane* and *Dakota Manuals* for Haynes Publishing. *(Crown Copyright/Cpl Andrew Seaward)*

⋀ Cpl Matt Thompson completes some routine maintenance work on the tail wheel of Spitfire PR XIX PS915 at Coningsby on 11 June 2012. *(Keith Wilson)*

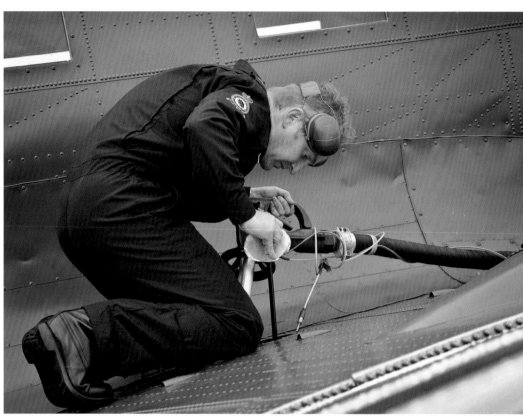

⋏ SAC(T) Daz Bell works on Spitfire IIa P7350 at Coningsby on 30 September 2012, ahead of its display during the Lincolnshire Lancaster Association Members' Day. *(Crown Copyright/Cpl Paul Robertshaw)*

⋏ Cpl Kev 'Fruitbat' Harnett refuelling Dakota ZA947 at Coningsby on 30 September 2012, ahead of its display during the Lincolnshire Lancaster Association Members' Day. *(Crown Copyright/Sgt Pete Mobbs)*

⋏ After landing and shutdown at Fairford on 8 July 2012, SAC Pete Harrison checks the security of all the panels and inspection hatches on Spitfire Mk Vb AB910. *(Keith Wilson)*

➤ Cpl Kev 'Fruitbat' Harnett working on the main undercarriage leg of Hurricane LF363/YT-W at Coningsby on 11 June 2012. *(Keith Wilson)*

With a final wave to the control tower, Smithy taxies out to the runway to start his final display flight in Spitfire Mk XIX, PM631, at the Lincolnshire Lancaster Association Members' Day on 30 September 2012. *(Crown Copyright)*

When the wind is strong, it is not unusual to place a couple of crewmembers on the tail of the Spitfire to keep it down during engine start-up, checks and, occasionally, taxiing too. At Coningsby on 30 September 2012, just before Smithy's last display flight, both Parky and Dunc provided the necessary ballast to the back of PM631. *(Crown Copyright/Sgt Pete Mobbs)*

Almost time to start. Cpl Richie Kear helps Smithy strap into Spitfire IIa P7350 at Fairford on 8 July 2012. *(Keith Wilson)*

At the end of his final display flight, Smithy leaped from the cockpit of Spitfire Mk XIX PM631. *(Keith Wilson)*

After seven years with the BBMF, the last three as Officer Commanding, Sqn Ldr Ian 'Smithy' Smith celebrates his last display flight on 30 September 2012, with a glass of Champagne, in the company of the Flight's new OC, Sqn Ldr Duncan Mason. *(Keith Wilson)*

The event saw seven key members of the BBMF Engineering Team take their leave of the Flight. Left to right: SengO WO Dave Marshall, Cpl Paul 'Bella' Macluskey, Cpl Kevin 'Fruitbat' Harnett, SAC(T) Phil Sprott, Cpl 'Lingy' Lingwood, SAC(T) Ed Cash and Junior Technician Ben Jones (Coningsby, 30 September 2012). *(Keith Wilson)*

A fond farewell to the Flight toasted with Champagne. For the Coningsby Station Commander, Gp Capt Sammy Sampson DSO and SEngO, WO Dave Marshall, the Lincolnshire Lancaster Association Members' Day was the last BBMF event for both of them. *(Keith Wilson)*

Supporting charities

The Battle of Britain Memorial Flight supports a variety of charities including the Royal Air Forces Association (RAFA), The Flying Scholarship for the Disabled, The Jon Egging Trust and the St Barnabas Lincolnshire Hospice.

In October 2011, at the end of the flying display season, Sqn Ldr 'Dunc' Mason organised the '400in4', a 400-mile (644km) cycle ride in four days, from St David's Head in Wales to Lowestoft in Suffolk. Members of the BBMF were joined by members of both the Red

Arrows and Blades formation display teams, as well as individuals from the fly2help charity, BAe Systems and Rolls-Royce. Each rider had to be sponsored for a minimum of £500 and it had been hoped that at least £50,000 would be raised – the amount to be equally split between the RAFA and the fly2help scheme.

One of the riders due to participate was Flt Lt Jon Egging but, sadly, Jon was killed when his Red Arrows Hawk crashed near Bournemouth on 20 August 2011. His place in the '400in4' event was taken by his wife, Dr Emma Egging, who completed the gruelling trip in his memory. Once the sponsorship pledges had been collected and counted, £95,000 had been raised: £25,000 each was donated to RAFA and fly2help, and the £45,000 surplus went to The Jon Egging Trust.

The next big charity event organised by Dunc Mason was the Lands End to John O'Groats Cycle Ride in June 2012. This time, Mason was supported by BBMF Lancaster pilot Flt Lt Tim 'Twigs' Dunlop as well as Emma and Luke Egging, wife and brother of the late Jon Egging, and Brian Jones from fly2help. On this event, the group of riders was raising money for The Jon Egging Trust, St Barnabas Lincolnshire Hospice and fly2help. The 1,009 miles (1,624km) were covered by the team in just 13 days and more than £20,000 was raised.

In December 2012, some members of the BBMF chose to spend their holiday walking along Hadrian's Wall, raising money for the care of people with multiple myeloma, a relatively rare cancer that starts in the bone marrow. Wg Cdr Fin Monahan, OC Operations Wing at RAF Leeming, was diagnosed with multiple myeloma three years ago and following treatment at the Royal Marsden Hospital is now in remission and continuing his Air Force career. Monahan joined the Flight's current OC BBMF Dunc Mason and former OC Sqn Ldr Ian 'Smithy' Smith, along with OC Ops Wing at Coningsby, Wg Cdr Paul 'Godders' Godfrey, and Gp Capt Tony Innes, the OC Ops Wing at RAF Leeming. The 84-mile (135km) walk took place over four days and the funds raised were divided between the Willow Foundation, Myeloma UK and The Royal Marsden Cancer Charity.

For such a small but dedicated group of people to work as closely together as they do, and to achieve what they do, on a regular basis, the BBMF demonstrates an incredible level of teamwork. Clearly, it is a case that the whole is very much greater than the sum of the parts.

⋀ **The LEJOG 2012 Cycle Challenge. On 31 May 2012, five riders set off from Lands End to ride to John O'Groats, the route taking them over 1,000 miles. The riders included two BBMF pilots: Sqn Ldr 'Dunc' Mason (far left) and Flt Lt Tim 'Twigs' Dunlop (second from right). They were joined on the trip by Dr Emma Egging (second from left), the widow of Jon Egging who was sadly lost when his Red Arrows Hawk crashed after a display at Bournemouth Airshow in August 2011; Luke Egging (centre), Jon's brother; and Brian Jones (far right) from the fly2help charity. In the front of the picture is Cpl Paul 'Bella' Macluskey – the indispensable support driver.** *(Via Dunc Mason)*

⋁ **Despite the often appalling weather, all five riders on the LEJOG 2012 Cycle Challenge made it to John O'Groats in just 13 days and raised around £20,000 for their chosen charities: The Jon Egging Trust, St Barnabas Lincolnshire Hospice and fly2help.** *(Via Dunc Mason)*

▼ Probably the most popular BBMF performer is the Avro Lancaster B1 PA474, seen here in 100 Squadron colours as the *Phantom of the Ruhr*. The sound of four Rolls-Royce Merlin engines in formation is something very special. *(Keith Wilson)*

the Programme

Ask most people to describe their experiences of the BBMF displays and they will almost certainly talk about the beautiful formation of Lancaster, Spitfire and Hurricane (even though it may have been two Spitfires). They may also mention the wonderful noise that the powerful Rolls-Royce Merlin engines make (although one of the aircraft may have actually been powered by a Griffon engine). Most will also add just how they actually felt at the time – a 'feeling' that most other display items do not produce. It is quite amazing the different ways that different people actually feel about the BBMF.

During the course of the display season, most people get to see the hallmark Lancaster, Spitfire and Hurricane display that usually opens with a three-ship formation arrival from behind the crowd centre. After a few three-ship formation passes along the crowd line, the aircraft separate and hold 'crowd rear', while an individual or pair of aircraft then display. Often, the Spitfire takes centre stage and performs a series of passes, including low-g vertical climb manoeuvres not available to the Hurricane. With a 2,500ft (762m) cloud base or better, the Hurricane can perform a series of Derry Turns, but if the cloud base is less than 2,500ft, both aircraft will perform a similar low-level display. Then, the Lancaster takes centre stage for its display. This usually consists of a series of 360° turns in front of the crowd line while demonstrating both the undercarriage retraction sequence as well as the cavernous bomb bay. With individual displays completed the formation re-forms before performing another couple of three-ship formation fly-bys along the crowd line.

If the Lancaster is unavailable due to serviceability issues, the Dakota can take its place, although the Dakota's slower speeds make the three-ship formation more difficult to fly. Thankfully, the Lancaster's excellent serviceability record ensures that the Dakota, Spitfire and Hurricane routine is rarely seen.

◁ For most BBMF displays, when the Flight is performing a three-ship routine of Lancaster, Spitfire and Hurricane, it is usual for the formation to arrive at a display from behind the crowd, as seen here during the practice PDA at Coningsby on 20 April 2012. (Keith Wilson)

⋀ Before the Lancaster separates from the fighters, the three-ship formation performs a series of passes along the crowd line. The roar of six Rolls-Royce Merlin engines in formation is phenomenal. *(Keith Wilson)*

⋁ To celebrate the 50th anniversary of the BBMF, a special formation was organised at Duxford on 5 May 2007 comprising the Lancaster, five Spitfires and two Hurricanes. Nine Rolls-Royce Merlin engines and two Griffons in formation – what a very special sound that must have been. *(Peter R. March)*

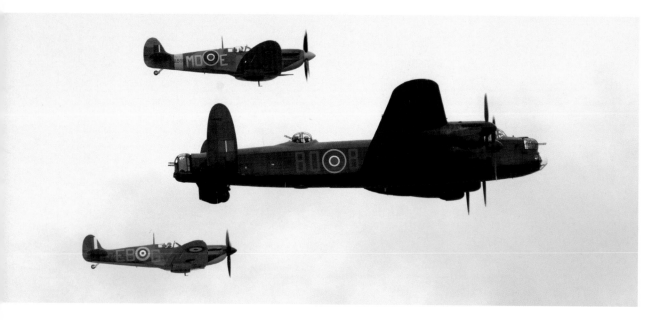

◁ **At the RIAT at Fairford on 8 July 2012, the fighters comprise a pair of Spitfires – Mk IIa P7350/EB-G and Mk Vb AB910/MD-E. After the three-ship formation passes, the fighters break away and perform their Synchro routine to great effect.** *(Keith Wilson)*

➤ **Another view of the Tail Chase routine at Coningsby on 24 April 2012. It provides good photo opportunities for the photographers in the audience.** *(Keith Wilson)*

Fighter displays

The fighters are able to perform a variety of routines. Aside from them performing individually, as Singles, the Tail Chase is exactly what it says: the Spitfire and Hurricane, or a pair of Spitfires, following each other around the sky, one behind the other. It provides the viewing spectators with some great formation flying and photo opportunities, as well as the sound of two Rolls-Royce Merlin engines growling around the sky together. The final fighter option is the Synchro, when the two fighters fly a series of opposition manoeuvres including some crossovers, like the Red Arrows and other jet-formation display teams.

One advantage for both the Synchro and Tail Chase routines is that they can be flown with two Spitfires. However, for each of these routines, both pilots must be current on that particular show sequence, whereas with the Singles routine both pilots only have to be current in the particular aircraft they are flying on the day.

In 2012, the Synchro was flown to great effect at both the Waddington Air Show in June and the Royal International Air Tattoo (RIAT) at Fairford in July. On each occasion the routine was flown impeccably by OC BBMF Sqn Ldr Ian 'Smithy' Smith and Flt Lt Anthony 'Parky' Parkinson – a display that both of them clearly

➤ **When the fighters perform the Tail Chase routine, it is exactly as described: one fighter chasing the other around the skies during a variety of elegant manoeuvres designed to showcase both aircraft to good effect. The Hurricane IIb LF363 and Spitfire IIa P7350 perform the routine during the PDA examination at Coningsby on 24 April 2012.** *(Keith Wilson)*

⋏ When the Synchro routine is displayed, both aircraft fly a series of opposition manoeuvres, much like the Red Arrows or other jet display teams use to good effect. Once again, it provides the photographers in the audience with great photo opportunities although you have to be sharp to press the shutter at the correct moment. (Keith Wilson)

⬋ During this Spitfire and Hurricane formation pass, as part of the Synchro routine during the PDA examination at Coningsby on 24 April 2012, it appears from the pilots' helmets that the Hurricane (flown by Sqn Ldr 'Dunc' Mason) is keeping a careful station on the Spitfire IIa (flown by Flt Lt Anthony 'Parky' Parkinson). (Keith Wilson)

The most commonly flown fighter routine is when both aircraft take it in turns to perform a series of solo manoeuvres, shown here to good effect by Flt Lt Anthony 'Parky' Parkinson in Spitfire Mk Vb AB910/MD-E. *(Keith Wilson)*

A Synchro routine was also flown at Fairford on 8 July 2012, by Spitfire Mk IIa P7350/EB-G (OC BBMF Sqn Ldr Ian 'Smithy' Smith) and Spitfire Mk Vb AB910/MD-E (Flt Lt Anthony 'Parky' Parkinson), where they are seen to be just about to pass across each other. *(Keith Wilson)*

It is normal for the fighter pair to take off in formation, ahead of their routine, as seen with Wg Cdr Paul 'Godders' Godfrey in Spitfire Mk Vb AB910/MD-E and Gp Capt 'Sammy' Sampson in LFIXe MK356/UF-Q on departure from Coningsby on 24 July 2012 during the PDA examination. *(Keith Wilson)*

enjoyed, and it showed. With both fighter pilots employed on a full-time basis with the Flight, it was a little easier for them to maintain currency on the routine.

While the 2012 display season was Parky's seventh with the Flight, it was his first in the admin role which provided him with a new perspective of the operation: 'Despite it being something of a difficult year with the often inclement weather, we flew an amazing array of different displays so we were able to offer lots across the season,' he said. On the question of serviceability he added, 'The Spitfires were absolutely amazing for serviceability. We achieved an 85% success

rate for the year, and after removing weather issues, the Spitfire had a 99% success rate.'

The Hurricanes are only allowed 120 hours per year combined. With PZ865 undergoing a major maintenance with the Aircraft Restoration Company at Duxford, the Flight did not want to put 228 hours on LF363 in 2011 and 2012 combined. It was flown hard in 2011 but achieved around only 60 hours in 2012; although it did have a few overheating issues during the season. Thankfully, PZ865 should be back with the Flight for the 2013 season so that LF363 can have a slightly easier time of things.

◁ During the course of its solo display routine, the Lancaster will usually offer the photographers in the crowd an opportunity to shoot the top side of the aircraft, as seen at the BBC *Children in Need* Airshow at Little Gransden on 26 August 2012. This manoeuvre was easier at Little Gransden as the display had a two-direction axis creating a natural turn towards the crowd for the Lancaster. *(Keith Wilson)*

Bomber displays

Both the Lancaster and Dakota display sequences differ from the fighters in that they are able to complete their display from either 'crowd left' to 'crowd right' or 'crowd right' to 'crowd left', regardless of how the display started. On the other hand, the fighters always finish their display from 'crowd left' to 'crowd right'. In other words, spectators see the fighters complete their display sequence from left to right only. The completion direction is driven by factors such as the runway in use, as is the case if performing a break downwind to land after the display. Otherwise, the completion direction is dictated either by display venue restrictions or, more usually, by the departure route to the next venue. Flying hours are a precious commodity and the cumulative effect of

minutes spent unnecessarily repositioning after a display can have a significant impact on flying hours' consumption for the season.

In a two- or three-aircraft display, the fighters normally display first with either the Lancaster or Dakota concluding the display routine. The Dakota is considerably slower than the fighters and it is not usual for the Dakota to be seen in close formation with them. Usually, the Dakota will depart for the display venue some time ahead of the faster fighters, which will, in turn, catch up and rendezvous with the Dakota at the venue. When the fighters start their display, the Dakota positions itself to hold 'crowd rear'. On completion of the Dakota display, rather than join in close formation, the fighters will 'tail chase' the Dakota on its final pass along the display line before the three

∧ A nice low pass from the Lancaster, right along the crowd line, flown by Bomber Leader Flt Lt Ernie Taylor at the RIAT Fairford on 8 July 2012... *(Keith Wilson)*

➤ ... before the aircraft turned away from the crowd and started to open the bomb bay doors. *(Keith Wilson)*

aircraft either break downwind to land or, if departing, separate and continue to the next venue or return to base individually.

The Lancaster is capable of both greater acceleration and higher speed than the Dakota, so it is more usual to see the fighters and the Lancaster arrive and depart from display venues together as three aircraft in close formation; normally for 2012, this was from 'crowd rear'. The Lancaster will lead the formation through a pre-briefed sequence of manoeuvres and position for the fighters to 'break' and commence their individual or two-ship routines.

The Lancaster pilot monitors the fighter display(s) from 'crowd rear' carefully and, knowing both the content and approximate duration of the fighter display sequence, anticipates the 'one minute' call to position the aircraft for the takeover. Then he moves the Lancaster into position and commences a series of passes designed to show all the aspects of the aircraft, including the cavernous bomb bay and its sturdy undercarriage – along with the spectacular sound of four Rolls-Royce Merlin engines operating in close formation.

↑ **Two images of the Lancaster, demonstrating its cavernous open bomb bay. The first is as the aircraft flies along the crowd line at the BBC *Children in Need* Airshow at Little Gransden on 26 August 2012.** *(Oliver Wilson)*

➤ **The second is as the Lancaster turns away from the crowd and starts to close the bomb bay doors.** *(Oliver Wilson)*

The Lancaster performs a slow, gear and flaps down, flypast of the crowd line at Little Gransden on 26 August 2012... *(Keith Wilson)*

... before it banks gently away from the crowd line and starts to retract the flaps and undercarriage, adding power to the four Merlin engines as it does so, producing a wonderful roar towards the crowd. *(Oliver Wilson)*

The Lancaster cockpit, as viewed over the right shoulder of the Navigator during the run-in to a display. Also visible are the shoulders of the Co-pilot and Air Engineer in the rather cramped confines of the cockpit. *(Crown Copyright/SAC Dan Herrick)*

The final pass for the Lancaster at Little Gransden on 26 August provided the photographers with another nice top-side pass as the aircraft manoeuvred around the split display axis. *(Keith Wilson)*

◄ Despite the aircraft's obvious appeal, it can be something of a handful to fly, especially during crosswind landings. At the Mildenhall Air Show in 1992, the aircraft left the runway and the stresses can be seen in the port-side main undercarriage. (EJ Van Koningsveld)

◄ The aircraft continued across the grass, heading towards the crowd line... (EJ Van Koningsveld)

◄ ... with the pilot still trying to get the aircraft under control. (EJ Van Koningsveld)

The pilot managed to turn the aircraft away from the crowd line and bring it back under control although the stresses and strains are still apparent on the Lancaster main undercarriage. Clearly, the crowd is not as close as it appears as the images were shot with a long telephoto lens. (EJ Van Koningsveld)

The aircraft was brought under control and safely stopped. After shutdown, the Lancaster was carefully examined and showed no signs of damage. (EJ Van Koningsveld)

△ The BBMF Dakota ZA947 taxiing past the Coningsby control tower at the start of an engineering flight test on 30 September 2012. The side door is open and the Air Loadmaster is standing by the doorway – a normal procedure for displays with this aircraft. *(Keith Wilson)*

∇ A nice view of the Dakota undersides and invasion stripes on this pass at RAF Coningsby on 16 May 2012. *(Keith Wilson)*

△ An undercarriage and flaps-down pass by the Dakota. The port-side undercarriage leg is just starting to retract, moments ahead of the starboard side. The Air Loadmaster, Flt Sgt Paul Simmons, can just be seen in the open doorway during this pass at Coningsby during the PDA examination on 24 April 2012. *(Keith Wilson)*

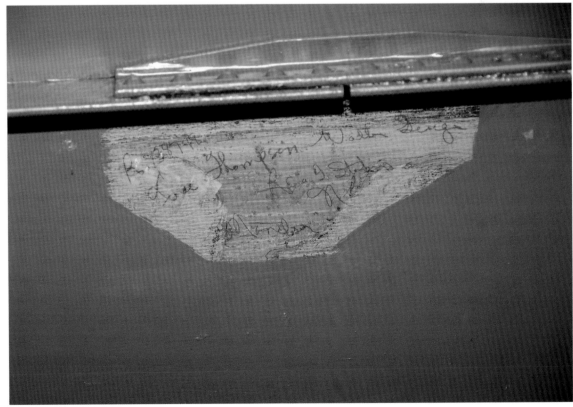

⅄ An impressive super wide-angle lens shot of the Dakota cockpit during a flight over the RAF Museum, Hendon, on 16 May 2012. The Captain in the left seat is Flt Lt Loz Rushmere with Navigator Sqn Ldr Tony 'Sluf' Beresford in the right. *(Crown Copyright/SAC Dan Herrick)*

➤ When the interior of the BBMF Dakota ZA947 was repainted, care was taken to ensure that the handwritten notes written on the sides of the fuselage by the troops being transported to the UK during the Second World War remained as a tribute to them. This is a close-up view of one of the many handwritten notes that remain along the side of the fuselage. *(Keith Wilson)*

◁ Occasionally, the BBMF aircraft are invited to display with another aircraft for a special event. At the 2010 RIAT at Fairford, the Flight's Spitfire LFIXe MK356, flown by Sqn Ldr 'Dunc' Mason, displayed in formation with a 29(R) Squadron Typhoon, flown by Flt Lt Rich Walton. *(Geoffrey Lee/ Planefocus GLD108797)*

➤ Cockpit and instrument panel of Lancaster PA474, seen here with the red ground locks securely in place. In this view it appears that only the pilot in command has a seat for the left-hand side of the aircraft, but the co-pilot sits on a fold-down seat (seen here in the closed position) – the space allows access to the bomb aimer's position in the nose of the aircraft. *(Keith Wilson)*

When the Lancaster is used for one of its poignant poppy drops, the fuselage is protected with a layer of fine mesh to keep the poppies out of the systems. The photograph was taken at Coningsby on 11 June 2012, just ahead of the aircraft's poppy drop onto the Bomber Command Memorial on 28 June. *(Keith Wilson)*

Poppy drops

Poppy drops are a unique aerial spectacle undertaken by the Battle of Britain Memorial Flight Lancaster to commemorate major wartime and related events, such as the unveiling of the Bomber Command Memorial in London's Green Park on 28 June 2012. The first BBMF Poppy Drop was flown as recently as 19 July 1995, when one million poppies were dropped over London during the 50th anniversary of VJ-Day.

Ʌ BBMF technicians load one million poppies by hand into the hold of Lancaster PA474 in readiness for the trip over the Bomber Command Memorial in Green Park, London, on 28 June 2012. *(Crown Copyright/SAC Graham Taylor)*

Invariably, poppy drops receive widespread media coverage and, although they appear simple in context, they are not quite as straightforward as is often perceived

There are two types of poppy drops flown by the BBMF: the 'over the top drop' and the 'on top drop'. The nature and location of the commemorative event will dictate the appropriate type of drop.

For most events, it is usually an 'over the top drop' that is used. As the Lancaster passes directly over the event or location, the bomb-bay doors are opened and the poppies come fluttering down. The spectacle of the trailing poppies provides onlookers with a remarkable sight, but, depending on the wind strength, the poppies rarely land on the event and can be blown some distance away.

For an 'on top drop', the poppies fall directly onto the event below, such as when used in 2012 for the opening of the Bomber Command Memorial in Green Park, London. To achieve this, the Lancaster will not fly directly over the event but will have to carefully position itself upwind at the correct distance from the drop zone to ensure the one million poppies fall on the correct location. Considerable planning is required, along with good weather forecasting and perhaps just a little luck, to get the poppies to fall exactly where they are directed.

A poppy drop is always an event to stir the soul, particularly for the Lancaster crew, and the spectacle of the plume being released and then falling to earth is always an emotive sight.

⋀ As the bomb doors start to open, the first of one million poppies leave the Lancaster, while below, the Queen unveils the Bomber Command Memorial in Green Park on 28 June 2012. The new memorial honours the bravery of the 55,573 RAF Bomber Command crewmembers who lost their lives during the Second World War. (Crown Copyright/SAC Graham Taylor)

◀ **A sequence of images taken from the tail gun position of BBMF Lancaster PA474. The first of one million poppies leaves the bomb bay on the occasion of the unveiling of the Bomber Command Memorial in Green Park, London, on 28 June 2012.** *(Crown Copyright/SAC Steve Buckley)*

◀ **... until a large cloud of one million poppies are visible.** *(Crown Copyright/SAC Steve Buckley)*

◀ **Poppies continue to fall...** *(Crown Copyright/SAC Steve Buckley)*

∨ **In just a few brief moments more than one million poppies have left the bomb bay of the Lancaster, falling onto Green Park below.** *(Crown Copyright/SAC Steve Buckley)*

◀ **... and the quantity of poppies continues to increase...** *(Crown Copyright/SAC Steve Buckley)*

Having arrived at Duxford in October 2010, Hurricane IIc PZ865 underwent a major maintenance at the beginning of 2011. In addition to its major maintenance, the aircraft would require a reconditioned mainplane centre section, tailplane and fin and it was agreed that these would be completed as close to the original as was feasible and using as much of the original structure as possible. Work was completed by March 2012 and the aircraft is seen with OC BBMF, Sqn Ldr Dunc Mason, outside the ARC facility, just about to undergo an engine run. She made an impressively fiery start due to a small problem with the priming pump which overprimed her, but the flames quickly cleared once the engine burst into life. (Keith Wilson)

Keeping them Flying

The BBMF's 12 aircraft are unique within the modern Royal Air Force and represent the last piston-powered 'tail-draggers' in regular use with the service. What does it take to keep a Lancaster, two Hurricanes, five Spitfires, two Chipmunks and a Dakota airworthy while rebuilding another Spitfire XVI in the team's spare time? A lot less than most RAF Squadrons demand, that's for sure! On Typhoon squadrons, the ratio of maintenance crew to aircraft is usually around 11.5:1; on the Tornado that number reduces to 10:1. On the BBMF, that ratio is just 2.5:1 meaning a total engineering strength of just 30 people – a lean and mean operation.

'Without the Flight Engineers the hangar doors wouldn't even open.'

Sqn Ldr Ian Smith,
Officer Commanding BBMF,
2009–12

SEngO

At the head of that small but dedicated team of engineers from 2009 to 2012 was the Flight's senior engineering officer, WO David 'Dave' Marshall. Marshall joined the RAF as a direct entrant propulsion fitter on 15 June 1976. Early postings included Coltishall (Jaguar) and Cottesmore (Tornado GR1) before moving to Coningsby for a four-year tour on the Tornado F3. After many years on a variety of squadrons, Marshall was moved to RAF Wyton to work in the Military Aviation Authority on Defence Equipment and Support, developing Airworthiness Policy. A glitch in the IT system prevented him from seeing that the SEngO position at the BBMF was vacant, but fortunately a drafter telephoned him with the news. Marshall contacted Sqn Ldr Al Pinner (OC BBMF) and introduced himself, and then visited RAF Coningsby the following day. After a four-hour interview he was offered the SEngO position.

A Two of the BBMF Engineering Team, Cpl Carl Broomhead and SAC(T) Ed Cash, checking for any sign of an oil leak after the engine test on Hurricane LF363. *(Keith Wilson)*

V Flt Lt Anthony 'Parky' Parkinson preparing one of the Flight's Chipmunks, WG486/G, for a flight test at Coningsby on 9 May 2012 while a BBMF engineer checks that the pitot static heating system is functioning. *(Keith Wilson)*

A During the 2012 display season, with PZ865 undergoing a major maintenance at Duxford, LF363 was the only Hurricane on the Flight's strength. Consequently it was in great demand. It underwent a scheduled oil filter change before being released back into service on 4 September 2012. A small amount of smoke can be seen emerging from the exhaust as LF363 is fired up for its engine run, with Sgt Adrian Smith in the cockpit for the test. Note the close proximity of the public viewing area where a couple of photographers are snapping away. *(Keith Wilson)*

◁ Shortly after the Chipmunk's flight on 9 May 2012, members of the BBMF Engineering Team, including Cpl Kev 'Fruitbat' Harnett, Chief Technician Paul Blackah MBE (back to camera) and Cpl Paul 'Bella' Macluskey, discuss the issues raised from the test with Parky (seated in the cockpit). *(Keith Wilson)*

◁ Chipmunk WG486/G up on jacks at Coningsby and with its main undercarriage completely removed, 11 April 2012. *(Keith Wilson)*

Engineering Team

There is a team of 30 engineers at BBMF. While most are regular RAF personnel, five are full-time members of the RAF Reserve: two chief technicians (Paul Blackah, the Airframe Specialist and Engineering Controller, and Paul Routledge, who heads the training/teaching process at the Flight) along with three corporals (Nigel 'Sticky' Bunn, one of the most experienced engine technicians on the Flight; Andy Bale, an experienced avionics specialist; and Norman 'Norm' Pringle, an experienced airframe repair technician). Between them,

the five have a combined experience of more than 60 years on the Flight – experience far too good to lose! They are all on a rolling four-year contract and do not get posted away from the Flight, thereby providing the long-term engineering stability absolutely required.

The remaining members of the Engineering Team comprise RAF regulars, who routinely serve between three and five years on the Flight, before they return to modern-day RAF operations. The entire BBMF groundcrew volunteer for posts on the Flight and there is a long waiting list for regular engineering personnel to be posted onto the BBMF.

➤ A busy day on the BBMF ramp at Coningsby on 16 May 2012. Both Spitfire PR XIXs (PS915 and PM631) and Hurricane LF363 are receiving attention from the Engineering Team while one of the PR XIXs, PS915, has already commenced its engine runs with its tail secured firmly to the ground. *(Keith Wilson)*

➤ With the engine running on Hurricane LF363 in the background, Cpl Richie Kear and SAC(T) Chris Cochrane work on the Rolls-Royce Griffon engine installation in Spitfire PR XIX PM631, ahead of engine runs on the aircraft. *(Keith Wilson)*

➤ Engine runs for Spitfire PR XIX PS915 at Coningsby on 16 May 2012 while SAC(T) Edward Cash monitors the engine from under the safety of the wing. *(Keith Wilson)*

A With the engine successfully run on Spitfire PR XIX PS915, it is a case of 'all hands to the pumps' to get the various cowlings and covers back onto the aircraft, 16 May 2012. *(Keith Wilson)*

◄ A long-exposure photograph taken on a long lens from a safe distance of Spitfire PR XIX PS915 while undergoing engine test runs at Coningsby on 16 May 2012. The image won Best Technical Photograph of the Year for SAC Graham Taylor in the annual Royal Air Force Photographic Competition. *(Crown Copyright/SAC Graham Taylor)*

V After having spent time in the hangar, the Lancaster receives a thorough inspection from the groundcrew, including Cpl Paul 'Bella' Macluskey (left) and Sgt Adrian Smith. *(Keith Wilson)*

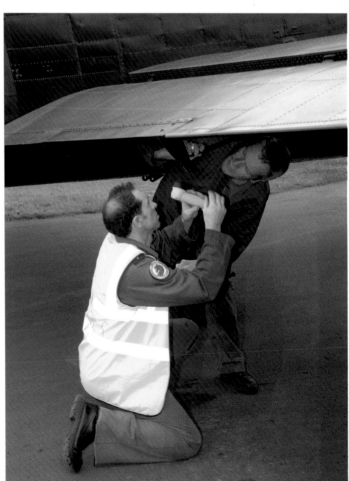

Engineering trades

The largest of the BBMF's aircraft engineering trades is the 18-strong Mechanical Team, which specialises in two main areas: aircraft structure and propulsion systems. Aircraft structure includes all aspects of the airframe as well as the flying controls, hydraulics and pneumatic systems. Propulsion systems includes all aspects of the aircraft engines and propellers, fuel, oil, ignition and cooling systems. Both the mechanical and avionic trades provide manpower for the Flight's Training and Standards Cell, which delivers essential training to the BBMF technicians on the Flight's five different aircraft types.

The six members of the small Avionics Team are responsible for all electrical and avionic systems on the BBMF aircraft. In addition to maintaining existing equipment, the technicians are also responsible for introducing upgrades. The equipment they maintain ranges from simple emergency magnetic compasses to modern retrofitted equipment such as the Mode S IFF transponders now fitted to the aircraft, as well as new radio and GPS systems. Although the BBMF's aircraft are not as

'electronic' as modern RAF aircraft, the work on the BBMF is unusual in that it includes maintenance on some items that previously would have been completed off the unit, in a specialist bay or at a third-party contractor. The BBMF now has its own bays for these purposes and the trades are involved in more levels of maintenance than is usual – particularly on key components including magnetos and generators.

With each member of the Flight having their own flying kit and helmet, a Survival Equipment Fitter is on the team. SAC Kelly Rhodes is the resident 'squipper' – a job she loves. Kelly joined the RAF back in 1998 and had been trying to get onto the Flight ever since.

Servicing the aircraft

All BBMF aircraft have an Out of Service Date (OSD), which is, effectively, a 20-year rolling life so the Lancaster is good to 2033. Next year the OSD on the Lancaster will be 2034 and so on. The Lancaster is due for a major service at the end of the 2015 season, which will include the replacement of the aircraft's tail spars.

After the test is completed satisfactorily, the Lancaster is carefully manoeuvred back into the hangar. This time Cpl Norman Pringle supervises the operation, keeping an eye on the wing tip clearance on the massive wing. *(Keith Wilson)*

Following the changing of the port-side engine, Dakota ZA947 is prepared for an engineering flight test at Coningsby on 7 September 2012. Here, SAC(T) Edward 'Ed' Cash and SAC Chris 'Corky' Cochrane move the ground battery unit just before the aircraft taxies away from the BBMF ramp. *(Keith Wilson)*

The Dakota suffered a number of 'technical issues' with its port-side engine during the 2012 season, which involved the removal and replacement of the offending unit. On 4 September, a 'new' engine is installed and prepared for a flight test. Seen here is a close-up of the replacement 14-cylinder Pratt & Whitney R-1830-90D Twin Wasp engine of 1,200hp. *(Keith Wilson)*

One of a number of key display boards that aid the smooth running of the BBMF Engineering Team. The second column from the left indicates the airworthiness of each aircraft; the third column shows the engineers what work is required for each aircraft. The photograph, taken at Coningsby on 11 June 2012, shows, at a glance, key information for all aircraft on that day. *(Keith Wilson)*

Another engineering control board is for the BBMF Tool Control System. It shows any aircraft that has tools being used on it and by whom. It plays a vital flight safety function as an aircraft with tools out on it may still be in work or, if not, there may be potential for loose articles. The rest of the board is a control centre for building keys. *(Keith Wilson)*

Another display board used to good effect by the BBMF engineers is the BBMF Engineers Flying Programme. As well as indicating the planned requirements, by aircraft, and the groundcrews required to prepare and assist with the engine starts, it also shows which members of the team are required to travel with the aircraft to a particular event. *(Keith Wilson)*

➤ The BBMF engineers' storage facility for the library of hard copies of all the various technical manuals used by the Flight. *(Keith Wilson)*

⋎ A tool cabinet used for servicing the aircraft. All tools are shadowed and a system of tags is used so that each tool is signed out, ensuring that all tools can be accounted for and that none are left in an aircraft. *(Keith Wilson)*

⋎ SAC Kelly Rhodes is the Flight's 'squipper' – Survival Equipment Fitter. Each pilot has their own flying kit and helmet, which needs to be fitted to them personally. *(Keith Wilson)*

To maintain the ultimate life of the aircraft, annual flying hours are severely restricted. The Spitfires are permitted 200 hours of flight combined each year, while the Lancaster is limited to 104 hours and the Dakota 180 hours. In support of this, the aircraft are regularly serviced, following a certain number of flying hours. For the fighters, they have an annual service after every 56 flight hours and receive a primary service every 28 flight hours. The primary service takes around two to three days to complete, requiring careful planning of the service programmes to minimise downtime. Similarly, the Lancaster has an annual service every 100 flight hours and a primary service every 56 flight hours, the latter taking around three days to complete. The Dakota's service intervals are 180 and 90 hours respectively.

The final airshow of the season is usually the Lincolnshire's Lancaster Association Members' Day, held at RAF Coningsby on the last Sunday in September, although the Dakota may undertake some events up to the end of October. Once the airshows are completed, the aircraft are moved into the hangar where the annual winter maintenance programme operates throughout the late autumn and winter months and all the BBMF display aircraft receive in-depth scheduled servicing. During the early part of October, most of the aircraft undergo pre-maintenance engine ground runs and they are then stripped down and inspected for any potential problems, including any cracks, wear or distortion.

The acquisition of any spare parts that are needed brings its own special challenges, although an extensive inventory is held by the Flight. If the required parts are not in stock, the Flight will approach specialist suppliers who can manufacture or overhaul these unique items.

The maintenance programmes proceed throughout the winter months and then the rebuilding process begins. By the middle of March each year the functional checks are being completed and then each aircraft undergoes full post-maintenance engine ground runs. Finally, each aircraft has to complete a full air test to confirm that all systems are fully serviceable, the aircraft handles as expected and its performance meets the flight test parameters. Only then are the aircraft allowed to participate in the pre-season practice displays and the full display season thereafter.

Careful engineering planning is crucial to the smooth running of the Flight throughout the airshow season. Once the Flight's participation and display programme has been agreed, the Engineering Team can look at the display schedule and plan ahead. 'It is absolutely imperative for the right people to be allocated to the correct task for a successful show,' says Dave Marshall. Accommodation is booked and aircraft are allocated. Bearing in mind the total number of hours each aircraft is allowed to fly annually and that they are suitably serviced, the length of the legs are considered along with the number of flypasts en route. 'As well as allocating the right people for the task, the correct aeroplane for each task must also be allocated in order to ensure success,' adds Dave.

While weekends are always busy with airshows, Monday mornings are particularly busy too. At 9am, the trade managers meet and discuss the status. The main engineering board – an excellent, easy-to-read, visual presentation of each aircraft's current status – is examined and all the Form 700s (flying paperwork) from the weekend are updated. Marshall says:

'We examine all the engineering issues from the weekend and see what lessons can be learned from them. Could we have done things any better? It is most important to learn lessons and implement changes to prevent future glitches. Then we look ahead to the following week. What do we need to prepare for, what aircraft are required? We also need to consider all the training sorties that will be required. We must ensure that all our display aircrew remain current.'

SEngO WO Kevin Ball joins the Flight

After four great years with the Flight, Dave Marshall retired from the RAF and left the BBMF in October 2012. On his final day at the post Dave said, 'I would like to publicly thank all the engineers who have worked for me during my time as SEngO. It is because of these dedicated people that the nation's iconic aircraft remain airworthy and a tribute to all those people that made the ultimate sacrifice in the name of freedom.'

However, Marshall's skills will not be lost to aviation as he is joining AsSystems, a contractor that carries out work on behalf of Rolls-Royce Aero Engines. His new role will be in the Cost Reduction Team concerned with the operating and maintenance of the Rolls-Royce Trent engine.

Marshall's replacement as SEngO of the BBMF is WO Kevin Ball. Ball's career since joining the RAF in 1980 has included serving on the Avro Vulcan, Tornado F3 and GR4, Merlin HC3, Puma HC1 and Harrier GR9/9A (see Chapter 2, The People). In 2011, he joined 32 (The Royal) Squadron at RAF Northolt to set up a Continuing Airworthiness Management Organisation for the Command Support Air Transport fleet of HS125, BAe146 and Augusta A.109E.

The BBMF Engineering Team comprises dedicated professionals who passionately support the belief that, although the debt of gratitude can never be repaid, as long as the Flight's aircraft are kept flying they will be a lasting memorial to those who have gone before. Dave Marshall summed up engineering at the BBMF: 'The aeroplanes belong to the country. We are just looking after them.' And what a great job the Flight is doing of looking after them for the nation.

'We are not on operations. If we don't get to an event, nobody is going to die. If we push too hard, somebody might!'

WO David Marshall,
Senior Engineering Officer BBMF,
2008–12

Engine repair and overhaul at Retro Track & Air

➤ The BBMF's Rolls-Royce Merlin engine from Hurricane PZ865 having been overhauled and repaired at Retro Track & Air (UK) Ltd, Gloucestershire, a few days before it was shipped back to Duxford to be refitted back into PZ865, 12 June 2012. *(Keith Wilson)*

⋎ Another Rolls-Royce Merlin engine undergoes a major rebuild at Retro Track & Air. *(Keith Wilson)*

◁ Rotating one of the Merlin engines in a specially designed cradle are Retro Track & Air's engineer Neil Smart and trainee Steve Walker. *(Keith Wilson)*

Hurricane PZ865's major maintenance at ARC

➤ With a minor maintenance required every three years and a major required every six years, Hurricane IIc PZ865's major maintenance was due at the beginning of 2011. ARC was chosen to complete this work and the aircraft arrived at Duxford in November 2010. After dismantling and a careful inspection, it became apparent that – in addition to its major maintenance – the aircraft would require a reconditioned mainplane centre section, tailplane and fin. It was agreed that these would be completed as close to the original as was possible and using as much of the original structure as possible. *(Keith Wilson)*

◄ By 26 April 2012, the top section of the wooden fuselage has been extensively rebuilt with the plywood covering already fitted to the cockpit area. Fabric covering would be added to the upper section at a later stage. *(Keith Wilson)*

⋀ A close-up view of the intricate woodwork of the Hurricane's fuselage.
(Keith Wilson)

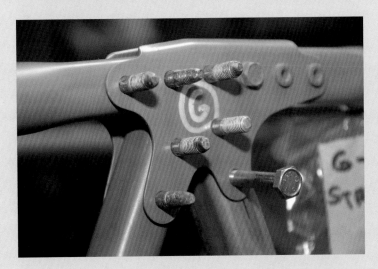

⋀ The complexity of the rebuild can be seen in this relatively 'simple' joint in the Hurricane's fuselage, just one of many in the Hurricane's tubular spaceframe structure. This joint consists of 26 separate components and all have to be correctly dismantled, cleaned and repaired before they can be re-assembled. It is a painstaking task. (Keith Wilson)

⋀ Compare the 'simple' joint (above left) with this rather more complex one. The level of workmanship during the rebuild has to be of the very highest quality. When the Hurricane was originally constructed, it was expected to last for about ten years; it was not designed to be dismantled, stripped and re-assembled, some 70 years later. (Keith Wilson)

By 1 August 2012, work on PZ865 is progressing well at ARC, Duxford. *(Keith Wilson)*

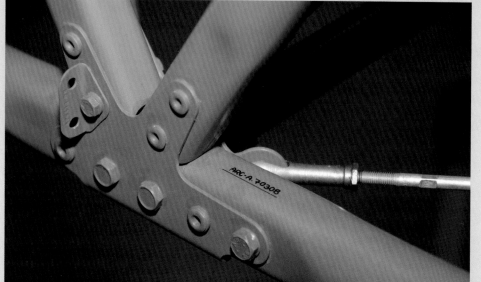

Another complex joint on the Hurricane's spaceframe construction – another set of problems! Where new components have been specially manufactured to replace original items, approval has to be obtained and the component and assembly clearly marked with the approval number. *(Keith Wilson)*

On 1 August 2012, the tail fin is refitted to PZ865. *(Keith Wilson)*

Work on the cockpit is progressing well, too. *(Keith Wilson)*

➤ By 26 September 2012, the aircraft is being re-covered with Irish linen using high-tautening red nitrate dope – exactly the same process and components as used in its construction 70 years previously. Husband-and-wife team Peter and Jean Johnson from Eastern Sailplanes complete the work at Duxford. Here, Peter is seen applying Irish linen to the top fuselage, just behind the cockpit area. *(Keith Wilson)*

Eastern Sailplanes' teamwork continuing on the Hurricane fuselage inside its special 'tent' in ARC's hangar at Duxford. *(Keith Wilson)*

◄ Coats of red dope were applied... (Billy Fletcher)

◣ ... before the silver dope is added to protect the red dope and fabric from UV light. The work takes place in the specially extended ARC spray-bake facility on 16 October 2012. The silver also covers the brush marks of the red dope at the edge of the fabric around the apertures for the various panels. (Billy Fletcher)

➤ By 18 October, the green and brown colours of PZ865's new South East Asia Command scheme have been applied, along with the light and dark blue roundel. (Keith Wilson)

 The Rolls-Royce Merlin engine installation on Spitfire Mk XVIe, TE311, at Coningsby on 9 May 2012. *(Keith Wilson)*

 The winter servicing programme was underway when this image of Spitfire LFIXe MK356 was taken at Coningsby on 2 October 2012. Once the display season is over, the engineers waste no time in dismantling the aircraft in preparation for the winter overhaul. *(Keith Wilson)*

↟ Spitfire Mk Vb AB910/MD-E was due to fly to ARC at Duxford at the end of the display season for its scheduled major maintenance, but a few technical issues caused a delay. On 2 October SAC(T) Ed Cash works on the engine and prop in preparation for the delivery flight which was eventually made by Dunc Mason on 7 October. *(Keith Wilson)*

➤ By 18 October, AB910 is already being dismantled by the ARC engineers at Duxford ahead of its major maintenance. *(Keith Wilson)*

A typical winter servicing scene at Coningsby, with Spitfire LFIXe MK356 up on jacks, the main undercarriage and wheels removed, all inspection panels removed and the cowlings off to allow access to the engine and propeller, 30 October 2012.
(Keith Wilson)

By 30 September 2012, winter maintenance work is well underway on the Flight's Lancaster PA474. All the engine cowlings have been removed to expose the engine for maintenance, while the port outer engine has been completely removed for overhaul, leaving just the radiator in place and the red oil tank behind in the subframe.
(Keith Wilson)

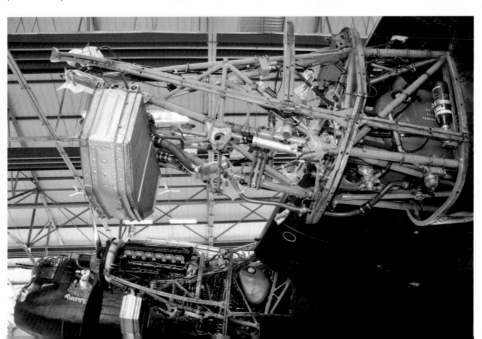

On the same day, Spitfire IIa P7350 undergoes similar treatment to MK356. Note how many inspection panels can be removed or released under the wings to allow a thorough inspection and lubrication of all relevant components.
(Keith Wilson)

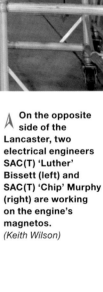

On the opposite side of the Lancaster, two electrical engineers SAC(T) 'Luther' Bissett (left) and SAC(T) 'Chip' Murphy (right) are working on the engine's magnetos.
(Keith Wilson)

◁ SAC(T) Matt Hannaford is seen removing the remaining undercarriage leg from Spitfire PR XIX PM631. *(Keith Wilson)*

➤ Work on Spitfire Mk XVI TE311 is progressing well for its first post-restoration flight, which was subsequently made at Coningsby on 19 October 2012 with Sqn Ldr Ian 'Smithy' Smith at the controls. Cpl 'Ned' Chamberlain is seen working on the aircraft in early October. *(Keith Wilson)*

◄ The busy winter servicing scene at Coningsby on 30 September 2012. Left to right: Spitfire PR XIX PS915, Spitfire PR XIX PM631, Spitfire LFIXe MK356, Spitfire IIa P7350 and Hurricane IIb LF363, with Dakota ZA947 just visible to the bottom right. *(Keith Wilson)*

Λ Cpl Kevin Harnett is seen working on the underwing inspection covers on Spitfire Mk IIa P7350, while Cpl Nigel Bunn works on the Merlin engine installation at Coningsby on 30 September 2012. *(Keith Wilson)*

➤ Over page: The Flight's Dakota, ZA947, at the start of its winter maintenance programme in the BBMF hangar at Coningsby on 30 October 2012. *(Keith Wilson)*

Often referred to by some members of the BBMF as the 'Warm-up Act', the Red Arrows perform during the Royal International Air Tattoo (RIAT) at Fairford on 8 July 2012 as Flt Sgt Martin Blythe and SAC Matthew Little prepare the BBMF Lancaster for its display flight. *(Keith Wilson)*

Showtime

Once the Public Display Authority has been signed and issued to the BBMF, the team members are able to don their all-black flying suits and prepare themselves for a busy season ahead. In 2012, the PDA examination was conducted by AVM Stuart Atha at the Flight's home base of RAF Coningsby. As a one-time member of the Flight, he knew what to look for; the programme exceeded his expectations and the PDA was duly authorised.

Airshow and event organisers who would like to invite the BBMF to perform, or would like a single Spitfire, Hurricane, Lancaster or Dakota to make a fly-by, have to place a bid for their appearance through an internet process managed by the Events Team at RAF Northolt. At the beginning of November the Events Team allocate the BBMF around 600–700 requests for displays and fly-bys. The decision on what flies where is based on a number of issues, but recruitment is considered by the Events Team as a major priority.

Against this, the team has to weigh up the number of fighter and bomber pilots available, as well as the number of hours each aircraft is allowed to fly during the season. These limitations are set to maximise the valuable engine and airframe life of each BBMF asset.

Once the Events Team has made its initial selection, the suggestions are passed to the BBMF Administration Team at RAF Coningsby which, working in conjunction with the OC BBMF, completes the detailed and meticulous planning process. The team was led by Flt Lt Jack Hawkins for the last 13 seasons; on Hawkins's retirement in May 2012, he was replaced by Flt Lt Anthony Parkinson.

Once Parky has the outline programme established for the year, he can consider all the fly-by requests that have been received and take a look at what might be achieved en route to and from the show location. If the BBMF trademark display of Lancaster, Spitfire and Hurricane are en route, he can normally consider up to seven fly-by venues; each aircraft can perform at up to five fly-by sites en route, but their fuel duration may restrict the number. While the Lancaster usually operates with a duration of up to four hours, Parky has to consider the maximum number (104) that the Lancaster can fly in one display season so that tends to limit the number of fly-bys. The Spitfire and Hurricane usually operate with a 1hr 45min fuel duration so that dictates what they are able to achieve en route. Typically, the three aircraft would take off separately, fly a series of fly-bys en route and then meet up at an RV point near the display location before displaying in their trademark manner.

Another limiting factor is the number of crews available to the Flight. Currently, there are only five fighter pilots to fly the five (soon to be six) Spitfires and two Hurricanes. Similarly, each fighter pilot is limited to the total number of hours they can fly in a year. For the OC BBMF, that number is 80 hours in a year, for all the other (mainly volunteer) pilots the limit is 55 hours. Despite the obvious limitations, things get very busy. In one four-day period in mid-September 2012, the Flight made a total of 75 appearances – some going!

By November 2012, Parky had started to allocate aircraft and trips, juggling appearances to maximise the fly-pasts of all the aircraft. 'The programme is always being tweaked to accommodate another fly-by – right throughout the year but, eventually, we have to say "No" to any more additions,' says Parky.

Parky creates a separate planning folder for each and every location, containing all the relevant timings, site details and crowd lines for any given sortie. Ahead of the actual day, the individual

➤ Hurricane IIb LF363/YB-W, flown by OC BBMF Sqn Ldr Ian 'Smithy' Smith, and Spitfire PR XIX PS915 *The Last!*, flown by Sqn Ldr Dunc Mason, alongside the cameraship as the Lancaster PA474 is cleared to join the formation. The photograph was taken en route to the Eastbourne International Airshow in August 2012. *(Keith Wilson)*

➤ It is not always possible for the Flight to perform with its hallmark BBMF three-ship formation of Lancaster, Spitfire and Hurricane. At RAF Waddington on 30 June 2012, due to serviceability issues with Hurricane LF363, the Lancaster leads a pair of Spitfires with Spitfire IIa P7350, flown by OC BBMF Sqn Ldr Ian Smith, to port, and Spitfire Vb AB910, flown by Flt Lt Anthony Parkinson, to starboard. *(Keith Wilson)*

fighter pilot or bomber navigator assigned to the task will collect all the relevant folders – sometimes as many as 16 may be in use. The fighter pilot or bomber navigator will then plan the exact sortie using the Advanced Mission Planning Aid facility. This navigation planning capability will refine all timings, turning points and key navigational locations ahead of the actual sortie and produce detailed maps and charts for the pilots on the day.

That said, flexibility is essential on the Flight and as Parky reported, '10% of last year worked to plan, but the often unseasonal weather in 2012 as well as unserviceability issues affected lots of shows. Crosswinds seriously affect planning issues due to the necessary very tight limits being imposed on the aircraft and individual pilots.'

Once a show has been performed, the feedback from venues is usually positive and enthusiastic. But not all of the telephone calls are easy: 'The difficult ones are to cancel appearances, due mainly to weather issues, and this is clearly the worst part of my job,' said Parky. 'However, the best bit of the job is to receive calls from people who love the aircraft and are clearly delighted with what we have achieved.'

⋀ **If the aircraft is slightly over-primed, the excess fuel burns momentarily in the exhaust pipes during engine start-up, as seen here at Coningsby on 16 May 2012, ahead of a display.** *(Keith Wilson)*

➤ **Lancaster PA474 with its tail up and the main wheels just about to break ground on take-off at the RIAT on 8 July 2012.** *(Keith Wilson)*

The engines are allowed to warm slowly, to prolong their life. During this time, one of the ground engineers stands nearby to inspect and observe proceedings. On 19 April 2012, ahead of a display practice, the task falls to Junior Technician Ben Jones. *(Keith Wilson)*

East meets west: as the Lancaster climbs away from Fairford at the start of its display routine, a Polish Air Force Mikoyan MiG-29A Fulcrum, serial number 111, taxies towards the runway at the start of its display. *(Keith Wilson)*

◄ An unusual long-lens close-up view of the *Phantom of the Ruhr* as it passes along the crowd line at Fairford, 8 July 2012.
(Keith Wilson)

⋀ With only the No 3 engine to shut down, the groundcrew start to attend to the Lancaster at Fairford, 8 July 2012. The three BBMF engineers are SAC(T) Matt Litton (far left), Sergeant Gary Millman (centre) and Cpl 'Lingy' Lingwood.
(Keith Wilson)

➤ It doesn't matter how tall you are, the special 'broom handle adaptor' is necessary to refit the pitot cover immediately after flight, demonstrated here by SAC(T) Matt Litton.
(Keith Wilson)

A smoky start with Spitfire IIa P7350 at Fairford, 8 July 2012. Smithy is in the cockpit. *(Keith Wilson)*

Slightly less smoke on start-up for Parky with the Spitfire Mk Vb AB910 at Fairford, 8 July 2012. *(Keith Wilson)*

Pairs take-off for Smithy and Parky ahead of the Flight's three-ship formation display routine with the Lancaster, followed by a spectacular Synchro Pair display for the two Spitfires at Fairford, 8 July 2012. *(Keith Wilson)*

⊰ Lancaster PA474 *Phantom of the Ruhr* takes off ahead of its display at the RIAT at Fairford on 17 July 2011, while the 'warm-up act' are still parked on the ramp behind. *(Oliver Wilson)*

⋀ Preparing the Lancaster for a flight at Coningsby on 7 September 2012. While the aircraft is refuelled, Cpl Norman Pringle cleans and polishes the perspex on the nose of the Lancaster. *(Keith Wilson)*

⋁ It is not just airshows at which the BBMF appears. On 4 August 2012, the Flight flew a series of flypasts over the Ramsey Golf Club in Cambridgeshire, while a 'Help for Heroes' Charity Golf Day was in progress on the course. *(Keith Wilson)*

◁ The best view was obtained from atop the St Thomas a Becket Church in Ramsey, Cambridgeshire, as the three-ship formation positions for another run over the golf course. The flypast temporarily halted all play on the course as everyone stopped to look skyward. *(Keith Wilson)*

◁ Recognise the celebration? Volunteers from the BBMF man the Flight's Roadshow caravan at major air displays around the country. Left to right: Cpl Matthew Thompson, SAC(T) Ian Fazey and SAC Dale 'Teapot' Whieldon. *(Keith Wilson)*

⋀ Under the watchful eye of their mother, a group of young aviation enthusiasts receive BBMF posters from Cpl Matthew Thompson at the RIAT, Fairford, 8 July 2012. *(Keith Wilson)*

⋀ Cpl Matthew Thompson distributes BBMF posters to a young enthusiast at the RIAT, Fairford, 8 July 2012. *(Keith Wilson)*

BBMF on the East Coast Main Line

In a dramatic and spectacular start to the Jubilee Celebrations, on Saturday 2 June 2012, TV star Carol Vorderman officially opened the Railfest 2012 event at the National Railway Museum in York. As part of that ceremony, she also unveiled a Class 91 locomotive, number 91110, named the *Battle of Britain Memorial Flight*, in a specially designed livery featuring the Flight's iconic aircraft, badge and logo. After presentations from the OC BBMF Sqn Ldr Ian Smith and the BBMF's former Bomber Leader, Stuart Reid, Vorderman addressed the huge crown gathered for the event at York and used her famous *Countdown* clock to time the unveiling. It all went spectacularly to plan and just as the curtain came down on the side of the locomotive, revealing its new special colour scheme, the BBMF formation of Lancaster, Spitfire and Hurricane flew overhead.

Locomotive 91110 was chosen for the honour because it currently holds the UK national speed record for electric trains, awarded when it ran at 162mph (260kph) along Stoke Bank, north of Peterborough, on 17 September 1989.

The locomotive operates on the East Coast Main Line and since the ceremony has been seen almost daily travelling from London King's Cross up to the north of England and Scotland, and back to the capital. On these journeys, the locomotive passes through Lincolnshire – aptly named 'Bomber County' – and close to RAF Coningsby. It is another fitting tribute to those brave souls who lost their lives in the Battle of Britain and Bomber Command, and is a living memory of the Memorial Flight set up to remember them all.

⋏ In a spectacular start to the Queen's Diamond Jubilee celebrations on Saturday 2 June 2012, TV star Carol Vorderman officially opens the Railfest 2012 event at the National Railway Museum in York. Vorderman addresses the crowd gathered for the event and for the train naming ceremony, using her *Countdown* clock to time the unveiling of 91110. *(Keith Wilson)*

⋏ At the appointed moment, the curtain comes down to reveal the new and spectacular colour scheme on 91110. *(Keith Wilson)*

⋎ 'Lest we forget': commemorative artwork applied to the left-hand side of 91110 – a tribute to those who lost their lives in the Battle of Britain and with Bomber Command. The right-hand side of the train features the BBMF's Lancaster PA474. *(Keith Wilson)*

A Spectacularly to plan, just after the curtain comes down on the side of the locomotive, the BBMF formation of Lancaster, Spitfire and Hurricane flies overhead. *(Keith Wilson)*

➤ Locomotive 91110 operates on the East Coast Main Line and regularly travels between London King's Cross and Scotland, passing through Lincolnshire ('Bomber County') and close to RAF Coningsby. It was photographed heading north through Huntingdon on 13 June 2012 with the BBMF crest on the front and the Lancaster artwork and message 'Lest we Forget' prominent along the side of the train. *(Keith Wilson)*

Engineers on the road

With busy weekend schedules and complex display programmes, organising the engineering support is quite a task. The Lancaster requires at least three engineers while each flight needs one. Consequently, at least five engineers are carried onboard the Lancaster, in addition to the four aircrew members. As members of the RAF, the Lancaster is allowed to carry out flypasts and displays with the engineers on board, and often does. Once the Lancaster reaches its first destination, the engineers are available to prepare all three aircraft for their next round of displays.

Occasionally, extra teams of engineers are dispatched to interim locations in one of the team's Sherpa vehicles, to assist and supplement the onboard engineers. At other times, when specific engineering issues occur, the Sherpa is dispatched with a team of engineers, along with replacement parts to fix the snags. In addition to their engineering duties, the team is available to speak with members of the public and share their enthusiasm and knowledge.

St Michael's Church, Coningsby. Located just a short walk from the main gate at Coningsby, St Michael's provides a landmark for the team's returning aircraft. Built in the 17th century, the church's one-handed clock measures 16ft 6in (5m) in diameter and the hand is almost 9ft (3m) long, making it the largest one-handed clock in the world. *(Keith Wilson)*

BBMF Visitor Centre

A partnership between the Royal Air Force and Lincolnshire County Council provides the public with a gateway to the home of the BBMF at RAF Coningsby. Since opening in 1986, the BBMF Visitor Centre has welcomed over 300,000 people through its doors, and paying visitors in the financial year 2011–12 showed an increase of over 11%. However, the Visitor Centre still runs at a slight loss, which is currently subsidised by Lincolnshire County Council.

Entry to the car park, exhibition centre and a well-stocked souvenir shop is free. Entry to the BBMF hangar is by guided tour only, lasting about one hour, for which a small charge is made. Visitors are led around the hangar by knowledgeable volunteers, and are given the opportunity to view the aircraft at close quarters and observe the small but dedicated BBMF engineering team at work. There is also a small viewing area outside where visitors may see aircraft being prepared for displays or undergoing engine runs, depending on the time and day.

The aircraft can be observed every weekday, 10am–5pm, with the exception of public holidays and two weeks over Christmas. The last guided tour starts at 3:30pm. For further information, contact the Visitor Centre, tel: 01522 782040; www.lincolnshire.gov.uk/bbmf.

An area in the Visitor Centre devoted to the Dam Busters raid on the Ruhr in May 1943. *(Keith Wilson)*

The well-stocked shop provides visitors with a wide variety of souvenirs. *(Keith Wilson)*

A small group of visitors takes one of the regular guided tours of the BBMF hangar at Coningsby. If the aircraft are parked nose-on to the visitors it indicates they are airworthy; if they are parked tail towards the visitors it indicates they are not. Hurricane LF363 was suffering minor cooling problems at the time of this photograph on 11 June 2012. *(Keith Wilson)*

Entry to the BBMF hangar is by guided tour only, lasting about one hour, for which a small charge is made. Visitors are led around the hangar by knowledgeable volunteer guides, and are given the opportunity to view the aircraft at close quarters. *(Keith Wilson)*

Former Bomber Leader and now volunteer guide Stuart Reid (left) with a group of visitors from the Starlight Children's Foundation – including Connor Lancaster, James Porter and Ben Richards – during a visit to the Flight on 2 October 2012. The Starlight Children's Foundation grants once-in-a-lifetime wishes for seriously and terminally ill children. *(Keith Wilson)*

An unusual silhouette-style image of Lancaster PA474. In the background, members of the public stand in the small viewing area, watching the Flight's aircraft and activities at relatively close quarters. *(Keith Wilson)*

◁ Another day, another group of visitors for Stuart Reid – this time a group from the RAF Museum, Hendon, are shown around the Dakota. (Keith Wilson)

⌄ Stuart Reid demonstrates to good effect just why the width of the D-Day invasion stripes painted on aircraft were the size they were. (Keith Wilson)

▷ The Lincolnshire Lancaster Association Members' Day at Coningsby on 30 September 2012 is, effectively, the last air display of the year for the BBMF. The Flight usually tries to make the day's flying a little special for the members, often featuring formations not seen elsewhere. One of the 'unusual' formations flown on the day was this routine with a pair of Spitfire PR XIXs (PM631 and PS915), the Hurricane IIb LF363 and Lancaster PA474, now flying as *Thumper Mk III*. (Keith Wilson)

Airshow appearances increase year-on-year

For many years after its formation, the Flight carried out relatively low-key operations, performing around 50–60 displays a year, up to the mid-1960s. By 1992, this number had risen to around 150 per season, which in turn rose further to 200 in 1995. By 1996, the number was 500 and this increased progressively in 2002 and 2003 when more than 600 appearances were flown. In 2004, the planned commitment was over 700 individual appearances, with the BBMF booked to appear at more than 60 airshows plus 300 other events – all this with just nine display aircraft.

By 2006, the number was up to 761 total aircraft appearances and rose steadily to 2010 when the number climbed over 1,000 for the first time and a total of 1,097 scheduled aircraft appearances were due to be made. The British weather hits the actual number of displays quite badly, particularly the crosswinds which affect tail-wheel aircraft significantly more than modern aircraft with a conventional tricycle undercarriage. Serviceability of aircraft has a very small impact, affecting an average of only 3% of appearances during the 2005–10 periods – a testament to the skills of the small but dedicated BBMF Engineering Team.

In 2012, the Flight had increased to 11 aircraft – one Lancaster, one Dakota, two Hurricanes, five (soon to be six) Spitfires and two Chipmunks. A total of 202 displays were flown, in addition to 566 flypasts; there were 768 individual performances.

'Lest we forget.'

◅ Participating aircraft are parked near the fence, allowing visitors a close-up view. *(Keith Wilson)*

➤ With visitors filling the viewing area close to the fence, the four-ship formation passes overhead. *(Crown Copyright /SAC Dan Herrick LBIPP)*

⋎ Members' Day attracts large crowds who are provided with a magnificent end-of-season display. *(Crown Copyright/SAC Dan Herrick LBIPP)*

An elevated view of the event from one of the cherry-pickers shows the BBMF hangar to the left, crowds along the fence and the close proximity of the parked aircraft as the BBMF four-ship formation passes overhead. *(Crown Copyright/SAC Graham Taylor)*

The traditional BBMF formation of Lancaster, Spitfire and Hurricane over Buckingham Palace to mark the Queen's official birthday on 14 June 2008. The flypast involved a total of 55 aircraft of 14 different types, from the BBMF to the Typhoon. *(Crown Copyright/Cpl Scott Robinson via Defence Image Database 451457876)*

Famous locations and formations

The BBMF is one of the world's foremost airworthy historic aircraft collections, maintaining the Lancaster, six Spitfires, two Hurricanes, a C-47 Dakota and a pair of DHC1 Chipmunk aircraft.

In the years immediately following the Second World War it became traditional for a Spitfire and Hurricane to lead the Victory Day flypast over London. Initially, the Historic Aircraft Flight was formed with three Spitfire Mk XIXs along with the last airworthy Hurricane, PZ865 _The Last of the Many_. During the following years, Spitfires were added while others were lost, and the Flight continued to carry out its duty of leading the annual Victory Day flypast over London, despite having to rely exclusively on volunteer engineers to keep the precious aircraft airworthy. Perhaps unsurprisingly, airshow appearances by the Flight's aircraft in the formative years were somewhat infrequent.

Banned from flying over London

The Flight suffered a major setback to its primary aim when Spitfire Mk XIV SL574 was involved in a flying accident at Martlesham Heath on 28 May 1959. Then, on 10 September, Spitfire Mk XIV TE476 was involved in a flying accident; the pilot landed back at Martlesham Heath after his radio failed and it appears he forgot to lower his undercarriage. As a consequence, the powers that be decided that 20 September 1959 would be the last occasion that single-engine fighters like the Spitfire and Hurricane would participate in the annual Battle of Britain flypast over London.

That decision was probably vindicated when SL574 suffered a complete engine failure during that very sortie. Harold Macmillan, the Prime Minister at the time, had just left Westminster Abbey at 4.30pm, after the service of remembrance for 'The Few'. Leading the Battle of Britain flypast were Spitfire SL574 and Hurricane LF363. After passing Horse Guards Parade, the Spitfire's engine failed and the pilot, AVM Maguire, was forced to look for somewhere to put the aircraft down. He chose what he thought was an empty sports field in Bromley. Fortunately, the OXO cricket team and their opponents, the Old Hollingtonians, were having tea. The Spitfire had just 200 yards (183m) in which to stop, and after hitting the grass one of its wingtips took out a set of stumps before it skidded 60 yards (55m) onto the outfield and came to rest.

All change over London

By the mid-1980s and with the Lancaster now part of its display routine, the BBMF continued to increase its display appearances across the UK. The ban imposed in 1959 on its single-engine aircraft was still in effect and prevented it from operating the Spitfires and Hurricanes over London, but that was to change in 1986. At precisely 11am on 5 March 1986, Sqn Ldr Paul Day flew PM631 across London and alongside Big Ben. It was the 50th anniversary of the first flight of the Spitfire, which took place at Eastleigh on 5 March 1936. The hour was chosen as a tribute to 11 Group which had borne the brunt of fighter operations during the Battle of Britain and was the controlling authority of which the BBMF was part.

Battle of Britain 50th anniversary

An event was organised to celebrate the 50th anniversary of the Battle of Britain on 15 September 1990. It included a display of static aircraft on Horse Guards Parade and a march of RAF personnel from Horse Guards Parade to Buckingham Palace. The highlight of the event was a flypast by 168 aircraft over The Mall led by five Spitfires and two Hurricanes of the BBMF. The permission required to carry out this formation of single-engine aircraft over Central London highlights the importance the event was given. Spitfire IIa P7350 led the formation (with AVM W.J. Wratten at the controls) along with Mk XIX PM631 (Sqn Ldr Paul Day), Mk Vb AB910 (Wg Cdr Dave Moss), Mk XIX PS915 (Sqn Ldr Chris Stevens)

◅ Dramatic wide-angle lens view of Hurricane IIb LF363/YB-W as it passes over Buckingham Palace and the crowds celebrating the Queen's Diamond Jubilee on 5 June 2012. The image was taken from the rear gunner's position in the leading Lancaster PA474. *(Crown Copyright/SAC Dan Herrick LBIPP)*

△ 'Hurricane over London': with Sqn Ldr Andy 'Milli' Millikin at the controls, BBMF Hurricane Mk IIc LF363/YB-W flies over London on its run-in towards Buckingham Palace as part of the Queen's Diamond Jubilee celebrations on 5 June 2012. The flypast also includes the BBMF Dakota flanked by two King Air. *(Crown Copyright/SAC Dan Herrick LBIPP)*

➢ Overleaf: Midway between VE-Day and VJ-Day, 10 July 2005 was designated National Commemoration Day and formed the culmination of a week-long programme of events and commemorations to mark the 60th anniversary of the end of the Second World War. The traditional BBMF formation of Lancaster, Spitfire and Hurricane approaches Buckingham Palace, preparing to drop one million poppies. *(Crown Copyright/SAC Scott Robertson)*

◄ PA474 carries out one of its poignant poppy drops along The Mall in London to commemorate the 50th anniversary of VJ-Day on 19 August 1995. *(Crown Copyright)*

➤ Prince William and Catherine Middleton were married at Westminster Abbey on 29 April 2011. This image, taken from a good vantage point on top of Buckingham Palace, shows the BBMF formation of Lancaster, Spitfire PR XIX and Hurricane IIb as it passes over The Mall and approaches the royal couple on the balcony of Buckingham Palace. *(Crown Copyright/Sgt Andy Malthouse ABIPP)*

and Mk XIX PS853 (Flt Lt Jim Wild). The two Hurricanes completed the formation: IIa LF363 (flown by Gp Capt Dave Widdowson) and IIb PZ865 (Sqn Ldr Allan Martin).

The various formations that followed consisted of masses of current RAF aircraft, including a 16-ship formation of Harriers. At the rear of the formation was Lancaster PA474 (with Sqn Ldr Colin Paterson as captain). After making their first pass over Buckingham Palace, P7350 and LF363 went to the rear of the formation. Once the Lancaster had flown over the Palace the Spitfire and Hurricane flew towards the RAF Parade and carried out a break in front of the Palace – a fitting conclusion to the 50th anniversary celebrations.

50th anniversary of VE-Day and VJ-Day

To commemorate the 50th anniversary of VE-Day (Victory in Europe) and VJ-Day (Victory in Japan) there were two flights over Buckingham Palace in 1995. The VE-Day celebrations ran from 6 to 8 May, and featured a large exhibition in Hyde Park. Real and replica aircraft were on display, including the RAF Exhibition Flight's Spitfire Mk XVI TB382, which would later join the BBMF, albeit on a temporary basis. The BBMF provided a three-ship flypast on the evening of Saturday 6 May when the Lancaster, Spitfire AB910 and Hurricane PZ865 carried out two passes over Hyde Park.

On Monday 8 May a huge crowd gathered at Buckingham Palace, much as it had done 50 years earlier. Once again, the BBMF trio of Lancaster, Spitfire and Hurricane joined the flypast over the Palace.

To commemorate the 50th anniversary of VJ-Day in 1995, Lancaster PA474 carried out one of its poignant poppy drops along The Mall and over Buckingham Palace on 19 August. Towards the end of a two-minute silence, the rumble of the Lancaster's four Merlin engines could be heard as it passed over Admiralty Arch at the top of The Mall. As the Lancaster approached the drop point at just 500ft (152m), the bomb doors opened, discharging one million poppies – each one symbolising a life lost. Later that afternoon, a Spitfire and Hurricane flew over The Mall and in the evening a Spitfire flew along the River Thames from Kew Bridge to Tower Bridge, where HMRY *Britannia* was anchored with the royal family on board.

Funeral of Her Majesty Queen Elizabeth The Queen Mother

The funeral of Her Majesty Queen Elizabeth The Queen Mother was held in London on 9 April 2002. The Queen Mother personified the wartime spirit that helped Britain through the Second World War and her funeral stirred the emotions of the nation.

Although outside the Flight's normal operating window (the Flight's principal operating season is from May through September), a spell of unseasonably good weather had allowed Sqn Ldr Paul Day, OC BBMF, to offer the Lancaster and a pair of Spitfires when approached by 1 Group on 4 April. The Flight was in the midst of its pre-season

Lancaster PA474 soars over the Derwent Valley Dam on 19 May 2008 to mark the 65th anniversary of the Dam Busters raids over the Ruhr. Lancasters of 617 Squadron trained in this valley to prepare for the mission flown on the night of 16–17 May 1943. Operation Chastise – the breaching of dams vital to the German war effort – resulted in the destruction of two dams. *(Crown Copyright/Sgt Graham Spark)*

An early formation shot during rehearsals for the Battle of Britain Flypast in September 1959, featuring the Battle of Britain Flight's Spitfire LFXVIe TE476 and Hawker Hurricane IIc LF363 in formation with Hawker Hunter F6 XF511/P of 74 Squadron and Gloster Javelin FAW7 XH958 of 23 Squadron. *(Crown Copyright/Air Historical Branch image T-1162)*

work-up period and the Lancaster had undergone a successful air test that very day. Two Spitfire PR XIXs, PM631 and PS915, were to join the Lancaster. Sqn Ldr Paul 'Major' Day led the formation in PM631 and was accompanied by Sqn Ldr Clive Rowley in PS915, and the Lancaster crewed by Sqn Ldr Stuart Reid (Captain), Flt Lt Andy Sell (Co-pilot), Sqn Ldr Brian 'Brain' Clark (Navigator) and Flt Sgt Ian Woolley (Air Engineer).

Large crowds had gathered at Coningsby to wave the Flight off and to greet them on their return, many of them patriotically waving Union flags. The crews took time to speak with the visitors gathered outside the perimeter fence after the flypast. The Queen Mother was synonymous with a time when people refused to leave London during the Blitz and instead, she offered her support to the victims. The appearance of the Flight in their historically significant aircraft added a special tribute to her. All of the Flight's personnel are rightly proud of the part they played in such an historic occasion.

The Queen's 80th birthday

To celebrate Her Majesty Queen Elizabeth II's official birthday on 17 June 2006, the largest RAF flypast over Buckingham Palace for many years was staged. Led by the BBMF, the flypast contained almost 50 aircraft.

The first wave was given the call-sign 'Memorial Flight' and was led by the Flight's Lancaster PA474 flanked by two Spitfires and two Hurricanes. Once again, the Lancaster was led by Sqn Ldr Stuart Reid, while OC BBMF Sqn Ldr Al Pinner MBE was in Spitfire Mk Vb AB910, Wg Cmdr Russ Allchrome in Spitfire IIa P7350, Sqn Ldr Clive Rowley MBE in Hurricane IIa LF363 and Sqn Ldr Ian Smith in Hurricane IIb PZ865.

'Memorial Flight' arrived overhead the Palace precisely on schedule at 13:00hrs, with all the aircraft flying at 1,500ft (457m). They were followed one minute later by 'Windsor Formation', comprising eight separate elements that overflew the Palace at 40-second intervals. At the rear were nine Hawk aircraft of the Red Arrows joined by an EE Canberra PR 9, making the type's farewell appearance after 55 years of service in the RAF. In total, there were 49 aircraft of 15 different types.

⋀ **A Lockheed CF-104 Starfighter, serial number 12846 of the Canadian Armed Forces, flanked by a Hurricane, LF363, and Spitfire Mk Vb AB910/ QJ-J of the Battle of Britain Flight in July 1966. Image records indicate that the photograph was taken during a sortie from RAF Leuchars.** *(Crown Copyright/Air Historical Branch image T-6499)*

➢ **An unusual formation featuring BBMF's Lancaster PA474 with nine red Folland Gnat aircraft of the Red Arrows, near Kemble on 12 April 1975.** *(Crown Copyright/Air Historical Branch image TN-1-7237-41)*

The wedding of HRH Prince William and Catherine Middleton

Once again, the BBMF was called upon to lead a small flypast of aircraft over Buckingham Palace on 29 April 2011, shortly after the wedding ceremony of HRH Prince William and Catherine Middleton had taken place at Westminster Abbey.

After the ceremony, William and Catherine were joined on the Buckingham Palace balcony by senior members of the royal family as Lancaster PA474 (flown by Flt Lt Ernie Taylor, Sqn Ldr Jamie Watson and Flt Lt Bill Williams), accompanied by Hurricane LF363 (Flt Lt Anthony Parkinson) and a Spitfire Mk XIX (Sqn Ldr Duncan Mason) flew over, to the obvious delight of the royal couple. A pair of Typhoons and Tornado aircraft completed the flypast.

Bomber Command Memorial

On 28 June 2012 Her Majesty Queen Elizabeth II formally unveiled the Bomber Command Memorial in Green Park, London. The memorial commemorates the personnel of Bomber Command who flew operations during the Second World War, some 55,573 of whom lost their lives. The memorial was officially opened in the presence of Bomber Command veterans and family members of personnel from all over the world.

Lancaster PA474 was to complete a flypast and poppy drop over the memorial. At the time, PA474 was painted in the colours of Lancaster Mk III EE139, coded 'HW-R', which operated with 100 Squadron and carried the nose art _Phantom of the Ruhr_. During the war, EE139 flew 30 operations with 100 Squadron before moving to 550 Squadron as code 'BQ-B'.

At the time of the aircraft's arrival with 100 Squadron at Waltham, the aircraft was handed to Sgt Ron Clark who, with his crew of NCOs, flew EE139 on 32 occasions, logging 165 hours in the aircraft, of which 147 were on night operations.

When it was announced that PA474 was to overfly the Bomber Command Memorial, it was also announced that Flt Lt Ron Clark would be on board the Lancaster. Clark would be making his first flight in a Lancaster for 67 years; in 1945 he had flown a Lancaster as part of the VJ-Day commemorations over London.

Captain on board the Lancaster on 28 June 2012 was Flt Lt Roger Nicholls with his crew of Flt Lt Loz Rushmere (Co-pilot), Sqn Ldr 'Russ' Russell (Navigator) and MACR Brendan O'Sullivan (Flight Engineer). When the Lancaster approached the memorial ready to release its symbolic payload, as the bomb doors opened and the poppies streamed behind the aircraft to flutter peacefully down over Green Park, Ron said on the intercom 'Lest we forget', which was echoed by the rest of the crew on board.

Next time you see one or more of the Battle of Britain Memorial Flight aircraft at a display, look up and enjoy the moment, but spare a thought for the brave souls who gave their lives to save others.

'Lest we forget.'

◁ During the RIAT at Fairford on 14 July 2007, the Red Arrows were joined by Hurricane LF363, Spitfire PR XIXs PM631 and PS915, and the Rolls-Royce Spitfire PR XIX PS853 to mark the 50th anniversary of the BBMF. *(Peter R. March)*

∨ 229 OCU Tornado F3 ZE785/AO in formation with BBMF Spitfire PR XIX PS853/C near Coningsby on 21 August 1990. *(Crown Copyright/Air Historical Branch image BRUG-7-32)*

◁ Tornado GR1 ZD788/CB of 17 Squadron, based at RAF Bruggen in Germany, in formation with Spitfire Mk Vb AB910/ AE-H of the BBMF on 26 May 1995, around the time of 17 Squadron's 80th anniversary. *(Crown Copyright/Air Historical Branch image BRUG-7-32)*

△ BBMF Spitfire Mk IIa P7350/YT-F in formation with Tony Bianchi's Sopwith F1 Camel (Replica) B-2458/ G-BPOB in 1991. Both aircraft types were used by 65 Squadron. *(Geoffrey Lee/Planefocus GL-9104335)*

◁ BBMF Spitfire LFIXe MK356 in formation with 100 Squadron Hawk T1 XX314/CN on 2 May 2004. The Hawk carries a '100 years of Flight' logo on the side of its fuselage. *(Geoffrey Lee/Planefocus GL-040217)*

➤ A pair of 100 Squadron Hawk T1s (XX314/CN and XX351/CQ) in formation with the BBMF Lancaster PA474/ QR-M on 28 June 2002 to celebrate 100 Squadron's 85th anniversary. While the Lancaster is seen here flying in 61 Squadron colours, the type was operated by 100 Squadron from December 1942 to May 1946. *(Geoffrey Lee/ Planefocus GL-020515)*

↖ 100 Squadron Hawk T1 XX285/CB in formation with the BBMF's Lancaster PA474/QR-M on 12 May 2005. *(Geoffrey Lee/Planefocus GL-050572)*

↙ An unusual formation mixing fixed and rotary wings: a 28 (AC) Squadron Merlin HC1 from RAF Benson in formation with a Hurricane IIb LF363/US-C and Spitfire PR XIX PM631 from the BBMF while in transit from Lowestoft to RAF Coningsby on 29 July 2005. The Merlin is being flown by its display pilot, Sqn Ldr Mark Beardmore, the Spitfire by Sqn Ldr Clive Rowley and the Hurricane by Wg Cdr Russ Allchorne. *(Geoffrey Lee/ Planefocus GL-054495)*

⋀ **BBMF Dakota ZA947/ A1 leads a Hercules C3 XV188 and a Hercules C5 ZH887 over the Wiltshire countryside on 1 September 2005 to celebrate the 90th anniversary of 24 Squadron. All three types have served with 24 Squadron at some time during the squadron's lifetime.** *(Geoffrey Lee/ Planefocus GL-055797)*

➤ **On 6 June 2007, No 5 (AC) Squadron is presented with a new standard. To celebrate the occasion, one of the squadron's Sentinel R1 aircraft (ZJ690) flies in formation with a 25 Squadron Tornado F3 (ZE342/FG) and the BBMF's Hurricane IIc PZ865/JX-E. Both the Hurricane (from July 1943 to September 1944) and the Tornado F3 (from January 1988) were types that had operated with 5 Squadron**. *(Geoffrey Lee/ Planefocus GL-072182)*

At the Lincolnshire Lancaster Association Members' Day at Coningsby on 30 September 2007, BBMF's Lancaster PA474/BQ-B joins alongside the Flight's Spitfire LFIXe MK356/21-V, Spitfire IIa P7350/XT-L and Hurricane IIc PZ865/JX-E. *(Crown Copyright/Sgt Gary Morgan)*

A very neat BBMF five-ship formation with the Hurricane IIb LF363 leading Spitfire Mk Vb AB910/RF-D, Spitfire Mk IIa P7350/XT-L, Spitfire LFIXe MK356/UF-D resplendent in the all-over silver colours of No 601 (County of London) Squadron, AuxAF, and Spitfire PR XIX PS915 – at the LLAMD, Coningsby, 28 September 2008. *(Crown Copyright)*

Five of the BBMF's fighters are joined by Lancaster PA474/BQ-B at the LLAMD at Coningsby on 30 September 2007. Nearest the camera is Spitfire LFIXe MK356/21-V, Spitfire Mk Vb AB910/RF-D, Spitfire Mk IIa P7350/XT-L with Hurricane IIb LF363/YB-W and Mk IIc PZ865/JX-E. *(Crown Copyright/Sgt Gary Morgan)*

⩗ For the 2010 flying display season, two Tucano T1s (ZF171/LZ-R and ZF317/QJ-F) from RAF Linton-on-Ouse were painted in camouflage to mark the 70th anniversary of the Battle of Britain. On 19 May 2010, they were joined for a photoshoot over North Yorkshire by the BBMF's Spitfire Mk IIa P7350/QJ-K, itself a veteran of the Battle of Britain. ZF171 was flown by Flt Lt Tom Bould from 72(R) Squadron and P7350 by OC BBMF, Sqn Ldr Ian Smith. *(Geoffrey Lee/ Planefocus GLD-105566)*

⩻ A special formation to mark the 50th anniversary of the Battle of Britain flies along the south coast on 13 June 1990 with a British Airways Concorde G-BOAA and BBMF Spitfire IIa P7350/ UO-T. *(Crown Copyright/Air Historic Branch TN-2-760-2a)*

⩺ No 41 Squadron celebrated its 95th anniversary in 2011. For the occasion, one of the squadron's Tornado GR4s, ZA600/EB-G, was painted in special markings and was joined by the BBMF's Spitfire Mk IIa P7350/EB-G also in 41 Squadron markings, for a photoshoot close to Coningsby on 8 September 2011. The BBMF Spitfire was flown by Flt Lt Anthony Parkinson and the GR4 by Wg Cdr R Davies and Sqn Ldr M Elsey. *(Geoffrey Lee/Planefocus GLD-118994)*

⋀ The 95th anniversary of 100 Squadron, formed at Hingham on 11 February 1917, was celebrated with a special anniversary photoshoot on 30 May 2012. Two of the current squadron's Hawk T1s (XX246 and XX318) from RAF Leeming were painted in a pseudo-wartime special commemorative paint scheme and were flown in formation with the BBMF's Lancaster PA474, itself flying with a 100 Squadron colour scheme applied to its port side, representing EE139/HW-R which flew at least 29 missions with the famous wartime squadron. _(Geoffrey Lee/Planefocus GLD-128490)_

➤ Shortly after the Lancaster had been in formation with two 100 Squadron Hawk T1s, it was joined by a pair of Typhoon FGR4s from No XI (F) Squadron (ZK323/DN and ZK305/DE). No XI (F) Squadron was re-formed at Coningsby in March 2007 as the second front-line Typhoon squadron. _(Geoffrey Lee/Planefocus GLD-128874)_

BBMF Hurricane IIb LF363/YB-W and Spitfire PR XIX PS915 fly alongside the camera over southern England on 11 August 2012. PS915 is marked *The Last!* as it was the last of the type to make an operation flight with the Temperature and Humidity Flight on 10 June 1957. *(Keith Wilson)*

Bibliography

Battle of Britain Memorial Flight Official Yearbook 1982, 1983, 1984, 1986, 1987, 1989, 1990, 1991, 1992, 1993, 1995, 1998, 1999, 2000, 2001, 2002, 2003, 2004, 2005, 2006, 2007, 2008 and 2012 (available from the Visitor Centre, RAF Coningsby, RAF Coningsby, Dogdyke Road, Coningsby, Lincolnshire LN4 4SY; tel: 01526 782041; www.lincolnshire.gov.uk/bbmf; and at BBMF Roadshows)

Blackah, Lowe, Malcolm V., and Blackah, Louise *Hawker Hurricane – Owners' Workshop Manual* (Haynes Publishing, 1st edn, 2010)

Blackah, Paul and Louise, *Douglas DC-3 Dakota – Owners' Workshop Manual* (Haynes Publishing, 1st edn, 2011)

Bowman, Martin, *The Immortal Few* (Halsgrove, 1st edn, 2010)

Cotter, Jarrod, and Blackah, Paul, *Avro Lancaster – Owners' Workshop Manual* (Haynes Publishing, 1st edn, 2008)

Cotter, Jarrod, *The Battle of Britain Memorial Flight – 50 Years of Flying* (Pen & Sword Books, 1st edn, 2007)

Ellis, Ken, *Wrecks & Relics* (Crecy Publishing Ltd, 21st edn, 2008)

Fisher, M.D.N., Brown, R.W., and Rothermel, T., *Chipmunk – the First Fifty Years* (Air Britain (Historians) Limited, c.1996)

Jackson, A. J., *De Havilland Aircraft Since 1909*, updated by R.T. Jackson (Putnam, 3rd edn, 1987)

Jefford, Wg Cdr C.G., MBE RAF, *RAF Squadrons* (Airlife Publishing Ltd, 1st edn, 1988)

Price, Dr Alfred, and Blackah, Paul, *Supermarine Spitfire – Owners' Workshop Manual* (Haynes Publishing, 1st edn, 2007)

Taylor, Bill, *The Battle of Britain Memorial Flight* (Midland Publishing Limited, 1st edn, 1995)

Thetford, Owen, *Aircraft of the Royal Air Force Since 1918* (Putnam Aeronautical Books, 8th rev. edn, 1988)

Winslade, Richard, *The Battle of Britain Memorial Flight* (The History Press, 1st edn, 2007)

Index

Green Design
Design for the Environment

First published in Great Britain in 1991
Second edition published 1997
by Laurence King Publishing
an imprint of Calmann & King Ltd
71 Great Russell Street
London WC1B 3BN

Copyright © 1991, 1997 Dorothy Mackenzie

A catalogue record for this book is available
from the British Library.

ISBN 1 85669 096 2

Designed by Area, London
Printed on minimum-chlorine-bleached paper
Printed in Hong Kong

Acknowledgements
Many people have made this book possible. I
would like to thank, in particular, Louise
Moss, Julia Engelhardt and Rochelle Martyn,
whose persistent research helped track down
so many of the examples featured in this book,
all the companies and individuals who provided information and photographs, and my editor, Jane Havell, who proposed the book in the
first place, and whose encouragement and
deadlines ensured that it came to fruition. I
would also like to acknowledge the influence
of John Elkington in the thinking behind the
book. His booklet, *The Green Designer*, published in 1986, set out important guidelines
and directions, which I hope this book ampli-
fies. Many other friends and colleagues contributed to the development of ideas, and my
husband Stephen provided support and help
throughout.

Dorothy Mackenzie

Green Design
Design for the Environment

Dorothy Mackenzie

Researchers
Louise Moss
Julia Engelhardt
Rochelle Martyn

Laurence King

Contents

Foreword

The contribution that design can make to improving environmental performance is increasingly being recognised. Over the last few years many companies have made considerable progress in improving the environmental performance of their manufacturing operations, but in many industries the major impact comes from their products in use, or when disposed of. Improving the environmental performance of products, through intelligent design, is now a major focus of interest.

A great deal of progress has been made in architecture, with many of our leading architects demonstrating their understanding of environmental priorities in showcase buildings. But the vast majority of new buildings remain largely untouched by concerns such as energy efficiency or the avoidance of toxic materials.

This book aims to recognise, through the use of case histories, the progress that is being made in many areas of design, and the interesting ideas and new directions which are beginning to emerge. None of the examples can claim to be completely "green", and there will inevitably be aspects of many of them which could be criticised. In some cases, cost or aesthetic motivations may have driven the design, with environmental improvement an accidental rather than intentional result. Some examples are given of improvements to products whose very existence may be open to question on the grounds of utility or harmfulness. It is, though, part of the task of designers to minimise the damage done by the products we currently use, while helping to create new, less harmful ways of addressing people's needs.

Despite the progress that has been made, there remains a need to demonstrate the significance of the designer's contribution to minimising environmental problems, by setting out the relationship between design decisions and environmental issues. The book is intended to help designers ask the right questions, rather than to deliver unequivocal answers.

Some background to major environmental issues is covered, although the book focuses on the implications of the issues for the design process. A wide range of excellent reference books is available, some of which are listed at the end, together with organisations which can provide further, more detailed assistance.

One objective of this book is to demonstrate that designs which take account of environment considerations can be commercially successful, functional and highly aesthetically attractive. There is little point in producing environmentally sensitive solutions if they are too expensive, inconvenient or unattractive for anyone to want to buy and use them. There is no reason why designing for minimal environment impact should produce drab, poor-quality results which give satisfaction only through guilt reduction.

The incredible rate of change in the solutions available and in the development of new thinking means that any book on this subject is always out of date. For that reason, detailed technical information on materials and production techniques has been avoided; it is always best to check directly with manufacturers or professional associations for the latest developments.

The need to build consideration of environment impact into the design process will pose enormous problems and challenges, but it will also be a stimulus for innovation and creativity. Above all, it will provide real opportunities for designers to demonstrate the value of their problem-solving skills and the breadth of their contribution.

Right
A wind farm near
Palm Springs, California
(see page 25).

1 Introduction

"In this age of mass production when everything must be planned and designed, design has become the most powerful tool with which man shapes his tools and environments (and, by extension, society and himself). This demands high social and moral responsibility from the designer." (Victor Papanek, *Design for the Real World*, 1970)

The idea that designers should take into consideration the environment impact of their work is not new. Thirty years ago Victor Papanek argued convincingly that the designer was in a powerful position, able to help create a better world, or contribute further to planetary destruction. His ideas – that designers should resist designing built-in obsolescence; that consumers' needs, rather than their wants, should be addressed; and that designers should strive to find ways of using their skills for socially useful ends, especially in developing countries – outraged much of the design establishment at the time.

Today, however, ideas which once seemed utopian and naive appear highly relevant and almost inevitable, given the unprecedented levels of concern being expressed throughout the world over environmental problems. Twenty years ago, environmentalism was regarded as an activity for the radical fringe; now, governments strive to demonstrate their environmentalist credentials, and problems attract high levels of popular concern. There is a growing consensus that problems affecting the environment cannot be ignored. As a result of dramatic scientific evidence of ozone depletion and new scientific agreement about the impending problems of global warming, a new sense of urgency has arisen.

Rising public concern is being translated into action in many countries: people are demonstrating their feelings through their voting preferences, by joining environment campaigning groups, by changing their behaviour to accommodate recycling or

energy efficiency, and by using environment criteria in their purchasing decisions as consumers.

We are entering a period when environment performance, together with a wide range of ethical and moral issues, will be on the agenda for business, government and individuals. New criteria will evolve for judging the acceptability of products and processes; new methods will emerge to calculate the true cost of activities; new regulations will control industrial and individual behaviour. Decisions about the nature of our society and economy may well be underpinned by a growing commitment to sustainable rather than uncontrolled development.

Are designers equipped to respond to the new demands which will arise from these changes? The answer is almost certainly no, as it must be for almost all professionals trained without reference to the environment impact of their activities.

In most places, design has not been taught in the context of its social and ecological impact. Many designers assume that their area of responsibility is limited to function and appearance. In some fields, most notably architecture, a broader view has sometimes been taken because of the scale of the direct impact of buildings on their local environment. But even here, little attention has been paid to the implications of the type of construction materials used or, for example, to the energy efficiency of the lighting system.

One might be able to argue that up until now designing with environment impact in

Below
Exterior of the corporate
headquarters of the NMB
Bank in The Netherlands,
designed by Alberts
and Van Huut for energy
efficiency and employee

satisfaction. The
natural environment
has proved hugely
popular with the staff
working there (for
a detailed analysis,
see pages 56-9).

mind was a matter of personal taste or individual moral responsibility. Now it is clear that it will become a commercial imperative. The value and role of designers will be substantially reduced if they cannot incorporate new concepts and new criteria into their work.

There is an opportunity for designers to show imagination and leadership, pioneering the way forward and solving real problems.

For many years, designers have been asserting their influence and demonstrating the power of design. The new demands of designing for minimum ecological impact will provide an ideal platform from which designers can justify their claims and acknowledge their responsibilities.

The role and responsibility of the designer

Why should so much responsibility fall to the designer? Design is one part of a holistic process, which involves a wide range of other skills. However, design is a pivotal part of the process.

Many environmental problems are caused by the pollution which results from the production and use of products and services, particularly mass-produced products. Most products and services use up natural resources, many of which are irreplaceable.

The method by which raw materials are extracted from the earth can cause severe local environmental problems. The manufacturing process itself uses energy, creates waste, and may result in harmful by-products. The product has then to be distributed –

Sustainable development

Sustainable development was defined by the Bruntland Commission (The World Commission on Environment and Development, published in 1987) as meeting "the needs of the present without compromising the ability of future generations to meet their own needs". The implication is that for development to be sustainable, it must take account not just of economic factors, but also of environmental and social factors, and must assess long-term consequences of actions as well as short-term results.

Some businesses are beginning to consider how they might become sustainable. At a minimum, they need to take the full environmental costs of their activities into account when assessing their investment decisions or their day-to-day performance. They will have to consider whether their supply of raw materials can be produced indefinitely, and whether their products and services actually contribute to meeting human needs in ways which have the minimum environmental impact. Concepts such as "eco-efficiency" – which means the delivery of the maximum benefit to the user, with the minimum use of resources and the least possible environment damage – are now being developed by major companies as a tool to help them progress towards sustainable business.

raising other environmental issues – following which it is used. Many products have a significant effect on the environment when in use – cars, for example, or detergents, or paints. And finally, the product may be disposed of, causing another set of problems.

The designer, as the principal determinant or creator of the product itself, has a direct influence on the amount of damage which will occur at each stage in the process. What materials will be used, and from where will these be obtained? How will the product be manufactured? Are particular processes required to give a specific effect or appearance? How will the product be used and disposed of – is it designed to be easy to repair, or to be thrown away? If it is to be disposed of, can parts of it be re-used or recycled? Designers, as creators or specifiers, are in a position to determine many of these issues.

But designers also influence environment impact indirectly, through their role as setters of styles and tastes. In some countries, most notably the UK, the Eighties saw a dramatic rise in the recognition of the importance of

good design. But by the end of the decade the word "designer" had become devalued almost to the point of becoming pejorative, because it had become associated with superficial glitziness, with a proliferation of expensive, unnecessary objects whose sole purpose was to convey social status upon their owners. Design was criticised as elitist, and was seen to be relevant to only a narrow area of activities – primarily industries making consumer goods. Designers have participated fully in the disposable society, creating new styles with increasing frequency, and therefore necessarily building in obsolescence. They have often been criticised by environmentalists for failing to use their skills and influence to useful purpose.

Until now, many designers may have felt that, if they wished to use their skills, they have had no alternative but to participate in the misuse of design. Now, however, as individual values and business priorities are beginning to change, they have the opportunity to demonstrate that environmental considerations, along with social and ethical concerns, occupy a central position within mainstream design thinking.

Designers can now speak from an authoritative platform in most countries, and they increasingly occupy key positions in major companies. The contribution that design can make to business performance is now widely recognised, and many governments have been active in encouraging industry to work closely with designers to improve the quality and competitiveness of their products and services.

"The effective use of design is fundamental to the creation of innovative products, processes and services. Good design can significantly add value to products, lead to growth in sales and enable both the exploitation of new markets and the consolidation of existing ones. The benefits of good design can be seen in:

- processes improved by gradual innovation
- redesign of existing products in response to user needs, new markets and competitor products
- development of new products by anticipating new market opportunities

The challenge is to integrate design into business processes." (UK Government White Paper on Competitiveness, 1995)

The role of designers as the link between the manufacturing process and the customer, between technical and marketing requirements, has given them an important position in many companies in areas such as new product development. Designers have an opportunity to demonstrate their ability to take on the complex and challenging issues which surround designing to improve environment impact. This will require thorough research before starting the design process, and an understanding of environment issues and the ability to know where to look for guidelines. However, unless the company is committed at the highest level to improving its environment performance, the systems and culture will tend to thwart all but the most determined designer.

The commercial imperative

Many businesses are beginning to realise that long-term commercial success depends on acceptable environment performance. Environmental problems such as resource depletion and pollution are disruptive and costly, and poor environment performance, such as industrial accidents, can call into question the social acceptability of a company. The suspicion which many people feel about "big business" is legitimised by any evidence of a careless approach to the protection of the environment. Poor environment performance can also considerably reduce the attractiveness of a company for investment purposes. Exposure to liabilities such as those created by responsibility for contaminated land can significantly affect a company's financial strength. Some major investors, such as public service worker pension funds in the US, adopt environmental and ethical criteria which influence their investment portfolio, and green investment funds have attracted an enthusiastic following – for their commercial as well as environmental performance.

Many of the large companies regarded as being the leaders in their fields are now incorporating environment criteria into their definition of "quality", through programmes such as Total Quality Management. Some have practised several aspects of good environment performance for many years, inspired by a desire to reduce waste. 3M's "Pollution Prevention Pays" programme (see page 15), and Dow Chemical's "Waste Reduction Always Pays", are good examples of companies identifying a commercial benefit in sound environmental practices.

Many of the most active programmes have been in industries at the forefront of environmental problems, such as the chemicals industry and the oil industry, but such programmes are now beginning to gain acceptance across a much wider spectrum. Up until now, however, the majority of companies which have considered environment issues at all have done so because they were forced by legislation to address problems they themselves were causing – such as river pollution or the emission of harmful gases – or because there were substantial cost savings to be achieved, or because of issues related to the health and safety of their workforce. Now there are a number of additional pressures, which will mean that environment issues will move increasingly centre-stage for industry.

Biologists examine the shore after the giant supertanker Exxon Valdez went aground in March 1989 in Prince William Sound in Alaska. More than 10 million gallons of oil escaped, polluting over 700 miles of coastline and killing millions of fish, birds and other wildlife.

The Valdez Principles

The code of practical guidelines for corporate behaviour was published in September 1989 by the Coalition for Environmentally Responsible Economies, a group composed of environmentalists and ethical investment organisations. The principles are intended to help industry develop its own policies and practices, and to guide investors on their decisions by identifying which companies subscribe to the principles. They are:

- Protection of the biosphere
- Reduction and disposal of waste
- Risk reduction
- Damage compensation
- Appointing an environment director and managers

- Sustainable use of natural resources
- Wise use of energy
- Marketing of safe products and services
- Disclosure of information
- Undertaking environmental assessments and annual audits

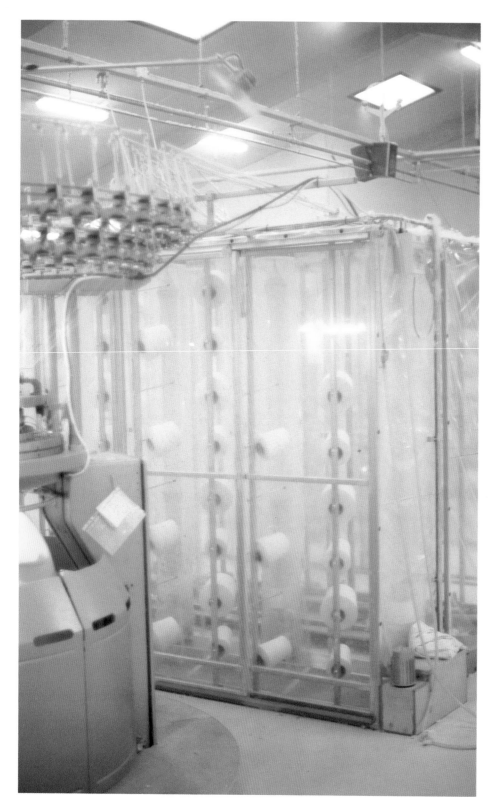

Above
Part of the factory producing Novotex "green cotton" in
Denmark (see pages 146-9). The glassed-in sections
protect workers from the health hazards associated with
cotton particles in the air.

3M

The US-based multinational company 3M has pursued a policy of trying to reduce pollution at source wherever possible, rather than relying on controlling it once it has been created. The "Pollution Prevention Pays" programme encourages individuals or groups of employees to identify ways of preventing pollution through modifying processes, developing improved products, re-designing equipment and finding new uses for waste. The programme has resulted in major cost savings for the company, as well as the avoidance of large quantities of pollution.

New legislative frameworks

Increasing public concern has led to demands for more and more legislation to control industrial activity. The extent of legislation varies considerably between countries, and even within parts of a country, but there is universal belief that the amount of legislation will increase. Already in some countries laws determine what materials a soft drinks container may be made of.

A number of clear themes are emerging from legislation being introduced all over Europe, North America and Australia:

- The polluter pays.
- The producer should bear responsibility for waste disposal.
- The public should have access to information on companies' environment performance.

Meeting new legislative demands such as these will require significant changes in some industries, and will change priorities especially in areas such as product design. A manufacturer charged with the responsibility of taking back used cars for final disposal will have an incentive to ensure that cars are designed in the first place for easy disassembly for recycling, or that no harmful emissions are given off if final residues have to be incinerated.

Employee pressure

Many developed countries are facing the prospect of a decline in the number of people making up the skilled workforce. Competition for the best employees will grow tougher, and companies will have to make themselves as attractive as possible to secure the right people. There is now a very high level of concern over environmental issues amongst younger people, particularly those in higher education, which means that, increasingly, companies' environment performance will be assessed by any potential recruits as a key issue when they are considering employment. Already, company recruitment literature is emphasising environment commitment in recognition that this may be a crucial deciding factor.

Maintaining the loyalty and commitment of the workforce will also demand that the goals and values of the company are compatible with the goals and values of individuals; as the latter are changing to place a higher importance on environment protection, so company values will have to change too, to avoid the alienation of employees. And, of course, many people working within companies who see themselves as determined environmentalists will gradually appear in senior management positions. The marketing director of one major multinational company, when asked which environmental campaigning group gave him the toughest time and presented him with the most challenges, replied that his toughest critics came from inside the company, from the junior members of his own department.

Market demand

In addition to financial, legislative and employee pressure, market pressure is playing a major role in encouraging changes in industrial behaviour. Some large organisations have introduced "Suppliers' Charters", setting out the environment performance they require from anyone supplying them with a product or service. Government departments and institutions in Germany, for example, are required to purchase products such as recycled paper; major retailers such as Wal-Mart in the US and B & Q in the UK are advising their suppliers on the development of lower-impact products, and on aspects of good environment practice such as energy efficiency. Retailers in several countries have been quick to respond

Personlig pleje uden PVC. Det virker både i dybden og i længden.

Irma har udviklet en ny hudplejeserie, der først og fremmest går i hudens dybde og virker efter de metoder, der i dag kendes som de bedste. Det er lette, milde cremer, og De kan vælge, om De vil pleje Dem selv med eller uden parfume.

Når den nye hudplejeserie også virker i længden, skyldes det den miljørigtige embal-lage. For nok er alt det, man har stående på badeværelseshylden en personlig sag. Men det er forurening af vore omgivelser til gen-gæld ikke. Hidtil er de fleste plastemballager

til hudplejemidler blevet fremstillet med PVC. Et stof, der blandt andet udvikler klor ved forbrænding.

Denne forurening vil Irma gerne være med til at sætte en stopper for. Derfor er em-ballagen til den nye hudplejeserie uden PVC. I stedet har vi brugt en miljørigtig plast, der ikke skader, men indgår i naturens kredsløb ved forbrænding sammen med det øvrige husholdningsaffald. Det fremgår også af det lille "indgår i naturens kredsløb"-mærke, som er præget i bunden. Og som i øvrigt sid-

der på flere og flere af vore emballager. I 1990 tager vi skridtet fuldt ud, og forbyder alle for-mer for PVC-emballager i vore butikker. Den tid, den glæde.

Velkommen i Irma.

Irma
Til alle, der tænker, før de handler.

---

to consumer pressure, and have often initiated their own specific campaigns. The commercial risk of failing to anticipate environmental problems can be considerable. Entire markets can now disappear almost overnight, as was the case with the market for CFC gases in aerosols. So it is very much in the interests of industry to follow the environment debate closely, and try to keep ahead of legislation at all times.

Environment pressures do not just create problems and commercial risks, however; they also bring about major new market opportuni-ties. Obvious examples are in the rapidly growing field of pollution-abatement technol-ogy, but improved environment performance provides an attractive new benefit in many sectors, and has led to significant competitive advantage for many companies.

What about the cost?

A frequent complaint about improving envi-ronment performance, and one of the main reasons given for failing to adopt high stan-dards, is the assumption that higher costs are always involved. In many areas additional cost is inevitable if, for example, the price of mak-ing good the damage done to water courses, seas or the atmosphere through the emission of waste materials has not previously been considered. The cost of safely disposing of products at the end of their life can also be high. Concerns are expressed about passing this higher cost on to the customer, particular-ly in markets facing competition from compa-nies or countries which do not adopt higher environmental standards and can therefore keep prices lower.

However, companies are increasingly embracing the concept of Eco-efficiency – the idea of achieving both economic and environmental benefits, through strategies such as waste minimisation, energy efficiency and risk minimisation. Of course, customers would prefer to have good-quality products, offering good environmental performance, at no extra cost: this is the new challenge for designers. Can products be re-thought so that they deliver the same benefit to the user, in a way that is environmentally better, but at no extra cost? In some sectors, the customer may be required to pay a higher price for the product, but the trade-off may be a longer-lived, more reliable product, or one that consumes less energy in use, thus leading to savings in the longer term.

Some companies have of course viewed the development of consumer interest in the environment as a short-term marketing opportunity. Taking advantage of consumers' lack of knowledge, they used minor improvements as the basis for dramatic "green product" claims. This inevitably led to considerable consumer confusion and scepticism, and in some cases to rejection of products with high-profile green claims. Green products were also perceived as being more expensive, and sometimes offering poorer functional performance – perceptions which were sometimes, but not always, justified.

The introduction of official environmental labelling schemes, such as the European Union scheme, should help to reassure consumers about both environmental legiti-

macy and functional performance, and may encourage consumers to demonstrate a higher level of interest in translating their continuing concern over environmental issues into practical purchasing behaviour.

Irrespective of whether consumers are overtly demanding greener products, manufacturers are realising that good environmental performance will increasingly be seen as a prerequisite of good management practice, and an essential component of quality.

So, for the designer, the ability to understand the environmental impact of design decisions will no longer be an optional extra, but rather an essential part of core design capability. "Green design" should not be seen as a sub-set of "mainstream design", but as an integral aspect of the design process. Environmental performance will be as important as producability, function and aesthetics.

Changing consumption

The 1980s saw the emergence of the "Green Consumers", people apparently eager to adopt green purchasing policies and greener behaviour. A rash of books and magazines were produced to inform their decisions, and many manufacturers launched new products or repositioned existing ones. Recycling household waste became popular. The emergence of a scientific consensus about the dangers of the destruction of the ozone layer, and

Below
L'Oréal's Plénitude skin care range was redesigned to reduce the amount of over-packaging, whilst retaining the premium look of the range. The packaging volume of each unit of finished product was reduced by half and the number of different materials used was reduced from seven to four. The number of units per pallet has increased significantly, and the weight of distribution packaging has been reduced by nearly half. The new design has been well received by both retailers and consumers.

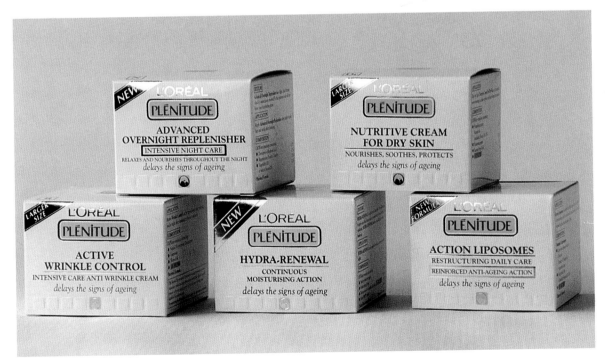

Right
The New Wave Plus 5 1500 autowasher from Hoover was the first European appliance to meet the criteria set by the EU Eco-label. It uses around a third less water, detergent and energy than previous machines, and achieves grade "A" energy labelling.

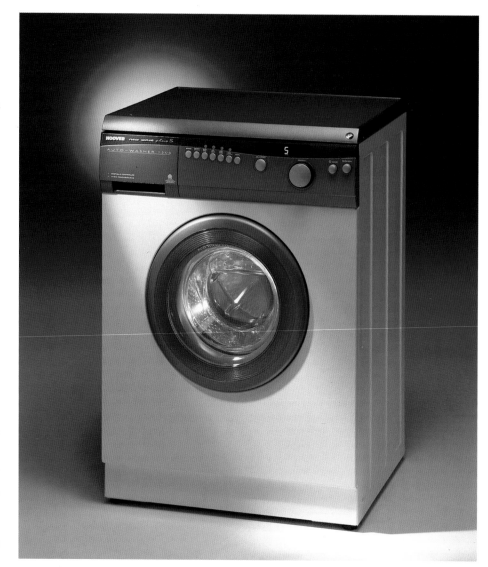

Below left & right
The Dutch Eco-label Stichting Milieukeur covers a wide range of consumer product areas, from carpets to chairs, paper products to refrigerators. The environmental standards set take account of all the stages in the product's life. In addition, products have to meet quality requirements to ensure they are fit for purpose.

the realisation that ozone depletion could increase the risk of cancer in humans, led to public interest in CFC-free products. However, the ready availability of acceptable alternatives in markets such as aerosols contributed greatly to people's willingness to switch. Some individuals wish to feel that they are taking on individual responsibility for addressing environmental problems, and the purchasing of products with lower environmental impact is a relatively easy way for them to feel they are "doing their bit". However, simply making small changes to day-to-day purchasing behaviour will not lead to the type of dramatic reductions in resource use in developed

countries that are likely to be necessary if the needs and aspirations of the rest of the world are to be accommodated.

Growing affluence in the developed world has created an opportunity for people to become interested in the quality of their lives, rather then simply in survival through the acquisition of basic necessities. The rapid increase in material wellbeing experienced by many during the 1980s did not necessarily lead to the perception that the quality of life had improved, and during the 1990s there has appeared to be some recognition that quantitative consumption goals may not lead to satisfaction.

Right
Compact fluorescent lightbulbs can last up to eight times longer than incandescent light bulbs and use about 80 per cent less energy to produce the same brightness. Replacing a 75-watt incandescent bulb with an 18-watt compact fluorescent bulb will, over the lifetime of the bulb, avoid emitting the equivalent of 1,000 lb of carbon dioxide and about 20 lb of sulphur dioxide from a typical power-generating plant in the USA.

Eco-labelling schemes

The growth of consumer interest in the environment performance of products has led some countries to introduce official "Eco-labelling schemes", to help consumers make informed choices. The German Blue Angel scheme (label, right) was established in 1978, and covers over 4,000 products. Canada, The Netherlands and Japan, among others, have national Eco-labelling schemes, and the Nordic Swan scheme covers products in the Nordic area. In 1993 the European Union scheme was established to encourage manufacturers to make products that do less damage to the environment, and to provide consumers with independent information. Criteria for the label are set on a category basis, using life-cycle assessments to identify the main areas of environmental impact.

Below
Advertisement for "eco-beer" from the Lammsbrau brewery in Neumarkt, Germany, which aims for a comprehensive approach to environment performance. The beer itself is made from organically grown ingredients, with no additives. The plant has a heat recycling installation, and solar energy is used to dry some of the ingredients. The product is distributed only in bottles, which are re-usable, and the labels contain only paper, without the metallic foil customarily wrapped round the neck.

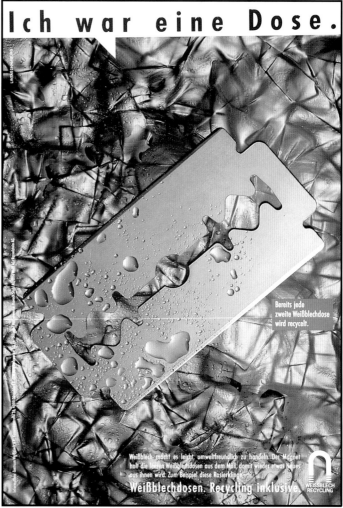

The new challenge must be to examine ways of making it possible for people to receive the products and services they need in ways which are much less resource-intensive – in other words, to move towards more sustainable production and consumption. Strategies such as dematerialisation, the use of shared rather than personal products, the extension of product life and the rediscovery of the value of simplicity will be explored in the innovation and design programmes of many companies in the future.

Marketing on green platforms

After an initial rush of enthusiasm for finding "green claims" which could be applied to products, manufacturers became more wary of making overt claims about the environmental performance of their products. However, there are many examples of products which have been successfully positioned on an environmental platform: recycled household paper; phosphate-free detergents; rechargeable batteries. Some smaller manufacturers have been able to establish their position in the market by offering a distinctive environmental benefit, while companies from countries such as Germany have been able to use environmental superiority as a tool for developing their presence in export markets.

But manufacturers face some risk when focusing on specific claims for individual products. In many areas, our understanding of what constitutes an environmental improvement is still developing, and opinions change over time. Consumers may find it hard to understand claims which rely on some technical or scientific understanding – but may be unwilling to accept banal generalisations. In

Ich war eine Dose.

Weißblech macht es leicht, umweltfreundlich zu handeln. Der Magnet holt die leeren Weißblechdosen aus dem Müll, damit wieder etwas Neues aus ihnen wird. Zum Beispiel dieser Fingerhut.

Weißblechdosen. Recycling inklusive.

addition, companies may find that their credibility is threatened if other aspects of their environmental performance are found to be poor. It may be more sensible in the long term for companies to ensure that their total environmental performance is excellent, and that they develop a reputation for good corporate performance, from which it is assumed that their products offer good environmental performance. Specific claims for individual products may be communicated more effectively through the use of official eco-labelling schemes. Companies should present environmental information relating to products clearly and convincingly, but it may be inadvisable to enter into, for example, competitive counterclaims based on the details of environmental performance.

Communication tools such as environmental reports will be an important way in which companies can inform some audiences about their environmental commitment and performance. The growing recognition of the importance of corporate reputation as an element of long-term business success will encourage more companies to be increasingly open about their environmental behaviour. Winning public trust and confidence will depend at least in part on convincing a suspicious audience that business is taking environmental concerns very seriously.

Above & above left
These advertisements, put out by the German Tin Information Centre, show products made from recycled tin. The headline reads "I was a can": in Germany every second tin can is recycled. Much of the recycled metal is used for high-quality products for which manufacturers have traditionally chosen virgin material, but they certainly do not suffer either in quality or aesthetic appearance.

Left
Guidebooks such as these give advice on issues from pollution to energy efficiency, Third World trade to animal welfare, identifying which products and brands represent the best, and worst, environmental options.

Right
The GE Generation 2 Battery Charger for New York-based consultancy Cousins Design recharges up to eight batteries in only one hour, and then reduces the current until it is ready for use again, using the minimum amount of energy. Rechargeable batteries help to reduce the problems caused by battery disposal, but the recharge time has traditionally been long and energy consumption high.

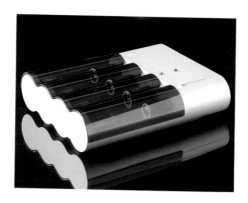

Left
Resource Revival, USA was founded to create fun and functional products from post-consumer recycled materials. Their range of furniture is made entirely from recycled materials. Stools have seats woven from old bicycle inner tubes with bicycle wheel-rim frames.

Right
Jetsystem Rinse Sensor was designed by Zanussi to reduce the levels of water, detergent and energy used by washing machines. The water intake is adjusted automatically according to the size and type of the wash load. Water is continuously recycled by a pump, and jet-sprayed back on to the laundry, so that water consumption is greatly reduced. The efficiency of water recirculation ensures that the detergent moves around more effectively, so that much less detergent is needed. The Rinse Sensor technology measures the amount of suds during rinsing and adjusts rinse water intake and spin accordingly.

Designing for environmentally aware consumers

Some of the earliest products which offered environmental performance advantages were significantly different from their conventional counterparts in terms of their performance. Many consumers found a reduction or change in functional performance, a loss of convenience, or an increase in price hard to accept. During the early stages of the introduction of greener products, those which met with most success tended to be those which performed very similarly to conventional products.

The production of less environmentally-harmful products which can compete directly with traditional products and even improve on their performance is a major challenge. However, there are examples of these already, such as refrigerators which use hydrocarbon coolants rather than CFCs, or vehicles which run on natural gas rather than petrol.

In some sectors, however, it may not be possible to deliver products which perform identically, and consumer expectations must eventually be modified. The answer may lie in a radical new solution which challenges convention by asking "why does it have to be like this?". It is in this direction that the real opportunity for worthwhile innovation lies.

2 The background to environment issues

Of the many important environment problems we confront, this chapter details the issues of which designers should be especially aware. The role of designers in addressing these issues goes far beyond the contribution that the actions of any individual citizen or consumer can make.

It is sometimes difficult to see how individual decisions by designers, about what appear to be rather minor issues – such as the selection of one material over another – affect global environment problems. But design can have an impact upon the environment in many different ways; through the extraction of raw materials; through the design of the manufacturing process; in how the product is used and distributed, and in what happens when the product reaches the end of its useful life.

The greenhouse effect, or global warming

Gases in the atmosphere insulate the earth, preventing some of the sun's heat, reflected from the earth's surface, from escaping into space. This is a natural effect without which the world would be frozen. But industrialisation and agricultural development have resulted in increases in the concentration of some gases in the atmosphere, trapping more heat. The main cause is an increase of 25 per cent in the last two hundred years in the amount of carbon dioxide produced by the burning of wood, oil and coal. Other gases, such as methane, chlorofluorocarbons (CFCs) and nitrous oxide are also playing a role. The effect of increasing concentrations of greenhouse gases could be to cause a significant increase in the global annual mean temperature: estimates vary, but even a 1 degree rise would have serious implications in terms of regional climatic changes, rises in sea levels and redistribution of areas of land suitable

for agricultural production. World energy use doubled between 1930 and 1960, and doubled again between 1960 and 1984,the vast majority of the energy supply coming from oil, coal and gas.

Discussions of ways to avert global warming have focused on the need to reduce emissions of carbon dioxide, for example by substituting low or zero carbon fuels such as natural gas in place of coal; on the importance of developing alternatives to fossil fuels; and on reducing the need for energy through improved energy efficiency, and the use of less energy-intensive products and processes.

The design decision
Opportunities exist for scientists and designers to design products and buildings powered by alternative sources of energy, but perhaps the single most important theme for design generally is energy efficiency. Jug kettles are more energy-efficient than the kettles they replace, because they can boil smaller amounts of water safely. Products designed to run on batteries use far more energy than those which use mains electricity, although clearly there are times when mains electricity would not be available or convenient.

The energy efficiency of the production process is important, too. Different mills making the same paper may use energy with very different efficiency. Up-to-date technology may lead to improved energy efficiency. The amount of energy used to manufacture different materials varies widely. Aluminium uses up huge quantities of energy, but can

Left
A wind farm near Palm Springs, California. Wind turbines are being used in some countries to generate electricity; large areas of land are required, although they could be built off shore. Wind power represents a relatively cheap, clean and simple form of alternative power, if enough can be generated.

Left
Tram belonging to
the Tramway de
l'Agglomération
Grenobloise (TAG) in
France. The system was
inaugurated in 1983 to
help reduce congestion
in Grenoble and revitalise
the city centre; trams run
on electricity and there-
fore help to reduce the
pollution from petrol
exhaust. These have
been designed to high
ergonomic, safety and
comfort standards, and
provide easy access for
people in wheelchairs.
Their introduction has
significantly improved
the quality of life in the
centre of Grenoble.

subsequently be recycled several times, with
low energy costs. Plastics are also energy-
intensive to manufacture, but this energy
is lost unless they are recycled or used in
schemes that generate heat from waste.

Designers can play a role in conserving
energy in several different ways:

- By designing products with improved
  energy efficiency.
- By designing products for recyclability.
  The energy required to manufacture a
  material originally is almost always greater
  than that required to recycle it.
- By specifying materials which have
  been produced efficiently. Many
  packaging manufacturers are now
  providing details of the energy cost
  of different materials.
- By using insulation materials, or solar
  panels, together with construction
  techniques that harness the warmth of the
  earth. This can dramatically reduce the
  energy requirements of buildings.
- By redesigning machinery and processes to
  reduce energy loss and to save production
  costs at the same time. Many industrial
  processes waste energy, simply because
  no one has really given energy efficiency a
  high priority.
- By encouraging more people to use public
  transport, through the design of attractive,
  convenient systems which can make people
  less dependent upon private cars.

The ozone layer

The ozone layer acts as a filter in the stratos-
phere, protecting us from harmful ultraviolet
radiation from the sun. During the 1970s
scientists realised that chlorofluorocarbons
(CFCs) were destroying stratospheric ozone,
as chlorine atoms were released when long-
lived CFCs began to be broken down.
CFCs are also powerful greenhouse gases.
In the mid-1990s ozone density in Europe
was recorded in spring at up to 20 per cent
below normal.

The Montreal Protocol, signed by governments in 1987 and subsequently updated,
aimed to cut production of ozone-depleting
substances. Production of CFCs is set to cease
by the end of the century. Manufacturers
responded by introducing hydrochlorofluoro-
carbons (HCFCs) and HFCs, which are
less significant, but still damaging, ozone
depleters. They are also global-warming gases.
CFCs have had a wide range of applications,
from blowing agents for plastic foams to propellants in aerosol sprays, from refrigerants to
solvents for cleaning electronic components.

The design decision
Alternatives to CFCs exist for almost every
use – even in specialist medical applications –
and designers are able to ensure that CFCs are
designed out of products.

- In packaging, alternatives exist for cartons
  previously made from CFC-blown foam, and
  no material made using CFCs need be used
  in any form of packaging.
- Alternative propellants are available for
  use in aerosols; the use of compressed air
  can reduce VOC emissions by a third and
  improves product safety. Pump-spray systems
  are also being developed as a complete alternative to aerosols, because of concerns

Right and below
Acid rain is caused when coal or oil is burned, releasing sulphur and nitrogen into the atmosphere. These pollutants combine with water in clouds and eventually fall as rain, snow or mist, often long distances away from their source. Over half of Germany's forests are thought to be dying or dead as a result of acid rain damage, and many historic buildings are literally being eaten away. *The Guide to Tree Damage* was designed by Gary Rowland Associates for the World Wildlife Fund.

over the high packaging use of aerosols.
- A wide range of insulation materials are now available which have not been produced with CFCs.
- Alternative refrigerants made from natural hydrocarbon gases or from ammonia are now widely accepted for domestic refrigeration and air-conditioning; their use in commercial refrigeration should also accelerate.

No new product which relies on CFCs should now be designed. Designers must fully assess whether alternatives can be used which are neither ozone depleters nor global warmers.

Tropical deforestation

Between the early 1960s and the mid-1980s, three quarters of a billion acres of forest were lost. Forests in temperate regions are relatively stable, although many trees are dying due to the effects of air pollution. The main cause for concern is the rate of destruction of the tropical rainforest. If the current rate continues, it is estimated that all rainforests will have disappeared within eighty years.

The effects of deforestation include the destruction of species, since rainforests contain a wide diversity of animal and plant life, most of it unique; the disruption of local climates, possibly leading to desertification due to changes in rainfall patterns; desertification, and the loss of habitat for local people. The destruction of vast areas of forest is also considered to be a significant contributory factor in the greenhouse effect and brings about global climate change, as forests act as absorbers of carbon dioxide.

Tropical deforestation is caused by a variety of factors. Population growth forces people to try to cultivate forested land; fuel is required to support the population's energy requirements; commercial logging is an essential generator of foreign currency in many countries and, in large areas of Southern America, cattle ranching has caused the destruction of rainforests.

The design decision

The strong demand in Europe, North America and Japan for tropical hardwoods is met by forestry practices which are not sustainable. A few companies claim to replant, and to cut down only a small proportion of trees, but the vast majority of felled timber results in loss of irreplaceable forest. Many species have become extinct and many more are now endangered.

Tropical hardwoods tend to be associated with high-value end-uses, such as furniture, musical instruments and durable boards for exterior protection of buildings. A great deal of it, however, is used for chipboard, plywood and window frames, and in other areas where other woods, or different materials altogether, would be entirely appropriate.

The simple design decision is not to specify any tropical woods, unless it can be proved that they are produced in a sustainable way. However, the issue is broader than simply tropical woods; many temperate forests are being destroyed, and much temperate forestry is currently unsustainable. Forestry practices often involve heavy use of pesticides and lead to soil erosion, a reduction in wildlife and contribution towards water pollution. It is therefore important to look for independent evidence that forests are well-managed. For example, WWF has been working with major DIY retailer B & Q in the UK to help them achieve their policy target of ensuring that all the timber they use will come from independently certified sources by 1999.

However, the problem remains of providing a livelihood, and foreign currency, for the countries where the rainforests are situated. It has been estimated that the value of the raw materials in rainforests – nuts, fruits, medicinal plants, natural ingredients for foods and toiletries – would, if properly cultivated, far exceed the once-off value of the trees. The development of these raw materials is only just beginning. Pharmaceutical companies, and recently the UK-based cosmetics company The Body Shop, are seeking new active ingredients for drugs and cosmetics. Other

Below left & right
In 1990 the UK-based Habitat furniture retailing company introduced a range of garden furniture and accessories made from rattan, sourced mainly from sustainable plantations in Indonesia. This is part of an initiative in rainforest management, to identify crops which can be extracted without harming the forest. In 1989 Habitat stopped selling any furniture made from tropical hardwoods such as mahogany.

Below
In North India, paper-makers use chapri, a paper mould made from grass stems strung together, which gives the paper its characteristic laid pattern.

Above
In Nepal, the lofka fibre — from the bark of a Himalayan plant — is used to make "washi" paper using a Japanese method. The lifted frame is seen with the wet sheet on its surface; this is peeled off when it has dried in the sun.

Handmade papers are produced in India using simple, low-cost equipment and local labour skills, but incorporating new techniques and materials. Sheet paper is formed by pouring a mixture of water and pulp into a mould: the water allows the pulp to spread evenly over the mould.

Left
In South India, papers are made from cotton rags mixed with tropical crop waste. Gunny papers are made from recycled jute sacking; banana paper from banana leaf fibre, and bagasse paper from sugar cane fibre. Other ingredients include rice husks, tea leaves, wool fibres and strings of algae. The papers here are being sorted before pressing, after which they are hung to dry.

Right
Mountains of rubbish buried under the soil in landfill sites can be unstable and dangerous because of chemical reactions that occur as materials decompose. Dangerous substances may also leach out of unlined sites into the soil, eventually seeping out into the water supply.

Left
Fertilisers that drain into rivers and seas can stimulate the excessive growth of algae, which can be toxic to marine life. In some parts of the world toxic chemicals and sewage sludge are dumped directly into the sea, threatening wildlife and humans.

substances may emerge which offer interesting potential to designers – natural dyes, for example, or leaves which can be used in the production of fine paper or packaging material.

Waste

The developed countries produce a billion tonnes of industrial waste each year, with the average household producing up to one tonne in household waste. Most of this ends up in landfill sites, some is incinerated, and some is simply dumped at sea. Each of these primary disposal methods has serious drawbacks, besides being a waste of valuable and often irreplaceable natural resources.

Landfill
In many areas, such as the North East coast of the USA, space for landfill sites is simply running out. Existing sites are full, and there is no room to create more, especially as no one wants a site near their home. Rubbish is often transported long distances to less heavily populated areas.

Rubbish deposited in landfill sites does not simply biodegrade into harmless substances, which become assimilated into the soil. Excavations of landfill sites have shown that even materials considered to be fully biodegradable, such as newspapers, do not decompose much in the airless atmosphere of most landfill sites.

Material in landfill sites often contains contaminants, such as metals or toxic chemicals, that eventually leach out into the surrounding soil, and then into rivers and streams, and end up in the water supply. The gases created by the decomposition of organic material contribute to the greenhouse gases, unless they are tapped and used for heating.

Incineration
Burning rubbish can generate energy, although the energy needs to be used close to the source, or it is wasted.

Because of the mixed nature of waste, and the types of materials included in it, incineration can release toxic gases into the air unless a very high temperature is reached. Plastics and chemicals such as pesticides can give off dioxins, one of the most toxic substances known.

Incineration also leaves behind a residue which can contain dangerous metal pollutants; this then has to be disposed of in special sites.

Dumping
Depositing rubbish out at sea may solve an immediate problem, but there is increasing evidence that it causes damage to marine life, and that there is a real limit on how much can be absorbed and safely broken down by the sea.

Right
Some types of plastic can be used several times. For example, soft drink bottles can be used as raw material for the manufacture of detergent bottles. Extending the life of plastic makes better use of a valuable resource, but the collection and separation of plastic waste demands an effective waste management infrastructure.

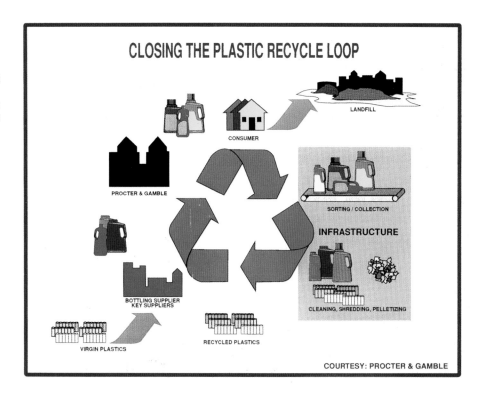

CLOSING THE PLASTIC RECYCLE LOOP

LANDFILL

CONSUMER

PROCTER & GAMBLE

SORTING / COLLECTION

INFRASTRUCTURE

CLEANING, SHREDDING, PELLETIZING

BOTTLING SUPPLIER
KEY SUPPLIERS

RECYCLED PLASTICS

VIRGIN PLASTICS

COURTESY: PROCTER & GAMBLE

Right
Sanara shampoo bottles by Wella made from Biopol, a degradable plastic made from the fermentation of sugars, introduced by ICI in 1990. On disposal, Biopol is broken down by bacteria into carbon dioxide and water in the same way as other organic matter. In use, however, it is durable, stable and water-resistant. It may be appropriate for use in products which are disposed of via the sewage system, or composting, where recycling or re-use is not possible.

Below
Swiss company Schupbach have developed the use of silicon-oxide-coated polyesters in response to the environmental concerns over the use of aluminium in complex laminates and the drive towards source reduction. The coatings provide maximum barrier properties for minimum resource use. Swissair are using this material on their refreshing tissue packs, and have found that the "glass" layer helps to give an improved shelf life for the product. An example of environmentally-improved packaging for a product of doubtful necessity.

The design decision

The most effective way of addressing the waste disposal problem is to produce less waste. This is an area where designers will have a crucial role to play, and where good design can really make a difference.

Increase in the life of a product
Products can be made more durable, or easier to repair. Often, however, a product is intended to last only for a specified period of time because of the rapid advance of new technology which quickly makes it obsolete, or because the desired market rate of growth can be achieved only by a high level of replacement purchasing. Consumer attitudes to new features and styles may change, and resistance may build up to short-life products, making it easier for manufacturers to build to last. The Swedish car manufacturers Volvo are beginning to make a virtue out of the consistency of their car styles. They claim that they never risk being out of fashion, because the designs of their most popular models hardly change over time, so that, with the cars remaining in such good condition, people find it hard to tell how old they are. Where there is a real reason to update models (as in the case of introducing energy-efficient appliances), designing for re-manufacture or recyclability in the first place can help minimise waste.

Reduction in the amount of materials used
Efficient use of materials, and imaginative component configuration or fabric pattern design, can reduce waste, as can miniaturisation. However, these moves, often inspired by cost-saving, can have a negative effect on the attractiveness of ultimate reclamation or recycling, because of the small amounts contained or because the reduction in the volume of materials has been accompanied by an increase in their variety and complexity. The move away from metals in automotive manufacture towards lightweight, easy-to-handle polymers reduced the attractiveness of the scrap car for the waste disposal industry. When choosing materials, therefore, and in particular when introducing a new material,

Right
Bottle banks and recycling bins can be large and unsightly. Busse Design in Ulm, Germany, have proposed this subterranean bottle bank, with an underground concrete container covered by a metal lid which can be walked on. The opening is easily accessible, and can form an attractive piece of street furniture.

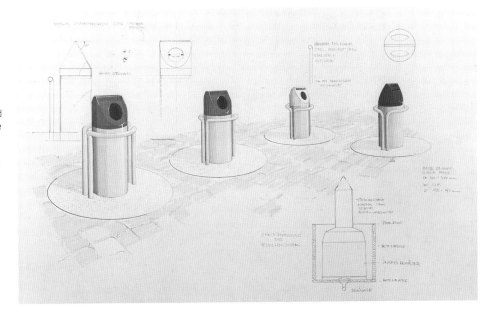

Above
Most breweries replaced the swingtop enclosure system years ago by the crown cap; however, it was retained by Grolsch, and is now a distinctive emblem. The top seal is recycled as well as the glass bottle, thus saving resources and reducing litter.

designers should take into consideration the likely impact of that material on the eventual disposal or recovery of the product.

Biodegradability of materials
Items which have to be disposed of, such as small components of surgical equipment, or products which consumers regard, wrongly, as disposable, such as pens or razors, might be manufactured from biodegradable material in the first place. This represents only a partial solution, as even biodegradable materials do not always biodegrade under landfill conditions. However, pens made out of paper may cause less of a problem and they certainly account for less waste than those made from plastic. Durability, rather than disposability, is the more appropriate longer-term solution, but this requires a significant change in consumer attitudes before it is acceptable.

Care must be taken about what happens to other components of the product. A cardboard camera introduced recently in Japan was severely criticised because of the risk that the batteries might be disposed of along with the camera; a special battery recycling scheme helped to make the product more acceptable.

Biodegradable plastics have caused much controversy. Early varieties, marketed as biodegradable, actually just disintegrated into fine particles of plastic, which cannot be absorbed into the earth. However, later products, such as ICI's Biopol, are produced entirely from natural materials such as sugar, and break down into carbon dioxide. Plastic

products which are disposed of into the sewage system could be made from this type of material, but biodegradable plastics cannot be introduced into a recycling stream.

Re-use, recycling and re-manufacture
In areas such as packaging, re-use will become increasingly important, with the development of returnable packs and refill systems. The environmental choice between re-use and recycling depends on many different factors, including the type of collection and distribution infrastructure, the energy cost of cleaning for re-use versus heating for recycling, and the number of times a pack may be re-used. The same considerations apply to products and to construction materials.

Clearly, there is little point in designing a product for recyclability if there is no market for the recycled material, so one of the most important contributions designers can make is, where possible, to specify the use of recycled materials. The use of recycled paper is increasing steadily, but there has been little demand for recycled plastics. It is pressure from designers on plastics manufacturers that will above all encourage them to develop a wide range of useful materials from recycled plastic. In some applications, clearly, safety requirements may make the use of virgin materials necessary, but there are many applications where recycled material would be fine.

Some general guidelines apply to designing for recyclability:

- Make the components easy to disassemble.
- Reduce the number of different types of materials used.
- Avoid using combinations of materials which are not mutually compatible.
- Avoid composite materials where possible.
- Consider how materials can be identified (in the long term, some form of chemical tracing ingredients may be used).
- Ensure that it is possible to remove easily any components which would contaminate the recycling process (e.g. microprocessors).

For major items, like household appliances, industrial equipment, boats and furniture, re-manufacturing or refurbishment may be a more effective form of reuse. Restoring used items has only relatively recently become unfashionable in the developed world, and is still widely used in the Third World. Designing for re-manufacture involves:

- Ensuring that parts are interchangeable between items.
- Making components repairable, or easily replaced.
- Allowing for technological components to be replaced, without affecting the overall frame of the product.
- Choosing a classic, timeless exterior design, or allowing for the easy update of a style through the replacement of a few key components such as panels.

Designing to minimise waste will require a good knowledge of the life cycle of the product, and good information about the performance of different materials within the re-use or recycling chain. It also raises fundamental questions about the wisdom of designing products which have a life expectancy far shorter than the life expectancy of the materials which go into making them.

Water pollution

The growth in population and the increasing use of water for industrial purposes mean that there is insufficient supply of clean water to meet demand. Water courses in developed countries are polluted with sewage, nitrates, chemical cocktails seeping from landfill sites and industrial discharges. In addition to possible dangerous effects on the drinking water supply, water pollution creates major

problems for wildlife and plants: many stretches of river in Northern Europe have "died" because of pollution.

Pressure is increasing for industry to aim for "closed loop" waste management systems where no harmful substances are emitted, but there are many processes that use very large volumes of water where cleaning it may not be practicable. The use of chlorine to bleach paper has been strongly criticised by environmentalists, and many paper mills are now moving away from chlorine towards hydrogen peroxide or other less polluting cleaning agents. Certain dyes, such as cadmium, may also cause harmful emissions, and many other dyes are considered not to be fully biodegradable.

The design decision

Designers and engineers may play a significant role in the redesign of industrial processes to reduce the need for harmful emissions; the development of pollution-abatement equipment also offers a rapidly growing opportunity for design skills. However, there are ways in which all designers can help to reduce water pollution and ease the shortage of clean water:

- The record of suppliers of raw materials and components should be examined to ensure that their manufacturing processes are not unnecessarily polluting. As a minimum requirement, suppliers should be able to demonstrate that they have not contravened local legislation concerning emissions.
- The processes by which specific ingredients are manufactured should be questioned. Titanium dioxide, used in a wide variety of

Above
Mark on the base of a soft drinks bottle identifying PETE, polyethylene terephthalate. More plastics will be identified in this way in future, to aid sorting for recycling.

products including paints and toothpaste, can be produced in different ways, with varying degrees of polluting effect. Paper produced by mills which use chlorine bleach should be avoided, in favour of unbleached paper, or paper bleached using hydrogen peroxide.

- The impact of dyes should be considered. Are they fully biodegradable? Could they cause a local pollution problem during manufacture? Could there be a contamination problem if dyed products end up in landfill sites?
- Saving water will be as important in some regions as saving energy. Designers can aim to design household appliances which use far less water. Imaginative devices for collecting and using rainwater will also be required.

Resource consumption

The conservation of natural resources and the responsible management of renewable resources lie at the heart of the concept of sustainable development, which will become an essential theme for politics and industry. The idea that we should aim to meet today's needs without harming the ability of future generations to meet their needs is a very simple one, but with fundamental implications. Using up non-renewable resources is an obvious concern, but simply increasing consumption of renewable resources may not be the solution.

The designer has an impact on this issue in three principal ways.

Choice of materials

Materials may be natural or synthetic, recycled or virgin, renewable or non-renewable. There are no clear-cut answers about which is least environmentally damaging. Naturally occurring materials may be in very short supply, so that to produce all dyes from natural sources, for example, would require vast quantities of plants which would have to be grown somewhere, possibly replacing more valuable crops. Growing trees for harvest can cause disruption of local eco-systems and soil erosion, as in the case of eucalyptus trees planted outside their natural growing areas. The use of plastics contributes to the depletion of oil reserves, but plastics can help reduce the weight and therefore the fuel consumption of vehicles.

Despite these difficult trade-offs, and the need to examine each case individually, there are some general guidelines:

- Materials which occur near to their point of use have the advantage that they require less energy to transport. The use of locally occurring construction materials is also

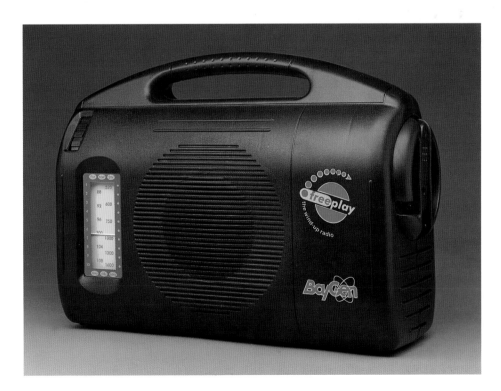

Right
The BayGen FREEPLAY Radio is the world's first clockwork radio, launched in the UK in 1995. The radio will be a vital communications tool in the Third World and developing countries. When wound for 25 seconds, electricity is generated and the Radio efficiently stores and distributes the power constantly over 30 minutes of playing time. It incorporates the Bayliss Generator, invented by Trevor Bayliss. The Radios are manufactured in Cape Town by a multiracial team of disabled workers, and have been widely endorsed by international humanitarian organisations.

becoming increasingly popular among architects, as a way of helping buildings to fit more comfortably into a location.

- Materials made from non-renewable resources should be re-usable or recyclable wherever possible.
- The extraction process of some raw materials, such as aluminium and gold, can cause severe damage to local habitats. While the designer cannot take responsibility for what happens at the very start of the supply chain, this is one area where information should be requested wherever possible from raw materials suppliers or intermediaries. Purchasing decisions should reflect a desire to support mining and extraction activities that cause the least damage.
- The specification of recycled and waste materials will very often be a sensible decision on both cost and environment grounds. Waste products such as steel, corrugated iron and driftwood have been used as materials for furniture and sculpture, and could find other high-value uses.

Energy content

A second area where the designer can make a major impact on resource consumption is in considerations about the energy used throughout the chain of extraction, manufacture, transit, use and disposal. Guidelines for energy efficiency are outlined above.

Environmental Fields \ Product Life Cycle	Pre-production	Production	Distribution (incl. packaging)	Use	Disposal
Waste relevance					
Soil pollution & degradation					
Water contamination					
Air contamination					
Noise					
Consumption of energy					
Consumption of natural resources					
Effects on ecosystems					

Reduction in the need to consume

Creating a fashion for minimalism is one approach, but another could be to design multi-purpose, highly functional products which, literally, reduce the number of objects, clothes or pieces of furniture one needs. Specific, single-purpose kitchen appliances could be replaced by machines which perform several different tasks.

Above
The cradle-to-grave approach requires analysis of a product's environment impact through each stage of its life. Charts such as this one prompt thought about every aspect of the life cycle; they are being used to assess products for eco-labelling schemes.

Left
A restrained use of materials is now common in exclusive fashion stores. At Junko Shimada in Paris, white walls and ceilings contrast with the black granite of the raised platform and the white granite of the floor.

Above
Interior of a house built into the rock on the cliffs of the Spanish island of Menorca. Designed by Javier Barba of Barcelona, it features naturally thick walls to keep out the heat, and local, natural materials for the interior.

Noise

Although noise pollution is not a life-threatening or ecology-destroying environmental problem, it is an increasing source of discomfort to people. Major improvements have been made in the reduction of the noise levels of many industrial machines, but noise can still be a real health hazard in some industries, particularly in heavy manufacturing. Noise from motor or air traffic is a serious problem for

those living near to busy routes, and even the noise from domestic machines such as lawn-mowers can cause considerable irritation and a real impairment of the quality of life.

The design decision
The selection of raw materials, and the construction techniques used, can greatly affect the noise levels of a machine or building. Sometimes the use of lightweight materials can reduce noise output; increased insulation can absorb sound; improving the efficiency of a machine may make it less noisy. By pursuing other improvements in environment performance, noise output may also be improved as a side effect.

The cradle-to-grave approach

Assessing the true environment impact of a product or construction can be done only if consideration is given to its effect throughout all the stages of its life. Focusing simply on its impact during use, or on one of its characteristics, such as recyclability or energy efficiency, gives only a partial and possibly misleading picture of its overall performance. The cradle-to-grave idea underlies the assessment systems developed for most official eco-labelling systems, and its use as a framework for product development and design can thus be expected to spread rapidly.

The cradle-to-grave approach acknowledges that environment issues may emerge at any stage, including raw material extraction; ingredients processing; manufacture or construction; distribution; use, and disposal.

The calculation of the exact impact overall may be almost impossible. Many research institutes and major manufacturers are attempting to develop objective eco-balance equations but, although it may be possible to measure energy consumption with some accuracy, other aspects of environment impact are harder to establish. Because there is no way yet of comparing different types of impact – water pollution and noise, for example – it is extremely difficult to make overall comparisons between different products with different environment profiles. For the moment, the cradle-to-grave form of assessment provides a useful framework and checklist for ensuring that every aspect of the product is considered. For practical purposes, though, it may prove necessary to focus attention on a limited number of areas which cause the greatest potential environment impact, while ensuring that performance in all other areas meets certain standards.

Right
Lamp made from discarded computer boards in the shape of a Thirties skyscraper by British sculptor and clockmaker Philip Hardaker, a member of Reactivart, an environmental-based art group. The group re-uses obsolete objects, especially hi-tech and industrial products, and turns them into decorative and functional works of art. Computer boards, in particular, have a very short functional life, the ones used here being only a few years old.

3 Architecture & interior design

Buildings are responsible for more external pollution than any other product. About half the greenhouse gases produced each year by industrialised countries are related to buildings, through the use of energy. Buildings also contribute directly to other global environmental problems, such as acid rain and the reduction in the ozone layer. The impact on the local environment can be negative, too – disturbing local habitats, generating pollution, contaminating the soil and defacing the landscape. The way in which a building is designed and built is therefore extremely important.

The ability of architects or designers to influence environment impact is directly related to how early in the planning of the building they are involved, and whether the work is an entirely new building or a refurbishment. As with most issues in this area, the earlier that environmental criteria are considered the better.

Finding ways of minimising the harmful effects of buildings may lead in two apparently contradictory directions: the development of highly sophisticated technology to help control the functions inside a building; and the use of entirely natural, very simple features, to ensure that the building makes the best use of its site, and is comfortable and attractive to live in.

Decisions taken at the design stage of a building have long-term consequences because they determine how the building is serviced – i.e. lit, heated and ventilated. They also determine how well the building will fit into the local area and community. It is therefore important to conduct a thorough investigation of the proposed development even if it is one modest building rather than a major project, to ensure that all factors have been considered.

The architect and designer have a major role to play in determining how well the build-ing will perform in terms of energy usage and human health and safety. They also have a role in promoting the use of materials which are produced in an environmentally sensitive way.

Energy efficiency

Increasing the energy efficiency of buildings is one of the most significant areas of opportunity for energy conservation. Architects and designers can directly contribute to reducing the risk of the greenhouse effect by creating buildings which consume substantially less energy. Although it is not possible to control the human activity within buildings that may involve care-less use of energy, the way in which the build-ing is designed can moderate the use of energy without the occupants having to be particularly aware of it. Designing for energy efficiency involves an integrated approach, from building structure and internal systems right through to interior furnishing.

There are two broad approaches. The first aims to minimise the impact of the external environment, through the use of good insula-tion, controlled ventilation and economic use of space. The second is to use directly the effect of the sun and natural ventilation to minimise the need for heating and cooling systems. This approach uses the siting of the building as a

Below
From a distance, this
house, designed by Javier
Barba and built into a
rocky cliff in Menorca, is
almost invisible.

major contributor to internal climate control. The different approaches will be appropriate in different situations. In each development, there has to be a balance between construction cost, technical feasibility, energy effectiveness and function.

Site analysis

The primary focus of site analysis is to ensure that the land is used efficiently, and that the building fits appropriately into the service infrastructure. The way in which a building is sited, however, relative to other buildings or to natural features of the landscape, can be a major determinant of its energy efficiency. In a climate where protection is needed from cold, the building can take advantage of natural shelter such as trees or banks. Windbreaks, in the form of trees or walls, can prevent the area immediately surrounding the building from becoming as cold as it might do if unprotected from the wind; the outside of the house, therefore, does not become so cold, reducing the need for heating inside. However, in a hot climate, it could be important to ensure that the prevailing breeze can blow

easily through the building, creating a natural cooling ventilation. In cities, the position of surrounding buildings is important, as this can determine the flow of wind currents, and therefore the temperature.

By making most use of naturally occurring climatic regulators, it is possible to reduce the degree of dependence on artificial forms of heating, cooling and ventilation. A study of the site, in terms of natural features, wind direction and positioning of other buildings, will build up a picture of the local climate, and how its features might be exploited or protected against.

Solar design

The use of solar power as a source of energy is not simply confined to countries with long hours of sunshine. Houses can be designed to capture and store solar energy, and this can make a worthwhile contribution to heating requirements even in very northerly climates.

Solar power can be actively collected by the use of solar panels which absorb heat; alternatively, the house can be designed so

Above
A major housing development in the UK, the Energy Park at Milton Keynes explores many different ideas that promote energy efficiency. The Spectrum 7 building, designed by The ECD Partnership in London, includes a well-insulated roof which admits daylight; a front elevation fully glazed for solar gain; automatically controlled low-energy lighting, and a water-cooled floor slab which functions as a summer cool store. This was one of 49 Project Monitor case studies coordinated and published by The ECD Partnership on behalf of Directorate-General XII of the Commission of the European Communities 1987-89 (see also pages 10-11, 42-43 and 156-157).

Right & below
This abandoned stone quarry in Barcelona has been transformed into a public park by architects Martorell Bohigas and Mackay in collaboration with A. Martinez. La Crueta del Col Park was completed in 1989.
The north slope was reforested, with facilities for picnics and an open-air theatre; terraces on the edge of the hillside provide sports areas. On the south side is a 100-metre wide lake, with a series of steps and terraces leading up to the rim of the crater. A gangway follows the crater rim, and sculptures add extra interest.

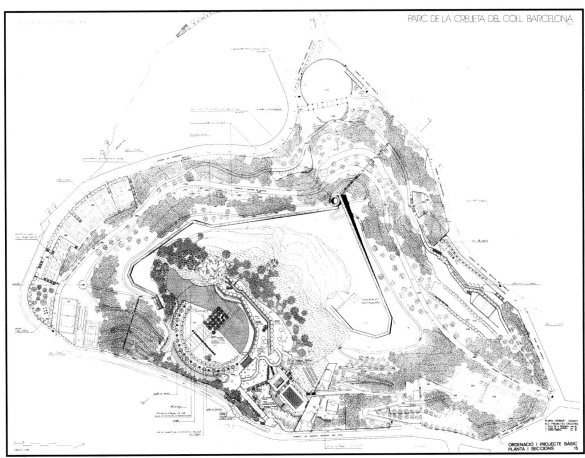

PARC DE LA CREUETA DEL COLL BARCELONA

that the structure of the house itself passively absorbs heat because of the nature of the materials it is made from.

Active solar heating systems

First the sun heats metal solar panels on a sun-facing roof. The heat is then collected by circulating either air or water around the hot panels. Air is passed into a thermal store such as a rock bed, before being distributed round the building through ducts with the help of fans. Water is stored in a tank, for use directly as hot water, or is circulated in pipes to provide radiated heat.

Solar panels are becoming a regular feature of new buildings, easily incorporated and aesthetically acceptable. The costs of installing them, however, can mean that the cost-saving payback is achieved only in the longer term, as the initial cost of materials and installation is relatively high.

Passive solar heating systems

Potentially, these offer a low-cost approach to the use of solar power, as the heating system effectively runs itself without the use of mechanical components. The sun warms the building directly through the windows, and the walls and floors act as heat absorbers; they store the heat until the air has cooled sufficiently to cause it to flow naturally out again.

Windows designed to capture heat effectively have to be large and south-facing, to ensure that more heat is trapped than lost. A conservatory or glass-covered balcony will increase the amount of solar energy collected: it will heat up quicker than the rest of the building, so warm air from it will flow through the rest of the building. During cool periods, the warm air left in the conservatory insulates the area of the building to which it is attached, and thus helps preserve the temperature inside. Large areas of window can be covered during the night by shutters, to prevent heat being lost through the glass. Reflective blinds can also be helpful in regulating temperature.

The heat let in through the windows must be absorbed by the walls and floors, which should be made of stone, brick, concrete, even earth.

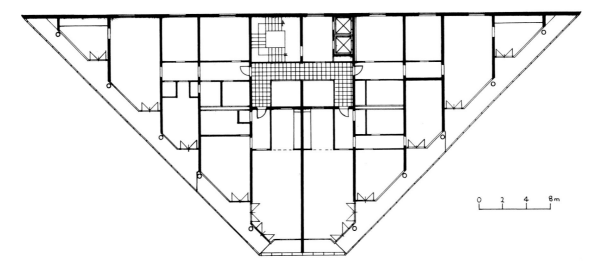

0 2 4 8 m

Above & left

The ten-storey Orbassano apartment block in Turin, Italy, was commissioned by the Unione Piemontese Svilieppo Edilizo as part of a programme of solar heating and low-energy schemes, which was used as a case study for the EC's Project Monitor (see page 40). The tower, a right-angled triangle with the angle trimmed off at 45 degrees, has two fully glazed sides facing south-east and south-west. All forty apartments have full-width "sunspaces" adjacent to the main living rooms, which are single-glazed to allow the heat to penetrate, and which have concrete floors to provide thermal mass for heat storage. Solar panels which heat the air supply nearly half the annual hot water demand and contribute to space heating, while high levels of insulation minimise heat loss. The heat requirements from other sources are only half those of similar blocks.

The thicker and more solid the floors and walls, the better they are likely to be at thermal storage. Thin board and carpets do not work in the same way. However, modern lightweight materials can be made more effective in thermal storage by "reinforcing" them with thick ceramic tiles or plaster. In addition, dark surfaces absorb the sun's heat considerably more than light ones.

Walls can be specially constructed to make them even more effective energy-storers. Walls made out of stone or brick, covered in special glass or glaze, can be used on the sides of the building most exposed to the sun; the heat absorbed can be circulated, in the form of warm air, throughout the building. Another approach is to use walls containing water, which is a most effective heat store. Water columns or water walls can either be hidden or used to provide an interesting design feature.

One indirect way of using solar energy is to make use of earth as a good moderator of temperature, and take advantage of the fact that it takes a long time to heat up and cool down. Building a house below the soil, or covering it partially with a layer of earth and grass, will help keep it warmer in winter and cooler in summer.

Heating systems

More effective insulation, and the use, for example, of passive solar heating, will help reduce the demand for large heating systems, but in most buildings there will still be a need for a source of heat which can be precisely controlled. Simply designing a system which can be flexible enough to allow for a variety of different temperatures can significantly improve energy efficiency.

It may be efficient for large buildings to have their own system for generating heat and power. Combined heat and power can reduce the amount of energy needed in heating the building. Gas can be used to fuel a boiler which generates electricity. The electricity is used in the building, while the hot water from the engine's cooling circuit can be circulated in the heating system, or used simply as a direct hot water supply.

Lighting and appliances

These features are often not regarded as an integral part of the building, but as the province of the interior designer. But both are major energy consumers, and offer opportunities for savings.

Lighting should be considered as a total system, where the aim is to develop the most appropriate combination of natural light and artificial light. Although as much natural light as possible is desirable, this might lead to too much sunlight and heat at times, unless it is possible to shade the windows effectively. The use of vast expanses of glass in modern office buildings often simply makes it necessary to have an air-conditioning system. Many new developments in glass aim to allow maximum daylight while keeping out excessive heat.

While it may be possible to supply most daytime lighting needs from natural light, electric light will of course be needed during the night, and for localised, more intense lighting requirements.

About half of the energy used in lighting is wasted. Incandescent light bulbs, the sort most commonly used, give off most of the energy they use as heat, not light. Energy consumption in lighting can be reduced by the use of longer-life, more efficient lamps. Changing from tungsten incandescent lamps to fluorescent lamps can reduce the amount of energy used by a factor of at least five. Modern fluorescents with high frequency ballasts minimise flickering and the problems of eye strain associated with it. Halogen lamps can also offer considerable energy savings, and can give a lighting effect that is very close to daylight.

Building materials

Designing for energy efficiency must also take into account the amount of energy that has been used in the manufacture of the building materials. There is little point improving the energy efficiency of a building if the materials needed to achieve this required more energy to make them than would be saved during the building's lifetime. Fortunately, many of the most energy-efficient materials, such as stone, are natural, and not highly energy-intensive to extract and use, unless they are transported over long distances. Sophisticated forms of thermal glass, however, although energy-intensive to produce, will justify their energy cost through subsequent savings.

Double glazing is a simple form of insulation, which can be highly effective. New designs are now incorporating special mirrors, which reflect back over-powerful summer sun, while allowing winter sun to penetrate the glass. Coatings can make it possible for light to enter the building, but not pass out again.

Well-insulated walls have traditionally been one of the major elements of designing for energy efficiency. Cavity walls, filled with heat-absorbent insulation material, can be effective. A wide range of substances, from waste paper to wool, is now being used in insulation materials, replacing foams manufactured using CFCs.

"Intelligent" building controls

"Intelligent" building controls allow heating, lighting and appliances to be switched on and regulated as needed, with the aim of using the minimum energy. Sensitive thermostats and light sensors, combined with a computer-based programme, allow temperatures to be monitored and heating needs adjusted accordingly. For example, pre-selected heaters will be activated for frost protection during the winter; water heating can be precisely controlled to meet occupants' requirements. Most automated systems will aim to achieve maximum energy savings, but they allow the flexibility of overriding programmes to ensure convenience and comfort.

Control systems are becoming increasingly sophisticated. They no longer monitor one service only, such as heating, but can now provide a comprehensive and integrated approach to regulating the entire internal requirements and energy needs of the building.

Above
The Parachute fashion store in New York, designed by Harry Parness, uses simple, rough materials and fittings to create a humorous, original effect. Wooden football benches, a painted concrete floor and original cast iron columns provide the backdrop, while recycled packing cartons and simple wire hangers form the display.

Right
Out of this World is a UK chain of shops, designed by The Fern Green Partnership, which promotes ethical and sustainable living. A bright, friendly environment has been created by using predominantly natural materials and organic forms. The layout emphasises the personal service and information which are essential parts of the shop concept. The materials used in construction are largely non-toxic in their production and use and are taken predominantly from sustainable and recycled sources. The flooring is marmoleum which is made from natural raw materials, and the walls and ceilings are decorated using a casein milk paint coloured with earth and mineral pigments. Freezer and refrigeration display units and the air cooling system use the refrigerant Care 50, a hydrocarbon product which does not destroy the ozone layer and has the lowest global-warming potential of any current refrigerant.

Above & left
The experimental workshop at Hooke Park College, UK, for the furniture designer John Makepeace applies sophisticated technology and engineering skills to roundwood — timber with a trunk diameter of 50-200 mm — which traditionally has been used only for low-quality applications. Instead of a post-and-lintel construction, the length of roundwood timbers and their flexibility when wet have been exploited. The trees are debarked, treated with preservative, and then bent into place. The shell action of the three-dimensional frame reduces the bending stresses. The shells are covered by a polymer membrane roof, with insulation sandwiched between; the membrane is both the ceiling of the workshop and the diagonal bracing to the shells. Computer analysis was used to establish the shape and predict the stresses as the bending took place.

Ventilation and air-conditioning

Air-conditioning systems are major consumers of energy, in addition to being a potential source of hazardous CFC emission. The growth in their usage could offset the energy savings being achieved by more efficient use of lighting and heating. Pressures to install air-conditioning units may well increase further, in anticipation of the effects of global warming. It is therefore important to consider how they could be made more efficient, and also whether any viable alternatives exist.

The use of "intelligent" controls will help reduce energy wastage but, from a design perspective, it is worth considering how the structure of a building can help to keep it cool, reducing the need for any artificial cooling.

Just as solar energy can be used to heat thermal stores to provide a source of heating for a building, so thermal stores can be used to help cool a building. Heat collected during the day is radiated off to the outside during the night, enabling the store to absorb the next day's heat. Solar energy can also be used to power refrigeration units, and so can provide a complete approach to heating and cooling; there is usually, however, a need to supplement the system with a complementary one, because of the unpredictability of weather.

Alternatives to air-conditioning may lie in the use of natural ventilation systems. A natural flow of air is created through a building because of the differences in pressure between cold and warm air. On the windy side of a building air will be cooler, and will flow towards the low-pressure side of the building away from the wind, displacing warmer air. Warm air will be lost upwards, through chimneys, for example, while cooler air is drawn in at a lower level. This form of natural ventilation creates a through draught of cooler air, and also allows moisture to escape.

Up until recently, most buildings were naturally ventilated, because construction techniques left many gaps through which air could leak. However, warm air lost in this way also represents a loss of energy, and so the challenge is now to retain the benefits of natural ventilation without the associated heat loss. The use of mechanically controlled ventilation, incorporating a heat recovery unit, can capture lost heat while ensuring that condensation problems are minimised.

Material specification

Architects and designers have a considerable opportunity to influence environment impact through the specification of materials. Understanding the environment issues surrounding the extraction of raw materials, the manufacture of construction materials, and their effects in use, is important to ensure that environment problems are minimised.

Natural materials

The general principle of using, wherever possible, non-toxic materials which are produced from renewable or re-usable resources can be taken as a guideline.

Wood is the obvious material in this respect, but it is not suitable in all applications. Opportunities may well exist for the incorporation into construction materials and fittings of new materials made from waste products such as paper and plastics. The selection of recycled materials has to depend on the performance requirements demanded, but could be significantly increased. The construction and furniture industries are major potential users of recycled plastics, and designers should aim to specify these in preference to virgin plastic wherever possible.

The use of PVC as a construction material has come under particular scrutiny because of the effects of hormone-disrupting chemicals such as dioxins which appear to be released in PVC manufacture and disposal. Environmental organisations are urging the substitution of other materials for PVC in construction, and a ban on the use of PVC in public buildings.

Timber choice

The use of tropical hardwoods in the building industry has been strongly criticised by environmentalists. Tropical timber is often used in building joinery, for front doors and in win-

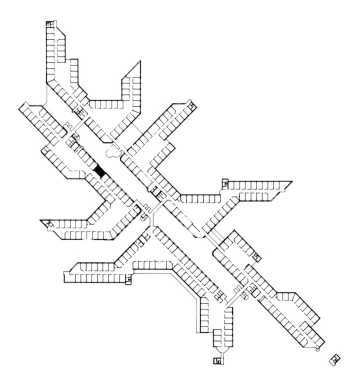

dow-frames. As most timber production is not carried out sustainably, its use contributes to the problems of deforestation, even though most deforestation is caused by the burning of forest to clear land for homes and agriculture. Tropical hardwoods, valued for their strength and appearance, have been used in applications such as plywoods and chipboard, where other materials would be just as appropriate.

Designers and architects specifying timber are now encouraged to avoid using tropical hardwood products altogether, unless it is possible to determine that the timber has originated from one of the few sustainably managed forests. Temperate hardwoods, such as cherry and alder, might be used instead; alternatively, softwoods may be suitable for some applications that have traditionally been reserved for hardwoods.

The use of hardwood veneers, as a way of greatly reducing the quantity of material used while still benefiting from its appearance, has attracted considerable controversy. The appeal of veneers has grown because it allows the use of low-grade softwood waste in place of solid wood, at a considerable cost saving. However, critics would claim that the veneer material must still come from a temperate hardwood or a sustainably managed tropical source.

Local materials

The amount of energy used to transport building materials from their source to the building site can be a major consideration. The transport of

Above
The headquarters of Scandinavian Airlines at Frosundavik, near Stockholm, was designed by Niels Tomp. One of the aims was to create a working environment that would be free from "sick building syndrome". Almost all of the 1,500 employees working in the building have their own daylit room, with individual controls for lighting and heat. Windows look either to the outside or to a central atrium.

Above
The residence of Leif
Nørgaard (who runs
Novotex, see pages 146-
9), in central Jutland,
Denmark, designed by
Jørgen Johansen. Difficult
to spot in the landscape,
its shape and situation
mirror the lines of the
land, and its structure is
low to avoid being obtru-
sive. The roof is covered
by a thin layer of grass
for further concealment.
The open-plan house
faces south, with large
windows to provide
passive solar heating.

large quantities of very heavy materials over
long distances can represent a very inefficient
use of resources, if there are materials available nearer to hand that would meet the
requirements.

The use of locally occurring materials is
becoming more popular because of the
emphasis now being put in many planning
considerations on how well the building fits in
to the local environment.

Chlorofluorocarbons

CFCs have in the past been widely used in the
manufacture of rigid polyurethane and extrud-
ed polystyrene foams, often employed in insu-
lating material. They have also been used as
refrigerants in air-conditioning systems, and
in fire protection equipment.

Many alternatives are now becoming
available, and architects and builders have to
explore which of many new approaches will be
most appropriate. Although CFCs will remain
in circulation for some time, it is no longer
desirable environmentally or economically to
specify any system which relies on CFCs.

Many insulation products are now using
non-foam materials, such as densely packed
waste paper, mineral fibre – even wool. In
some cases increasing the thickness of the
walls may provide significant additional
insulation. New types of triple-glazed
windows with low emissivity can also provide
good insulation.

Air-conditioning systems are now being
developed which run on alternative refrigerants,
such as hydrocarbons. From the architects' perspective, the starting point may well be to minimise the need for air-conditioning systems,
through the use of natural ventilation or shading. But if a refrigeration plant is necessary, a
wide range of options will increasingly be available. The architect will clearly have to work
closely with suppliers in this area to ensure that
state-of-the-art systems are incorporated wherever possible. Poor design and maintenance of
air-conditioning systems have been a problem
in the past, resulting in leakage of CFCs.
Consideration must therefore be given to ease
of maintenance of alternative systems.

Hazardous materials

The potentially dangerous side effects of materials commonly used in construction, decoration
and furnishing have recently become a cause of
concern. The carcinogenic effect of asbestos has
led to its removal from many buildings, and to
prohibition of its use in some countries. The use
of lead in paints is being reduced or abandoned,
because of the dangers it can cause to children
if ingested.

However, concern is now being expressed
across a much wider range of substances. Many
of the modern products taken for granted in
building and decoration – such as formaldehyde, epoxy and acrylic resins, and fungicides –
are criticised not just for the pollution caused

by their manufacture, but also because of concern that they can act as allergens, causing conditions such as asthma, hay fever and skin problems.

As with so many environmental issues, trade-offs have to be evaluated. The use of chipboards made from waste materials offers many benefits, but the glues in the manufacturing process can be toxic in production and use. Products are becoming available with a low formaldehyde content, and these should be specified in preference. Timber is frequently treated with pesticides and fungicides designed to protect the wood from infestation and rot. The chemicals used, and their quantities, can result in toxic fumes which are dangerous to human health for some time, and there is pressure to ensure that chemicals banned in all other situations are not used in the building industry. The selection of appropriate materials, and the design of effective ventilation systems, can reduce the need for protection with large quantities of chemicals.

Good ventilation will reduce the risk to human health of emissions of toxic chemicals

from furniture, construction materials and paints. Water-based paints, and paints made from plant materials, offer alternatives to the traditional resin-based paints, although they do not always provide the same level of protection.

There has been a recent increase in the tendency to relate ill health to buildings. "Sick building syndrome" is a term applied to a range of symptoms, including headaches, congestion and lethargy. Flickering fluorescent lighting, poor ventilation and low humidity have been blamed, and there is evidence to suggest that the incidence of these problems is lower where people can control their immediate environment, rather than have to rely totally on sealed systems.

Designers and architects can help reduce risks to human health through care in the specification of materials, minimising the use of toxic chemicals, ensuring good indoor air quality and temperature control, and selecting appropriate, flicker-free lighting systems, with lighting positioned to meet users' specific tasks. Large quantities of plants in offices and

Left & right
Architect Gustav Peichl has succeeded in concealing much of the building development which accompanies this telecommunications satellite dish in Alfenz, Austria. The objective was to minimise disturbance to the landscape by locating offices and houses under the ground. The circular designs mirror the shape of the satellite dish to create a harmonious blend of technology and nature; from down the hill, the development is well concealed. Rooms are positioned around central holes in the ground which form courtyards lit by natural light.

homes can have a beneficial effect on the atmosphere, helping to maintain the quality of the air, in addition to contributing to the aesthetic appeal of the building. However, the use of insecticides must be strictly controlled.

There is some evidence to suggest that radon, a naturally occurring radioactive gas produced by the decay of uranium in the soil, can accumulate into high concentrations in buildings located near a source. Assessments are now beginning to be made of soil conditions to try to detect the presence of radon, and steps can be taken to prevent its accumulation. Special floor linings or fan systems may offer some protection.

Town planning and countryside protection

It is beyond the scope of this book to address in any detail the important area of urban design; clearly, the environment impact of a building cannot be considered in isolation from its surroundings. Many major advances have been made in the design of large urban areas, with the aim of improving the quality of life for their inhabitants, as well as encouraging efficient use of energy, good public transport systems and street layouts which are appropriate to climatic conditions. The zoning of buildings can improve energy efficiency, for example by planning residential buildings in areas which can benefit from solar gain, while storage buildings or parking areas are located in areas receiving little sun.

Landscape design should be carefully considered at the planning stage of buildings. Often regarded as merely a cosmetic afterthought, landscape design can make a significant contribution to improving the environmental impact of a building or urban area.

Energy-conscious design requires careful analysis of the natural benefits and problems of a site, and the incorporation of features such as slopes, trees and hedges into the building plans. The increased use of large areas of trees is to be encouraged, not just for their visual appeal and protection properties, but also because of their ability to absorb carbon dioxide.

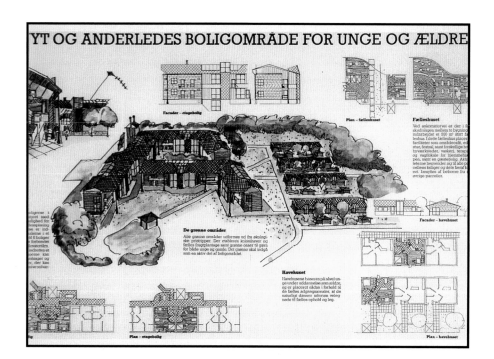

YT OG ANDERLEDES BOLIGOMRÅDE FOR UNGE OG ÆLDRE

Left
Thorsted Vest is a major housing project in Denmark, extending the town of Horsen. The aim is to provide a healthy environment, designed to meet the needs of the population and set a positive relationship between town and countryside. The elevation shows the mix of built-up areas and open spaces.

Environment impact assessment

Many countries already have planning requirements which demand a formal assessment of the environment impact of any development at the planning stage. This is often confined to large developments which are proposed for conservation areas, but there is an increasing tendency for environment impact assessments to be regarded as part of "good practice" requirements from developers. Broadly, the assessment should consider the direct and indirect effects the development has on people, soil, water, landscape, air climate, wildlife, plantlife and cultural heritage.

The intrusiveness of a development, in terms of its visibility in the surrounding landscape, is also a concern of environment impact assessments. Increasingly, attempts are being made to find imaginative ways of making buildings blend in with the surroundings – even, in some cases, to the point of complete invisibility.

Issues such as pollution, accessibility, density of development and disruption of local habitats are also included. Transport and communication requirements are being given increased attention in many countries, where the provision of adequate mass transport systems is regarded as a prerequisite for any major developments, in order to discourage dependence on private cars.

Environment impact assessments are generally regarded as a "one-off" review, conducted at the planning stage. They should,

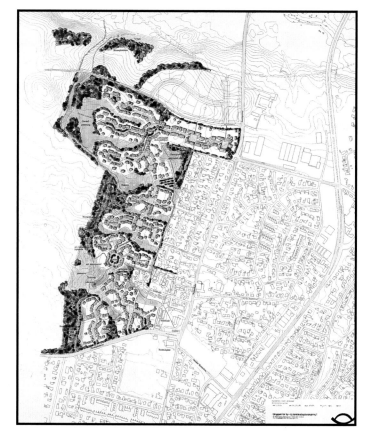

Above
The site plan of Thorsted Vest, showing the integration of housing and forest. The area is criss-crossed with winding paths.

however, be regarded as a regular activity,
used to monitor whether the building or
development does actually perform as predicted. How does the actual environment impact
compare with the assessment made initially?
Could improvements be made to it? Most
importantly, reviewing performance after time
can provide feedback to help the planning
process in future design.

There is considerable debate still about
the extent to which living and working areas
should be integrated. Developments in technology now mean that many factories and
offices are "clean" enough to be incorporated
within housing developments. Reduced travelling distances between work and home give
obvious environmental benefits. The growth in
tele-commuting may also affect people's work
and leisure requirements.

Re-use of existing buildings

The use of an existing building, in place of the
construction of a new building, can lead to
obvious environmental benefits. Energy can
be saved, and existing materials used rather
than wasted. The existing building may also
have value aesthetically, or because it fits into
the style of the surrounding area.

Recognition is growing of the environment
benefits of extending the life of an existing
building, and of designing new buildings so
that they will have an extended life. Flexibility

of usage may have to be incorporated into
original designs, or at least some anticipation
of changing user requirements. For example,
now that recycling has become widespread,
private homes and offices need to be equipped
with areas where materials can be segregated
and stored for collection.

A holistic approach

The Baubiologie – literally, "building biology"
– movement which emerged in Germany in
the mid-Seventies has been heralded as a new
concept in architecture. Pioneered by
Professor Anton Schneider, Baubiologie aims
to design buildings with a healthy environment which promotes physical and spiritual
well being through ensuring that the materials
used cause minimal harm to the environment
in their manufacture and use, and that they
allow the house to "breathe". The house is
likened to a living organism, with the same
control and regulatory functions; the aim is to
create a harmonious, balanced, self-sustaining
environment which is relaxing and easy to live
in. Baubiologie uses a scientific, rather than
mystical, approach to determining materials
use and layout, but sets out to influence life
style, believing that environmental impact and
health depend crucially on people's attitudes
and way of life, rather than on purely technical considerations.

Simonds Farsons Cisk Brewery, Malta

Left
Large windows on the north side allow daylight into the building without the risk of solar heat gain. The north vent chamber emerges from the roof, gaining height to encourage the stack-effect ventilation.

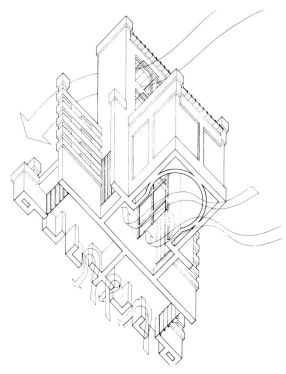

Above
Plan looking upwards
through a ventilation
chamber on the south
side. The vents are
shown open, as for night
operation. Glazing roof
lights admit diffused light
during the day.

Buildings in the Mediterranean and Middle East have for centuries
exploited the phenomenon of convective cooling. In Malta, traditional
houses are made from local limestone, a stone with high thermal capacity which stores heat during the day. The internal temperature is regulated by shuttering the windows and by the massiveness of the stone. At
night the shutters are opened, to draw in cool night air. This simple and
highly effective approach has not often been reflected in contemporary
architecture. Farsons Brewery, designed by Alan Short and Brian Ford
of the UK architectural practice Peake, Short and Partners, relies on
passive cooling systems to maintain the cool indoor temperature
required for the brewing process. No air-conditioning is used.

The limestone building consists of a central core, the process hall,
surrounded by a "jacket" of corridors through which air can circulate.
Night ventilation occurs through a stack effect. Three towers high
above the jacket provide exits for the circulating air. On summer nights,
the temperature in the towers is higher than the temperature on the
ground; as a result, cool air is drawn into the building. Vents into the
process hall, opened at night, allow air to move through and remove the
heat stored within the roof. The roof consists of a concrete deck with
insulation on the upper surface. This "inverted" roof protects against
solar heat gain during the day; its high thermal capacity provides a
time-lag of several hours so that the peak internal temperature is not
reached until well into the evening. By this time the night ventilation
is already working to reduce it.

Maltese summers are characterised by a large diurnal range in
temperature, and extreme heat can occur from time to time. The effectiveness of the system was tested on a computer model, to predict how
the building would react to typical and extreme weather conditions.
Average August temperature in Malta is 33.3°C. The model predicted

Left
Very small glazed
openings on the east
side minimise solar heat
gain, while vents in the
wall supply air to the
"jacket" space.

Below
A view of the roofline, showing the vents and roof lights standing above the roof plane.

Above
A view of the interior, looking to the north-west chamber, with the vents open. Ample light is provided from the large windows on the north side.

Left
The 12-metre high fermentation vessels in front of the south side.

that the peak temperature in the brewery would be 25°C, rising above 27°C only on very extreme days. The brewery will therefore provide comfortable working conditions without the need for expensive air-conditioning.

In addition to saving energy through its ventilation system, the building also makes use of natural light through perimeter roof lights. To minimise solar heat gain, light entering the building is reflected off the jacket wall into the process hall.

The architects believe that the principles adopted for Farsons Brewery could be used on a wide range of industrial buildings.

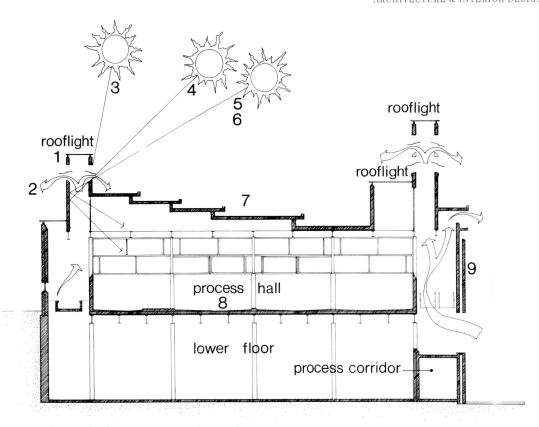

Diagrams showing the way the system works.

1 The process hall, indirectly lit from roof lights.
2 The "jacket", freely vented all day.
3 Temperature at noon on 21 June 25.5°C.
4 Temperature at noon on 21 October 6.1°C.
5 Temperature at noon on 21 December -1.1°C.
6 Low-altitude winter sun penetrates the building and is reflected from the back wall.
7 The roof mass provides a temperature time lag of about eight hours.

8 Predicted peak temperature 27°C.
9 The outer wall shades the inner wall, and the stack-induced air movement cools people on the walkways.
10 Air movement is encouraged by continuous slats on either side of the walkways.
11 Roof surfaces cool at night by radiation.
12 Interior surfaces cool convectively.
13 Tiled walls provide high thermal capacity.
14 Predicted minimum temperature 24°C.
15 Open volume allows cross ventilation.
16 Fresh air enters through "jacket" and into the lower floor.

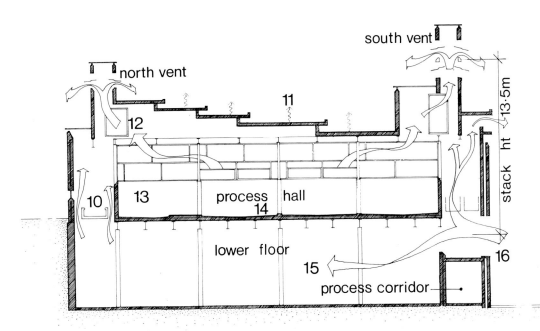

NMB Bank, The Netherlands

The new corporate headquarters for NMB, the largest bank in The Netherlands, represents one of the most imaginative attempts at bringing together human and environmental concerns with those of flexibility, efficiency and low operating cost. A working environment has been created which is attractive and successful for its users.

Located in the south-east of Amsterdam, the bank has a dramatic appearance, externally and internally. Its walls slope, there is no air-conditioning in the conventional sense, and it contains a profusion of plants which are watered with purified rainwater fed from sculptures.

The building is the result of close collaboration between a team of engineers, landscape designers and architects, led by Amsterdam architects Alberts and Van Huut. Unusually, all the participants in the project were invited to contribute their ideas at the start, rather than being called in after the architects and clients had decided on the scheme. This allowed an integrated approach, where every element fitted sympathetically together.

The building is a series of towers, strung together in an "S" shape. Each has a different colour, providing distinct identities for different departments. Each floor of the tower houses between twenty and forty employees, giving an intimate feel to working areas. Noise from passing traffic is deflected by the sloping walls, which also deflect wind, so reducing the loss of heat from the building. The separate towers emphasise the organisational structure of the bank, but an interior street plays an important connecting role, and creates a common area: all the building's general services are along this street, as are restaurants and small shops. The street passes through a series of sunlit atria, open at all levels of the building.

Energy efficiency has been a high priority in the design and servicing of the building: it is considered to be one of the most energy-efficient in the world. There is no air-conditioning system, but rather a heat-recovery air-circulation system. Cool air is taken in during the night, passed through energy-transfer equipment and recirculated during the day; the concrete mass of the building is used as cold storage. Large solar energy collectors supply heat to supplement the gas-fired central heating system which provides about 80 per cent of power requirements. The windows on the south-facing walls also act as solar collectors, and the heat is taken to the shadow side of the building. Large water-tanks provide temporary heat storage, and the entire interior environment is regulated by a sophisticated computer.

Natural light is enhanced by the use of light-reflecting and dispersing materials in the window openings and work areas. Even though windows cover only 25 per cent of the wall surfaces, artificial light is needed during only 30 per cent of office time. Windows can be opened, to allow individuals to control their immediate temperature and ventilation.

Right
Broad staircases provide opportunities to meet, as well as encouraging fitness.

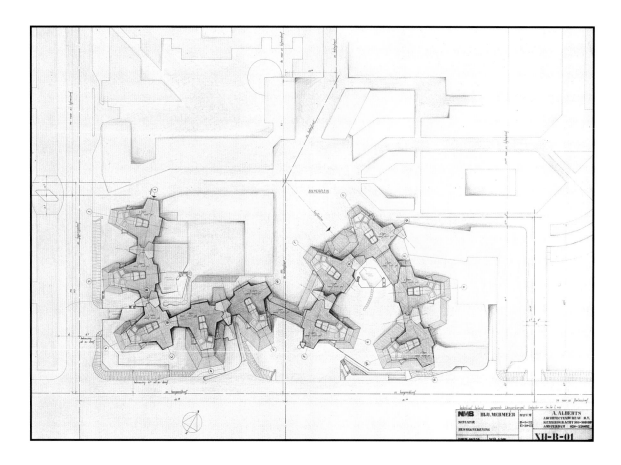

Above
Plan of the development, showing the series of towers which form an "S" shape. Each tower can have its own identity, but forms part of the whole chain.

Plants and gardens play a major role in the building, helping to give indoor areas an outdoor feel. The parking areas are covered with vegetation, and there are frequent views of the gardens from the central street. The extravagant use of the plants inside helps maintain a clean and pleasant atmosphere.

The central stairways are important features. Employees are encouraged to use the staircases rather than lifts for health reasons, but also to provide opportunities for social contact. The number of lifts was minimised, thus reducing construction costs.

Natural materials – such as wood, marble and copper – are used throughout the interior to create a warm effect. One notable feature is the lack of right-angled shapes: the architects believe that these discourage creativity and harmony, and therefore they have been avoided.

While the results of this design can be measured scientifically in terms of energy efficiency and noise levels, it is difficult to measure the impact of the building on employee health and satisfaction. One indicator, however, is given by the company: absentee rates have fallen, and prospective employees cite the new building as one of the major reasons for wishing to join the company.

Left
The unusual shapes and strong colours of the exterior of the NMB Bank create a dramatic effect. The sloping walls help to deflect wind.

IBM Headquarters, Kuala Lumpur

The Menara Mesiniaga in Kuala Lumpur, the headquarters in Malaysia of IBM, was completed in 1992. It demonstrates that a consideration for energy consumption and environmental needs can lead to dramatic, innovative architecture. Designed by Dr Ken Yeang, of T. R. Hamzah & Yeang Sdn. Bhd, Malaysia, it uses orientation, planting and natural ventilation in a bio-climatic approach. According to Yeang, one of the basic concepts for an energy-efficient building is that its orientation should be in the optimum direction to take advantage of existing natural factors such as wind, rain and sun.

As tall buildings are exposed more directly to the impact of external temperatures and radiation heat, the overall orientation of the building has an important bearing on energy conservation. This building is designed so that its main and broader openings face north-south, which helps to reduce its solar insulation and air-conditioning load.

Solar shading is required on certain building faces to control the quality of light entering the transitional spaces. In temperate zones, these can have adjustable glazing at the outer face so that the balconies or recesses can collect heat positively, in the way that greenhouses do.

Right
The building encourages windflow into internal spaces through balconies and atriums located in the upper section.

Right
The orientation of a tall building has an important bearing on energy conservation. An appreciation of existing natural factors enables the development of an energy-efficient design solution.

The external walls of the building are regarded more as a permeable membrane with adjustable openings. In temperate climates, the external wall has to serve both cold winters and hot summers. Therefore the external wall is filter-like, with variable parts that provide good insulation in cold periods and have a cooling function during hot weather.

The lift lobbies, stairways and toilets are given natural ventilation and an outside view wherever possible. They are situated at the periphery of the usable floor space which results in energy savings, since these areas do not require mechanical ventilation. This also reduces the need for artificial lighting. By placing these areas on the periphery of the building, they benefit from natural sunlight, and also provide pleasing views. Mechanical pressurisation ducts for fire-protection purposes are also unnecessary.

Below
External walls are filter-like with variable parts that make the building flexible to changing climates.

In addition to responding to commercial needs, the building reflects the pattern of life and culture of the place and climate. This requires an understanding of the way people work, and the way culture arranges privacy and community. Planting and landscaping is used not only for its ecological and aesthetic benefits but also as one way of cooling the building. Plants absorb carbon dioxide and generate oxygen, giving them a cooling impact which benefits the building.

Balconies and atriums are open, and transitional spaces located in the upper section of the skyscraper encourage wind flow into the internal spaces. "Wind scoops" are used at the edges of the skyscraper to use the high wind speed at the upper levels, where it is channelled into ceiling plenums to ventilate inner recessed spaces.

Below
Balconies and atriums
generate natural
ventilation and provide
pleasing views.

Woodlea Primary School, Bordon, Hampshire, UK

Woodlea Primary School, designed by Nev Churcher and Sally Daniels, is a school for 245 children, built in a natural woodland bowl. The aim was to set the building and its surrounding recreation areas into the landscape with the minimum possible disturbance, to ensure a balance between conservation and the provision of a practical educational environment for the local area.

The school is a series of low-level wood-framed structures, centring on a hall and curving round to form a rough semicircle. All classrooms lead on to a wooden deck where children sit out in good weather. The pitched roofs are covered in cedar shingles, and the flat roof links are finished with natural slate granules.

The intention was that the school should be flexible and attempt to break down the barrier between internal and external environments. Natural light has been maximised by large areas of glazing in the roof. The building is heated by gas-fired low-pressure hot water which feeds radiators, fan-assisted convectors and ducted fin-tubes with flush floor grilles. The siting and layout of the building took full account of micro-

Above
The building curves round to form a rough semicircle, centring on the hall.

Below
Wood is the main material used, and high standards of natural lighting have been achieved.

climate and passive solar-energy management, and these, together with very high standards of insulation, produce a very low energy-consumption figure.

The project demonstrated the concept of "Learning Through Landscape", which promotes the development, appreciation and use as a learning resource of the landscapes surrounding schools. Woodlea is surrounded by a very rich natural site, with a wildlife pond, garden and a large area planted with locally occurring species.

The school has won several prestigious architectural awards, and in 1994 won the BBC Design Award for Environment and Architecture, demonstrating that it is possible to develop radical, attractive and popular buildings which are highly practical and functional, while giving a high priority to environmental criteria.

Left
The school is surrounded by woodland; the natural environment becomes an important part of the school's working and recreation area.

University of Northumbria

This project was the first large-scale UK demonstration of the integration of a photovoltaic system into a commercial building.

The Northumberland building, a five-storey block housing several academic departments, needed refurbishment because the existing precast concrete cladding was failing. The south face was fitted with a new cladding system with integrated photovoltaic modules, which will generate around thirty per cent of the building's annual electricity needs. The modules are incorporated into the rainscreen overcladding, which provides a barrier to rain penetration. The panels and components are made from aluminium, and are hung into aluminium channel tracks, fixed to the existing concrete frame and which also drain the rainwater.

Temperature control for the modules is assisted by means of a ventilated air gap between the building and the rainscreen. The cladding is inclined to give better solar collection. Shading is provided to reduce solar gain through windows during the summer.

In high-latitude countries the use of solar radiation for power generation is not ideal, because of the low solar altitude in winter and the mismatch between peak supply and peak demand. However, the University of Northumbria building demonstrates that photovoltaic cladding is worthwhile even in a northerly, city-centre area.

Incorporating photovoltaics into the fabric of new and refurbished buildings could provide energy at a cost comparable with that from conventional sources, and could make a very significant contribution to a country's electricity supply capacity. The widespread introduction of this technology would make a major contribution to the reduction of CO_2 emissions from energy generation.

Below
View of the south face of
the Northumbria building.

Above
Close up of the
photovoltaic façade.

4 Product design

The traditional definition of a well-designed product is one that performs its function successfully; is manufactured efficiently, using appropriate materials and techniques; is easy to use; is safe; offers good value for money, and looks attractive. The relative importance of these criteria will vary from product to product. New definitions of good product design will include an environmental consideration: is the product designed to minimise the impact it has on the environment, during the whole of its life cycle?

Designers can make a significant difference to the effect of a product because they are responsible for influencing the key decisions. These determine the choice of materials; how long the product will last; how effectively it uses energy, and how easily it may be reclaimed and re-used. The aims of the environment-conscious designer are to use the minimum resources throughout, to get the maximum possible use and value out of the least quantity of materials or energy, and to minimise pollution created during the manufacture and life of the product.

The pursuit of these objectives may clash with other demands: making a product quieter or cleaner may result in its being heavier or less efficient. Minimising the weight of materials involved may make the product less easy to recycle. The designer has to balance these competing demands, and ensure that the product is both saleable and also environmentally acceptable.

Much effort will be devoted to improving the environment performance of existing products. As part of an evolutionary process, products will be adapted, new materials used, energy efficiency improved, harmful side-effects minimised. In the longer term, however, there is plenty of scope for designers to look for a more revolutionary approach, where the conventional way of approaching a particular user need is challenged, and entirely new solutions emerge.

Product life

Many products which used to be designed to last for years are now intended to have only a short lifespan. Disposability has been presented as a consumer benefit. Disposable lighters, pens, even watches, have been made possible by advanced technology reducing manufacturing costs, and there is often little incentive for the consumer to look after a product to ensure that it lasts, as it can so easily be replaced. Product life may be limited by changes in technology which make it obsolescent; by parts of the product simply wearing out through use, or by changes in fashion or style which make it old-fashioned and unattractive. Extending the life of a product is an obvious way of reducing waste. There are many different ways of achieving this, from improving reliability and durability so that it lasts longer, to making it recyclable so that the materials used to create it can have an additional life in another form.

Extending useful life
The desire to reduce costs to make items such as kitchen appliances available to the mass market has led in many cases to products which are not robust enough to survive high usage. Often, different parts of the product deteriorate at different rates, but it is difficult to obtain and fit replacement parts, with

Right
Commissioned by the manufacturers Junghans from the design consultancy FrogDesign in Germany, this clock uses 58 solar cells as an energy source. It produces 4,000 times more energy than the quartz movement consumes, the surplus energy being kept as a store for when light is unavailable. A radio link maintains the clock's accuracy, so that it does not need manual adjustment.

the result that the entire product has to be discarded.

One way of extending a product's life is therefore simply to design it so that it can easily be maintained and serviced, by making those parts which are more susceptible to failure accessible and replaceable, and ensuring that the product is easy to disassemble and reassemble. With advanced products, repairs and replacements tend to have to be carried out by specialists, which means that product servicing becomes an important part of the total product offer. Agfa Gevaert have developed a photocopier designed to last for about ten years – twice as long as most copiers – and all repairs are carried out by Agfa as part of the hire arrangements.

Durability can also be achieved through the use of different technologies. New energy-efficient light bulbs last many times longer than traditional incandescent bulbs, for example.

Design for re-manufacture
Product life may be extended simply by repairing small components over a period of time; however, if a product is difficult to service, or where several components may need replacement, the solution may lie in "re-manufacturing". This means that the product is disassembled, refurbished and re-assembled, incorporating new parts – or parts in better condition retrieved from other machines. The same approach can also be used where the product is technically functioning well, but the exterior appearance has deteriorated badly, or where major changes in colour requirements or surface finishes have rendered the product unfashionable. Major improvements in technology may also be incorporated into the product through remanufacturing. The introduction of a more intelligent microprocessor system, which makes a domestic appliance more energy-efficient, may make it worthwhile to have the machine "upgraded", especially if its mechanical components are in good working order.

The restoration of used items is widely used in Third World countries where there is a shortage of indigenous manufacturing facilities, and where the labour costs involved in repair and re-manufacture are low relative to the cost of the materials involved. Products designed in the first place for eventual disassembly and re-manufacture need not involve high labour costs, however, although frequent design changes may inhibit re-manufacturing

due to the difficulty associated with parts which are not interchangeable.

One of the dilemmas in designing for long life is the possibility that advances in materials or technology will make it possible to produce a new product which gives a greatly superior environment performance. Replacement of existing products may be a very desirable objective, but could result in considerable waste of resources unless the materials used can be recycled or adapted.

Design for recyclability
Products eventually wear out or become obsolete. A high proportion of the cost of most manufactured goods is the cost of the raw materials, many of which are made from non-renewable resources; however, difficulties in retrieving and re-using these materials have often led to disposal in landfill sites. The cost of collection, transport, separation and recycling may well exceed the monetary – and even the environmental – cost of disposal. But with disposal costs steadily increasing and a growing demand from governments and consumers for the creation of systems to facilitate recycling, pressures are likely to increase substantially in support of designing with eventual recycling in mind.

Above
The redesign of an existing vacuum cleaner was used by Electrolux to explore new directions for improving the environmental impact of a typical popular model. The base of the Z2571 Eco has been made from reclaimed and recycled materials; colour pigments have been avoided in the body upper and all internal cables and wires are PVC free.

Right
This Xerox copier meets German Blue Angel standards, with low ozone emissions, and the potential for power savings. The copy cartridge and toner cartridge are designed for recycling. It comes with minimal packaging.

Left
JAM is a group of designers who use waste products and materials in unusual contexts to give them new value. "RoboStacker" is a storage system designed from stainless-steel washing-machine drums, supplied by Whirlpool. Discarded cinematic film is used to make a table lamp.

Left
French designer Thierry
Kazazian, a member of
the O2 design group,
created this lamp,
"Mazurka", from used
household objects –
a steamer, whose
overlapping segments
can be used to change
the intensity of the light,
and a coffee filter that
houses a low-energy
halogen bulb.

Recycling can be more viable for large items, which can easily be collected and where the quantities of materials involved are significant. Ease of mechanical disassembly is important, with a minimum combination of different materials requiring separation. Zanussi's Nexus range of washing machines and dishwashers have a structure which is based on five modular sub-assemblies. A high proportion of the structure is moulded out of carboran, a recyclable advanced polymer which is also used to construct many of the functional components. The machines consist of fewer individual parts than usual, and additions like modular wiring and snap-on fixings make it easy to dismantle them for repair or recycling.

The reduction in the number of different materials used, and the use of single rather than composite materials, helps avoid the problem of material contamination. Recycled materials which are made from a mixture of different substances – particularly mixtures of different polymers – have unpredictable

behaviour characteristics, and can therefore be used only in restricted applications. In the longer term, it may be possible to develop highly sophisticated separation techniques through incorporating built-in tracers within the material, which might mean that guidelines for recyclability can be less restrictive.

Ideally, toxic materials should be replaced with non-hazardous alternatives; if this is not possible, they should be designed for easy identification and removal before the rest of the product is recycled. Batteries, for example, must be clearly identified so that they can be removed and safely disposed of before the product is recycled.

The sheer complexity of some products, however, precludes reclamation, as discarded products may contain only very small quantities of recoverable materials. This is apparent in the miniaturisation of electronic products, where tiny quantities of valuable materials are incorporated within a case composed of several different, hard-to-recover, low-value materials. Miniaturisation has the advantage

Above
Dorian Kurz, then a student at the Academy of Arts in Stuttgart, Germany, designed this larder to provide cooling and protection properties to rival those of the refrigerator. The free-standing aluminium-framed larder has three sections. The top section, shown here, uses terracotta to keep food cool. Water in an enam-elled tray in the bottom of the section evaporates due to the flow of air through the ventilation slots: absorption and evaporation of the water by the porous clay keeps the unit cool. The ripple detailing increases the available surface area of the terracotta.

of reducing the quantities of materials needed in the first place, but it can make recycling impossible. It is unrealistic to believe that every product can be recycled, but this could prove an important part of the life cycle of large items such as cars, domestic appliances, furniture and industrial equipment.

Imposed lifetime

Designers have been accused of fuelling thoughtless consumerism by building in obso-lescence, and encouraging replacement rather than repair, and disposal rather than re-use. "Newness" has been promoted as having an intrinsic value, and this has often been sup-ported by real improvements in technology which make it possible to move to higher and higher levels of performance, as seen in the progression, for example, from tape cassette to compact disc to digital audio tape.

Increasing consumer demand for quality, and concern about waste, may result in a favouring of "classic" design approaches which do not date. Owning a product which

is several years old may become a desirable self-statement, not something to be ashamed of because it indicates that the owner cannot afford to replace it.

However, advances in technology will continue, perhaps now fuelled by the need to improve environment performance. The introduction of CFC-free fridges will no doubt stimulate the replacement of existing fridges before they have reached the end of their useful life.

Material selection

The material used has a major impact on the environment performance of a product, influencing its energy efficiency in manufacture and use, how easily it can be recycled, or whether it represents a hazard when eventually disposed of. There has been a huge growth in the number of materials available, with complex materials now specifically tailor-made for particular purposes.

Consideration of materials should begin at the earliest stage of the design process, with selection made in the context of how the product will be used, whether recycling is feasible, and what performance characteristics are demanded. A variety of different solutions may be appropriate.

Quality specification

The over-specification of performance criteria may result in a heavier or higher-grade material being used than is necessary to meet the true functional requirements of the product. Without, of course, sacrificing safety criteria, the designer should aim to use a material which is appropriate for the way in which the product will be used. Sometimes high-quality materials are specified because of their attractive appearance, but innovative design can create unusual and appealing images through the use of low-grade material which may be more appropriate to the product life cycle.

Against this must be set the danger that lower-quality materials will simply encourage disposability. One Japanese company, Papyrus, has produced a clock made out of corrugated cardboard. Does this encourage the clock to be disposed of after a short period of time, or will the durability of corrugated board give a result that lasts a realistic amount of time,

after which the materials can be recycled or can biodegrade?

Use of recycled materials

Some materials, such as glass and aluminium, offer almost identical performance and appearance characteristics after recycling, and are therefore already used extensively in recycled form as a standard raw material. Others, however, deteriorate or simply change in chemical composition during recycling, making them difficult to use again for their original purposes.

This is true particularly if different types of plastic are recycled together, as may be inevitable with reclamation from household waste. The resultant material is unlike any virgin material, but may have interesting properties in its own right. Increasingly, designers will be faced with the challenge of finding significant uses for recycled plastics. O2, a group of European designers, have produced a range of experimental products from fragmented, pressed plastic obtained from a collection of bottles, plastic bags, old toys and packaging materials. Pure recycled material, for example from PET bottles, is likely to become a mainstream ingredient of packaging material, just as recycled paper is.

Designers should always consider whether a recycled material might perform the

Below
Yemm & Hart Green Materials from Marquand, USA is dedicated to broadening the applications for environmentally-responsible materials. The main aim is to raise the awareness-level of designers, so that they determine the specifications for products and thus are instrumental in creating market demand for recycled materials. The company is involved in all stages of the recycling process, and aim to make recycled materials look and feel desirable. One material manufactured by the company is Origins, made from post-consumer detergent bottles. It is offered as a decorative material because of its attractive colourways.

function just as well as a virgin material, and should request a good selection of recycled materials from suppliers.

There is a "cascade" effect in the recycling of plastics: high-performance plastics, after recycling, cannot be used for their original application. After several passages through the recycling "loop", applications will be limited to very basic products, such as park benches or fence posts. This means that uses have to be found for recycled plastics in order to stimulate the development of a recycling infrastructure.

Use of recyclable materials

There is little point in selecting a material which can be recycled if no mechanism exists, or is likely to exist, to enable it to be recycled, or if the product has not been designed with easy recycling in mind.

Materials which are difficult to recycle may have other benefits, such as greater energy efficiency. The replacement in the automotive industry of easily recyclable steel and iron by hard-to-recycle plastics helped improve fuel consumption because of the savings that could be achieved in the weight of the car. However, the inclusion of higher quantities of plastic made it more difficult for scrap merchants to retrieve the metal parts, thus increasing their costs and diminishing the

value of the metals recycling process. Efforts now being made to develop plastic components which are easy to dismantle and separate, and which can be recycled themselves, may reduce this problem.

Advanced materials

Much of the effort in materials development recently has been towards the creation of new materials which have unique properties, made through the integration of chemically different substances. To counteract the substitution of metals by plastic composites, metal producers have laminated or coated metals with plastic – making metal more difficult to recycle. Composite plastic materials have been developed to combine high strength with clarity, or heat resistance with flexibility. With ever-increasing numbers of new materials being produced, monitoring their environmental impact becomes almost impossible. However, the efforts being made to produce complex materials may also result in a greater understanding of how the materials can be separated out into their component parts for recycling.

Some advanced materials can give clear environmental benefits. Ceramics, such as silicon carbide and silicon nitrate, when mixed with aluminium, provide good solutions in applications where high temperature

Left & below
Treske specialise in the production of furniture from English hardwoods. They follow an environmental policy which considers a very wide range of ecological factors. These include proper woodland husbandry; avoidance of insecticide spraying; the use of non-polluting drying and curing methods; energy conservation and the design of high-quality, solidly-made furniture which will last for generations.

resistance enhances energy efficiency and therefore energy conservation. Super-strong, fine fibres made of graphite can be used as a construction material because they combine strength with light weight; they also produce less waste in manufacture than some of the alternatives. Advanced plastics can be valuable in medical applications, because they do not corrode like metal.

There is a tendency, however, for new materials to be developed simply in order to be different. A new material can be highlighted in the design of a car as an attractive "hi-tech" feature, when in fact the material offers no real improvement in performance. Unnecessary proliferation of material types – particularly of advanced composites – is not something the environment-conscious designer should encourage.

Biodegradable materials

Many materials which were thought to be easily biodegradable have proved not to be when buried in landfill sites; even organic materials such as paper may take a long time to decompose. But natural substances such as wood and cotton are inherently biodegradable, and may therefore be preferable in many applications to plastics, which will not biodegrade.

The development of truly biodegradable plastics (see Chapter 5, "Packaging Design") may be useful for items which have to be disposed of after limited use, such as small

components of surgical equipment. They have also been suggested for use in products regarded by consumers as disposable, which end up in the sewage system. However, a better alternative might be to encourage the use of re-usable products instead, or to discourage disposal of plastic items through the sewage system.

Avoidance of hazardous ingredients

Designers should not specify any substance without first considering whether it has any

Bottom
BMW are now designing cars so that they are easier to dismantle, repair and recycle. This includes examining how the number of different materials used can be reduced. The Z-1 sports car has recyclable thermoplastic doors, bumpers and panels which can be quickly removed from the chassis.

Below
The BMW 3 series: parts coloured blue are made from recycled materials; parts coloured green can be recycled.

dangers in use, such as a possible health risk, or whether it could create dangers in disposal. The use of polyurethane foam in soft furnishings is risky because of the toxic smoke produced when it burns; formaldehyde, often used in chipboard furniture, may be carcinogenic; heavy metals in paint can lead to problems if these are leached out into groundwater in landfill sites. The use of PVC may increasingly be considered unwise because of the controversy surrounding its environmental and human safety.

The Swedish automotive manufacturers Volvo aim to avoid the use of harmful substances as far as possible in all their vehicle production. Their objective is to eliminate completely the use of asbestos and mercury, for example.

Sometimes the hazardous substances are associated with secondary materials, such as

paints and adhesives. Solvent-based paints should be replaced with water-based wherever possible, because solvents contribute to atmospheric pollution as well as polluting the working environment.

It is not always possible to identify easily the harmful side-effects of products – especially when these occur at the disposal stage of the product's life, rather than in use. It is important to ensure that the composition of materials is known fully, so that checks can be conducted on safety.

Minimum use of material

A reduction in the amount of material used is desirable because of cost savings, in addition to the environment benefits of saving resources. A variety of approaches can be used.

Simplification
It is often the case that the simpler the design the less material it needs – provided that there is no hidden waste in the way materials are cut. Simplification may be achieved by clever component design, by the avoidance of purely decorative features or by making structures lighter in weight.

Miniaturisation
The reduction in size of electronic components has allowed items such as computers, televisions and calculators to be reduced in

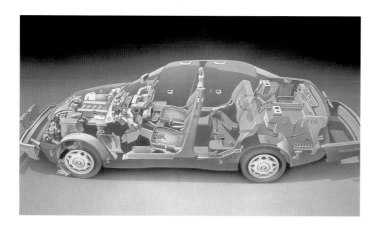

size, using smaller quantities of resources. As product shapes in many fields are no longer dictated by their mechanical components, new opportunities will emerge for the design form. Miniaturisation, however, tends to make it more difficult to reclaim the smaller quantities of material.

Multi-functionalism
One approach to minimising overall resource use is to develop products which can perform a number of different functions, making proliferation unnecessary. Many kitchen appliances now combine at least two functions within one casing. The danger with this approach is that the multi-purpose object may perform each function slightly less well, or may perform a large number of trivial or even unnecessary functions. But the concept of the versatile, intelligent, multi-functional product must be an attractive one, and it offers major opportunities to the designer.

Use of energy and water

One of the main contributions designers can make to improving the environment performance of products is in the area of energy use. They can design products which use energy efficiently, and which use as little energy as possible, and they can explore opportunities to use energy from renewable resources. Conservation of water supplies is also increasingly important, so opportunities to reduce water wastage should be sought.

Energy efficiency
Legislation in the USA and Europe requires appliances to be labelled with their energy consumption, stimulating the design of more efficient products. Significant savings can be achieved – sometimes by extremely simple design changes. Designers at AEG in Germany have developed an oven which saves energy by the use of a removable divider so that only part of the oven needs to be heated up at a time. The build-up of ice on refrigerator and freezer walls causes the use of excessive energy; many freezers are now "frost-free", which tends to improve energy efficiency.

Sometimes, energy wastage may go completely unnoticed. Televisions with remote control devices and "instant on" standby features consume electricity even when they are not being used.

The incorporation of microprocessors into domestic appliances can help save energy. A tumble drier which can detect how much water is left on clothes can choose the correct setting in order to minimise the amount of electricity used. Timing controls allow appliances to be used during the night, when energy needs can be supplied more easily.

Energy efficiency is important during the manufacturing stage, too. Many materials are highly energy-intensive in production – aluminium, for example – but that energy cost may be justified by energy savings delivered in use, and by length of life through recycling.

It has been suggested that considerable energy savings, as well as cost savings, can be achieved by allowing the end user of a product to assemble it. Assembling and transporting goods such as furniture and domestic appliances are costly; producing simple and easily assembled components would reduce manufacturing and transport costs.

Alternative energy sources
The contribution made to national power supplies by renewable forms of energy such as solar, tidal and wind power is likely to increase steadily in many countries. For most powered products, mains electricity or gas is likely to be the most practical source of energy, but there may be opportunities to use solar or wind power directly. The solar-powered calculator is an example of an everyday item with low power requirements, for which light is a very efficient and convenient source of power. Solar power is particularly valuable in areas where no other form of energy is readily available.

Batteries offer a convenient but very inefficient way of storing energy. Mains power should be used wherever possible. Recent developments making batteries renewable help to minimise the problems caused by battery disposal, but do little to improve overall energy efficiency.

Water use
Mechanical changes to products can reduce the amount of water they use. By increasing mechanical pressure, and ensuring that water is directed to where it is needed, it has been possible to develop a washing machine which uses significantly less water.

The redesign of the toilet cistern can also reduce water consumption, as in a design from Swedish manufacturer Ifö Sanitär (see pages 82-3).

The Kambrook Group in Australia worked with the National Key Centre for Design at the Royal Melbourne Institute of Technology to develop an energy-saving kettle, which also has potential for end-of-life disassembly and recycling. Research found that most people reboil kettles even when there is no need to – wasting large amounts of energy. The kettle's double-wall design reduces heat loss, and a water-temperature indicator signals whether the water is still hot enough to use. These features minimise reboiling. Recyclability is facilitated by the use of minimal, similar materials, and fewer components, many of which are stamped with identification codes.

Minimising pollution

Air, water and noise pollution can be reduced and prevented by designers carefully considering the selection of product materials, and by looking for alternatives to conventional approaches.

The automobile is one of the worst polluters. One way of addressing this problem is to try to produce cleaner cars by using power from electricity, methane or other cleaner fuel sources and by developing new types of engine, such as the leanburn, which use sophisticated electronics and modified cylinder heads for a fuller combustion and a destruction of the potential air pollutants. A more fundamental solution is to develop efficient alternatives to car usage, in the form of public transport systems. This is increasingly winning approval in major cities, where the use of cars causes major problems of congestion and noise in addition to pollution.

Noise is a form of pollution which is often overlooked, but which causes discomfort and

irritation. Many kitchens are used as living areas for the family, and the noise generated by appliances is continuously tackled by designers. New materials can virtually eliminate the internal resonance within the appliance cabinet, through their vibration-absorption properties. Mechanical devices, such as pneumatic dampers fitted in suspension units, and insulated suspension springs, can further minimise noise transmission.

Reducing the impact of pollution

Although the ideal is to prevent the risk of pollution in the first place, there are still many areas where pollution has to be addressed after it has occurred. The catalytic converter chemically cleans up car exhaust emissions once they have been produced, converting fumes into water vapour and less harmful emissions. Such "end of pipe" approaches to reducing manufacturing pollution have been criticised by environmentalists as only a partial solution. In the short term, though, designers and engineers will be asked to develop more effective ways of controlling emissions, and better ways of disposing of waste materials, through finding new uses for them.

The impact of new technology

New technologies can make more effective use of resources. The development in the telecommunications industry of fibre optics, made from glass, a renewable resource, will reduce demand for copper, of which there are only limited supplies. Fibre optic systems should be safer, more effective and less costly in terms of resource consumption.

The microwave oven uses far less energy than a conventional oven; intelligent home-management systems can ensure that heating systems are used efficiently, and sophisticated electrical spraying devices can mean that very small amounts of pesticides can be used to cover large areas of crops, as the product is dispersed accurately and evenly.

Of course, any new technology brings with it some uncertainty, because the long-term consequences of its use are unknown. However, it seems clear that the incorporation of appropriate advanced technology into products and processes can make a significant contribution to improving their environment performance. It is up to the designer to be well informed about the possibilities of new developments.

Herman Miller

Herman Miller, Inc., based in Zeeland, Michigan in the USA, is a leading multinational manufacturer of furniture and furniture systems. The company has a strong research base and has been the source of many major innovations in furniture for office environments.

The firm is currently working to ensure that all new products are made from "earth-friendly" materials and are designed for disassembly, to ensure that furniture parts can be reused or recycled. The company's environmental efforts are becoming an important aspect of how they differentiate their products in the market place.

The Avian chair is designed for recyclability – from its foam pads to its casters. Even its sturdy plastic frame can be recycled or reclaimed. After its useful life is over, it can be broken down into its component materials and reused in a new product. Manufacture and disassembly is made easier by the reduction in the number of parts.

A graphic with an exploded view of the chair is moulded into the underside of the seat to identify the various parts along with their appropriate material identification codes to assist in separation and recycling. In addition, the chair itself uses recycled materials. Over 60 per cent of its total weight is recyclate.

Below left & right
The Avian chair is designed to be dismantled and reused or recycled at the end of its life

Right & below
The Aeron chair
combines good ergo-
nomic performance with
attractive aesthetics
and lower resource
consumption.

The Aeron chair is a radical departure from traditional office chairs. It is intended to be more comfortable for more people than other office chairs, and more versatile. It has an aluminium and polyester structure and uses a breathable membrane known as a pellicle instead of fabric and foam. The pellicle adapts to the shape of the occupant, then returns to its original shape when vacated. The Aeron consumes less energy in manufacturing than conventional foam and fabric seating. It is also sparing in its use of resources, and is designed to be durable and repairable, and at the end of its life easy to disassemble.

Herman Miller is aiming to reduce the environmental impact of its packaging, by offering alternatives to traditional corrugated card and Styrofoam. Packaging is minimised, and alternative techniques include wrapping furniture in blankets for transportation.

Ifö Acqua toilet, Scandinavia

Right
Presentation drawing showing the internal workings of the cistern.

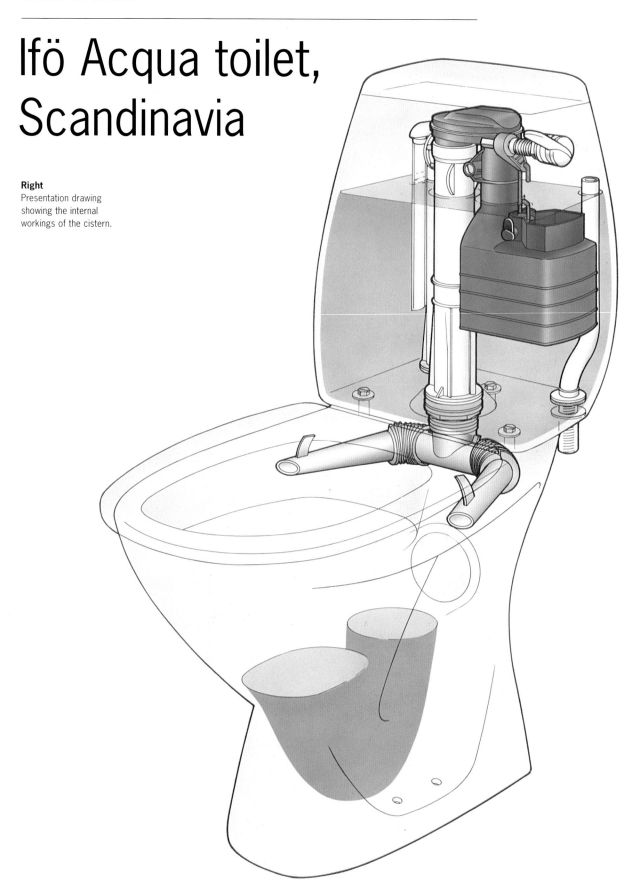

About 30 per cent of the water consumed by a household is used to flush the toilet – an obvious waste of processed, drinkable water. Ifö Sanitär of Sweden set out to develop a toilet which could operate with a much lower quantity of water, aiming to save over a third of the water used by traditional products.

Merely reducing the amount of water flushed from the cistern, however, was not the answer. The entire product had to be considered to ensure that it was effective. The design of the bowl and rim, the rate of the flow of water, the performance of the gravity drainage system – all had to be thought through to develop an integrated solution. The six-litre single flush system was achieved by the use of a special twin diverter flush tube which ensures efficient, effective use of a reduced quantity of water.

The redesign of the mechanics of the product was accompanied by an attempt to produce a more attractive sculptural form, which would have a classic, long-lasting appeal. Knud Holscher Industrial Design of Denmark developed an elegant, durable shape to meet this need. The product has also been designed for easy maintenance; repairs can be carried out without the need to dismantle the cistern or any major components. The compact, free-standing design gives flexibility to bathroom layouts, helping the efficient use of space.

Right
The innovative interior mechanical design of the Ifö Acqua was accompanied by exterior styling which positions the product as an attractive, contemporary object. It was important, however, for the product not to look out of place in a conventional bathroom.

A T & T Lucent Technologies

A T & T is prominent among major companies for its commitment to a "Design for Environment" process, and the incorporation of environmental criteria into the mainstream of the design and innovation process.

Lucent Technologies, the design and manufacturing part of telecommunications equipment within A T & T, worked with the University of Michigan to review the design of the 7401 business telephone terminal, to identify areas for improvement and to implement these through design changes in a replacement model, the 8403 terminal.

Business telephones, because of their significant value, are often returned to the manufacturer as part of trade-in arrangements when users upgrade their systems. They may then be refurbished and resold, or, if they are older or in poor condition, scrapped and recycled. The knowledge gained from refurbishment and recycling is fed back into the design process through the company's Design for Environment programme.

The main focus for environmental improvement was the housing of the terminal. Environmental requirements for the manufacturing stage specify that housing material be recyclable and non-toxic and that moulding scrap is minimised to reduce waste. Environmental requirements for the end-of-life stage specify that the housing be reusable, reconditionable, or, at the very least, recyclable.

The material used for the moulding for this model is ABS resin, a thermoplastic with good recyclability; the type specified contains no heavy metal stabilizers or colours formulated with heavy metals. The resin does not incorporate polybrominated flame retardants.

7401 TERMINAL	8403 TERMINAL	
Feature	**Improved Feature**	**Impact/Effect**
High-gloss surface	Textured surface	Moulding waste reduced
Rubber feet glued to stand	Rubber feet snapped on	Rubber contamination removed
Polycarbonate sheet used as light diffuser glued to housing	No light diffuser used	Contamination of plastic housing minimised
Housing material not identified	ISO marking code moulded in	Plastic type identifiable by any potential recycling centre

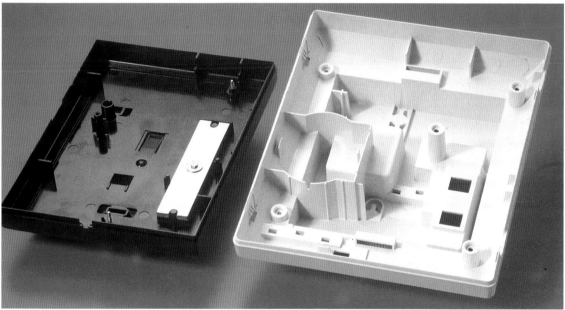

Above
The new 8403
terminal has an
improved environ-
mental impact over
its predecessor,
because of
its improved
recyclability.

The table sets out some of the specific features of the housing of the terminal which have been changed, and summarises the impact of these changes in terms of environmental improvement potential.

The textured surface hides minor moulding flaws better than a high-gloss smooth finish, and therefore the amount of imperfect, wasted product is reduced. Textured surfaces are also more scratch-resistant, which may help extend the life of the housing.

The other features make the housing material more recyclable. By designing the housing to require no glue joints, and by ensuring that minimal other materials are used which are difficult to separate from the base polymer, the recycled material is more likely to end up as high-value, uncontaminated regrind material with near virgin performance characteristics.

Greenfreeze

Left
Siemens were one of the first manufacturers to introduce hydrocarbon refrigerants. Their 0°C Electronic Storage Centre is one of their Greenfreeze models. Siemens have also improved the insulation of their fridges, and ensure that the materials used can be recycled.

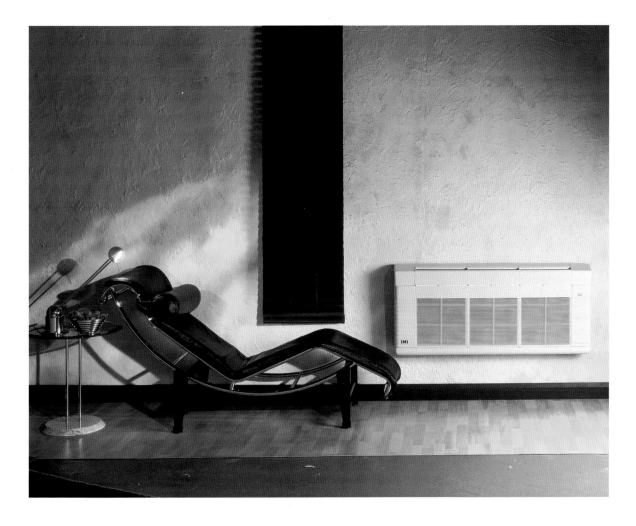

The development of Greenfreeze is a dramatic example of innovation in technology and design driven by environmental campaigning group Greenpeace. Frustrated by the apparent inability of industry to introduce refrigerants which did not damage the ozone layer or contribute to global warming, Greenpeace intervened directly in the market to launch a new product, commissioning a German manufacturer to develop and manufacture a fridge which used "Greenfreeze", a combination of hydrocarbon gases. Consumer and political response to the new product was very positive, stimulating the major manufacturers to move quickly to develop their own versions. Siemens were one of the first major manufacturers to launch a product using hydrocarbon refrigerants.

UK manufacturer Calor Gas launched a new business division selling hydrocarbon refrigerants for refrigeration and air-conditioning – for domestic and commercial purposes.

The design of refrigeration and air-conditioning units will increasingly be influenced by the use of the new technology. Hydrocarbon propellants can use less energy and may cost less than CFCs and HCFCs.

Greenpeace's initiative proves that real environmental solutions exist and can become a reality very quickly, and that engaging directly in the design and innovation process may be a valuable and legitimate way for a campaigning organisation to effect radical change.

Natural Gas Vehicles

Natural gas offers environmental benefits as a vehicle fuel when compared with petrol or diesel, while matching mobility and driving performance.

Significant reductions are achieved in emissions of carbon dioxide, carbon monoxide, nitrogen oxides, benzene and other substances, providing benefits both at street level and in the upper atmosphere. For example, formation of ground-level ozone is greatly reduced, and global-warming potential is lower, when compared with petrol or diesel. Vehicles powered by gas are also generally quieter than those powered by conventional fuels.

Worldwide, the number of natural gas vehicles is forecast to rise to two million by 1998, with the largest numbers being in North America, Italy, Argentina and the former USSR.

Both Volvo and BMW are introducing natural gas cars. The Volvo Bi-Fuel 850 can run on either petrol or natural gas.

Existing vehicles can be converted to run on natural gas by adding pressurised gas cylinders, although in future, once production volumes increase sufficiently, vehicle design for gas will incorporate gas storage areas as an integral component. Natural gas is safe to use because it has a higher ignition temperature than petrol and diesel, and, in the event of leakage, disperses instead of forming dangerous pools.

Below
Unlike liquid fuels, natural gas is supplied to the vehicle under pressure, through a sealed system. The nozzle is attached to the vehicle, and the process is then hands-free until the container is full. The process is therefore clean and safe.

One major commercial challenge is the development of infrastructure, in the form of gas refuelling stations. In the US and Canada, natural gas is available alongside petrol and diesel on public forecourts. In other countries, where natural gas is used primarily by depot-based commercial fleets, refuelling stations can be built at the depots to ensure ease of refuelling.

British Gas is a world leader in research and development in natural gas vehicles, bringing together refuelling and vehicle technology. They are converting part of their own fleet to run on gas, and are contributing to the design of new vehicles and refuelling infrastructure.

Below
Existing vehicles can easily be converted to gas by fitting a gas container and a gas/air mixer.

Above & left
A wide range of vehicles now use natural gas.

5 Packaging design

Packaging designers have demonstrated a great deal of ingenuity and inventiveness over the last few years, helping manufacturers deliver convenience and freshness to customers, and finding new ways to "add value" to the product through aesthetic or practical benefits. The way in which a product is packaged is often one of the major influences on whether people notice it and buy it, particularly in markets such as perfume and cosmetics where image plays a crucial role. The cost of packaging can be more than the cost of the product inside.

We are increasingly aware, however, of the impact that packaging has on the environment. Both the quantity of packaging, and the use of particular types of material, are being questioned. The visibility of packaging in the waste stream has prompted consumer concerns: it accounts for around one-third of household waste in most countries in Europe and North America, and is a clearly recognisable component of litter. As packaging materials become more sophisticated and elaborate, disposing of them after they have been used only once appears to be a waste of valuable resources. Producing and disposing of packaging can cause environment problems just like any other product: pollution in the manufacturing process; the consumption of energy and non-renewable resources, and the dangers of hazardous ingredients being dispersed into ground-water or the air during disposal through landfill or incineration.

Under the current structure of our manufacturing, distribution and retailing chain, and with current consumer expectations, packaging has a variety of roles. Its main function – to ensure that the product inside reaches the consumer in good condition – is often taken for granted, but it ensures that as little as possible of the product is wasted or damaged during distribution and storage. Packaging also delivers the benefits of hygiene and safety, which are increasingly important to consumers because of fears of contamination or tampering. It enables the product to be handled easily, stacked, stored and transported. And, of course, packaging helps consumers identify the product in the store – an important function in self-service stores with vast ranges of merchandise. Finally, it is a major communication vehicle, providing information and usage instructions.

Many environmentalists are calling into question the environmental cost of this type of production and distribution structure. They propose a return to more locally based economies, where the chain between producer and consumer is shorter, reducing the need for so much packaging. However, within the current structure, there are many ways of reducing the environment impact of packaging, often without compromising consumer and producer demands for functional performance and visual appeal.

In many countries, legislation will influence changes. The EC waste management strategy requires industry to minimise waste overall, with packaging identified as a specific area where there is room for improvement. The hierarchy of reduce, re-use, recycle continues to underpin the EU approach. The

How to wrap 5 eggs

Meguro Museum of Art, Tokyo
目黒区美術館

5つの卵はいかにして包まれたか

日本の伝統パッケージ展

Packaging and Packaging Waste Directive set targets for recycling, which will stimulate the development of infrastructure for the collection of used materials.

The shortage of landfill sites in the US has stimulated a variety of local laws. These include deposits on soft drinks containers to encourage their return, and the requirement that householders separate out waste so that it can be recycled.

The combination of consumer concerns and legislative pressure will ensure that environment impact becomes an essential criterion in the design of packaging material. In this area, as in other design areas, new ways of working will be required, and new aesthetics will evolve. The challenge for designers is to produce packaging that sells the product, and protects it effectively, but creates less environment damage.

Designing packaging for minimum impact requires an understanding of the complete life of the pack, from the production of the material through to manufacture, distribution, end use and disposal. While the overall objective should be to use the minimum resources, the best solution depends largely on context. What type of product is it? How will it be used? Where will it be used? The designer will have to consider a complex range of options to identify the best solution.

The material used in packaging, the way the pack is constructed, and the way it is merchandised in the store will be particularly important considerations for the packaging designer. Graphic designers, who often take the lead in packaging design, will have to place more emphasis on technical issues related to production and to the properties of materials if they are to play a leading role in

Above & left
Industrial ingredients are often distributed in dry granular form in steel drums, which can lead to high storage and transport costs. This alternative, made from corrugated board, was developed by Reed Corrugated Cases with Sams Design. The hinged plastic lid, incorporating an anti-tamper device, provides a waterproof seal. The square box gives better space use than a round steel drum, and the boxes can be stored flat before and after use, saving on storage space.

innovation to improve environment performance. Close collaboration between graphic designers, industrial designers, technologists and materials scientists will be important. Producers of packaging materials will find it essential to provide clear, objective information about the performance of their products, in areas like energy efficiency, recyclability and additives.

Products have very different packaging requirements. Delicate items of medical equipment have to be treated quite differently from shampoo, and washing machines differently from food, so generalisations about material usage and packaging construction are difficult to make. Improvements in environment impact can be made in a wide variety of ways – it is up to the designer to determine what may be appropriate, feasible and desirable for a particular product.

The selection of material may depend entirely on where the product will be used.

A refillable glass bottle designed for several re-uses may use less energy than a plastic bottle. However, if these bottles are miniatures, as used on airlines, their weight is important. Because glass is much heavier than plastic, using plastic results in a saving for the airline in terms of fuel consumed during flying. This energy saving therefore has to be set against the energy lost when the bottles are disposed of. It is clear, therefore, that the equations can be highly complex.

Avoiding over-packaging

A frequent criticism of packaging is that more is used than is really needed to meet the requirements of functional performance. This is particularly true of luxury items such as confectionery and cosmetics, and of products packed in single-serve units or blister packs. Significant reductions in the amount of packaging used for some products may be achievable only with some trade-off in consumer convenience, or with changes in usage patterns, or in expectations about product appearance. There may be opportunities for designers to adopt a radical departure from conventional norms. Packaging an expensive perfume, or selection of chocolates, in a box made from simple corrugated board may actually be interesting and attractive to consumers!

An elaborate and sophisticated pack may deliver a marginal benefit to the consumer, but simpler alternatives may be preferable from an environmental viewpoint. Aerosol packs are an example of over-packaging, where a small quantity of product is contained within a large pack. The performance characteristics of aerosols may make their use necessary in certain specialised applications – such as medicine – but they may no longer be considered appropriate for everyday uses when good alternative delivery systems exist. If aerosols could be easily recycled they might cause less environmental concern, but so far recycling appears to be difficult to achieve.

Some companies are beginning to set targets for improving their packaging/product ratios, by examining how much packaging is required to deliver a unit of product. They do not accept changes in packaging which lead to a worsening in this ratio, and encourage the achievement of ever greater efficiencies.

Using minimum amounts of material

Manufacturers have a strong cost incentive to reduce the amount of packaging materials used. Not only are raw material costs reduced with lighter or smaller packs, but distribution and storage costs are also saved. A re-design of the aluminium soft drinks can to reduce the diameter of the opening end allowed a reduction in the amount of material used per can. Removing the base cup of a bottle made of PET lightened it by nearly one third. However, lightweighting has to be considered in the context of the entire life cycle of the pack: creating a very light pack may not be desirable if it is possible to use the pack again, when strength would become important.

In packs which are "one-trip", or which go into the recycling system, reducing the quantity of materials is usually beneficial, because of savings in energy and in materials. The shape of a pack can have a significant impact on the amount of energy used in transportation. The use of a square-sectioned package rather than a circular pack gives a more

efficient way of transporting products like milk, as more unit product can be contained in the allotted space. An octagonal corrugated box used by one home-delivery pizza chain uses 10 per cent less material than the usual square box, and also delivers a more appealing product because toppings no longer smudge on the pizza lid.

Reduction in the quantity of materials used may also be achieved by considering the packaging requirements in the context of merchandising and in-store dispensing opportunities. A protective outer display at point of sale may reduce the need for a layer of secondary packaging.

Above
Courtin Packaging have developed a novel dispensing pouch for shampoo, shower gel and liquid soap. The pouch, made from PE/PET, uses far less material than normal dispensing containers, but is easy to use and convenient. The pouch incorporates a pump chamber, valves and an outlet nozzle which closes after use, making it especially suitable for older or infirm users.

The creation of unusual bottle and cap shapes can use more material than necessary. A double-walled cap on a shampoo bottle uses more material than a small screw cap; a complex, novel shape tends to be less efficient than a standard cylindrical shape. The desire to create a novel appearance – to give extra impact or to reflect the image the product wishes to convey – may be at odds with materials minimisation. Striking graphics can add interest to simple, standard containers. It is possible, as consumers become more critical of the environment impact of packaging, that they will become more approving of simple, straightforward packaging structures, and less likely to place novelty and distinctiveness quite so high on their selection criteria.

In some sectors, additional layers of packaging have been introduced to protect the product from being tampered with. Incorporating a tamper-evident feature into a closing device may be an effective and less wasteful solution.

Material quality

Another form of over-packaging is the specification of high-quality materials where functional performance and consumer taste do not require them – for example, the use of virgin white card in outer cartons.

Very often, material composition or weight is specified by habit, rather than by a real examination of the needs of the job. The increased use of recycled materials in the packaging industry can play a significant part in reducing overall resource consumption, and thus every effort should be made to specify these where their use is acceptable in terms of functional performance and aesthetic appeal.

Re-use and refill

Resource conservation may take the form of the re-use or refilling of containers, thus extending their functional lifetime. After minimising the use of resources in the first place, this route appears most environmentally attractive. However, the process of re-using and refilling has an environmental cost too, which must be considered. The energy cost of collecting and cleaning containers should not outweigh the energy value of manufacturing them in the first place, and packs may have to be re-used many times before the initial investment in energy is recouped, so dura-

bility will be important. Containers also have to be designed so that they can be cleaned easily.

There are a variety of ways in which a refillable system can work. The container can be returned to the manufacturer for refilling; the user can take the container to a refilling point; or the user can purchase a refill pack from which a more durable container can be refilled. Whether any of these approaches is appropriate and beneficial will depend on the manufacturing and distribution systems involved and, of course, on the nature of the product itself.

Returnable, refillable systems

Return systems that operate in a closed loop between manufacturer and user have traditionally been widely used in the beverage industry. In the UK doorstep milk delivery depends on consumers returning empty bottles quickly. In the food service trade, bottles and casks are returned to the manufacturer and many food items, such as bread, are supplied in re-usable crates. Where it is possible for the delivery system to double up as the collection system, with outlets relatively close to the manufacturer or distribution centre, this system can be highly efficient. Difficulties arise, however, if products are internationally traded; then, return systems work only if there is standardisation of packs, with every manufacturer participating in the re-use process.

While the collection of packs for re-use can be relatively easy if large numbers of packs accumulate at one point, as in a restaurant, it becomes more difficult for products consumed at home. Increasingly, however, retailers are accepting returned containers – particularly glass bottles – and in some countries this is becoming the normal system as bottle deposits are introduced via the retailer.

Consumer refill points

Many years ago, shoppers would take along their own containers to be filled directly in the shop from sacks or casks of product. In France and other countries, table wine is still sold in this way. This approach can be highly attractive in terms of environment considerations, particularly as there are savings in energy cost by avoiding the "return" route. Although containers need to be durable, they do not need to be able to survive numerous circuits through the distribution system.

The original container may be purchased with the first purchase of the product and replaced when necessary, or a variety of alternative containers might be offered separately, allowing the consumer to choose whatever is the most convenient size, shape, etc. The only important criterion is that the container should be able to protect the product effectively and should be easy to clean.

Consumers obviously have to be willing to accept a trade-off in terms of convenience, although the refilling process could be offered as an intrinsic part of the attraction of the product. In the case of the UK-based franchise The Body Shop, for example, refills are offered at a discounted price compared with the original packaged product.

Refill packs

In the short term, refill packs may offer the most practical way of achieving re-use in many categories. One durable container appropriate for storing the product and using it, is sold. Additional product requirements are supplied via refill packs, which need have only a short life expectancy, and can therefore be made from a small quantity of lighter-weight or lower-quality material. The refill pack can also be easier and less heavy for the consumer to take home. Soft-sided, collapsible refill packs take up considerably less room in landfill sites.

With detergents, shampoos and other household products which are in very regular use, refill sachets or cartridges could allow the original pack to be more attractively and more intelligently designed, because the extra cost of this will be spread across a much longer life, and packaging costs overall are reduced by avoiding the need to throw away significant quantities of material.

Refill packs must be easy and clean to use, rather than messy and inconvenient. Pouring spouts and easy-to-tear openings can be helpful.

Material choice

There is considerable confusion about whether some materials are inherently less damaging to the environment than others. Some may consume more energy or non-renewable materials in their production, but perhaps have a longer life span. Some are easier to recycle, while others are believed to degrade easily and harmlessly. When disposed of by incineration, some materials are valuable because their energy content can be

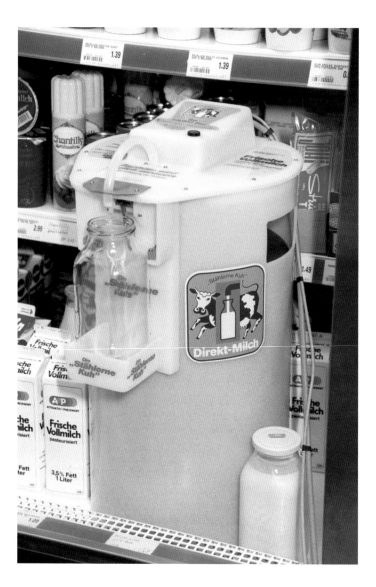

reclaimed, but there may be concerns about the substances released into the atmosphere during the incineration process. No one type of material can claim overall environmental superiority. Material selection has to be considered, therefore, as part of the total manufacturing and design process, taking into account the entire life cycle of the product and pack.

Use of recyclable material

Packaging uses valuable materials which could be reclaimed and re-used rather than dumped in landfill sites. The contribution made by the use of recyclable materials depends entirely on whether there is an end use for the materials once reclaimed. Glass may be recycled and re-used to make containers that are indistinguishable from the originals. Other materials, however, such as

Above
A self-dispensing milk refill machine, used throughout the Tengelmann supermarket chain in Germany since 1988. Glass and recyclable plastic bottles containing one litre are purchased at the store and filled with milk at the machine. When emptied, they are cleaned and brought back for refilling by the customer without limit to the number of times they can be used. In Munich alone, the system resulted in the saving of 3,700 tonnes of packaging waste in one year.

local areas are experimenting with curbside collection schemes. The high participation rates achieved demonstrate the public commitment to recycling, but there are still problems in sorting, grading and reusing many materials.

Designing for recyclability is worthwhile only where there is a recycling infrastructure, or where the manufacturer makes arrangements to collect the used packs. There also has to be an end use to which the recycled material can be put.

Recycling is assisted if composite materials or multiple layers of different materials are avoided. The use of one single material throughout avoids the problems of contamination and unpredictable performance which can arise from mixed materials.

Identification of the type of material can also be important in sorting. This may be done by consumers at home, or by a mechanical sorting process in a municipal waste site. Clear visual symbols will help consumers, while in the long term the incorporation of "tracers" within the material itself may allow selection and sorting to be carried out mechanically.

While collection and recycling systems are quite well established for glass and cans, plastic is far behind in most places, making it look relatively unattractive as a packaging material if glass is a realistic alternative. However, if plastic can be recycled, its high energy efficiency and other benefits change the picture significantly.

Use of recycled material
Packaging materials have used recycled ingredients for years. Cans are manufactured from material which contains a high proportion of secondary, reclaimed metal; outer packaging such as corrugated board uses waste-based pulp. The production of aluminium cans is made economic by using waste aluminium, as producing virgin aluminium has very high energy costs. The issue for designers now is whether more recycled materials can be used, as part of the process of stimulating demand and encouraging efficient recycling.

Paper and card
Recycled papers and card are used widely in packaging now, and frequently offer performance and printing characteristics which are only marginally different from virgin material. Some packs make a feature out of being self-

Above
Premier Waters developed a collapsible recyclable PET bottle for Evian, the mineral water from Danone. The empty bottle can be crushed to one-fifth of its original size. The PVC originally used was replaced by PET, which has made a lightweight solution possible. Around 37 per cent material savings are achieved for the 2 litre bottle, and damage during transit, storage and distribution is claimed to be reduced significantly.

plastic, are more difficult to recycle, and the recycled substances may have very different properties and appearances from the original, making them unsuitable for re-use for the same purpose. Recycled materials have to have a market, and this depends on a variety of factors, including the cost difference between recycled and virgin materials.

Most reclaimed materials come from industrial and commercial waste, where there are large quantities of identifiable materials which can be collected and processed efficiently. Most packaging ends up in household waste, with small quantities of different materials widely dispersed, posing a huge challenge for collection and sorting. Major effects are being made to encourage the reclamation of household waste. Bottle and can banks are now common in many countries, and many

consciously "recycled"; a gritty, grey look can contribute towards a feeling that the product is produced on a small scale, or that the product inside has convincing environment credentials. In some countries, such as Germany and The Netherlands, people expect recycled paper materials to be off-white, with a slightly rough texture. However, in others, such as the UK, recycled paper and card appears to be more acceptable and mainstream if it is very similar in appearance to virgin material.

Plastic

Most plastics are not difficult to recycle if they can be isolated, but changes in chemical structure do occur, and the recycled product may perform unpredictably, making its use rather difficult in applications where precise characteristics are required. The products generally associated with recycled plastic tend to be low-quality items such as builders' sheets, garbage bags and flower pots. However, there may be increasing opportunities to use recycled plastic in packaging materials. PET (polyethylene terephthalate), a clear, high-quality plastic often used for soft drinks containers, can be recycled. Material made from post-consumer PET waste has been used by Procter and Gamble in the packaging of household cleaning products. Designers should be open to the use of recycled materi-

als of all kinds, where these materials can meet the essential performance requirements of the pack.

The cost of using recycled materials relative to virgin materials varies widely. Difficulties in obtaining high-quality waste, and the small scale of many recycling efforts, can make recycled materials expensive. In the longer term, however, the increased use of recycled material should lower packaging costs. In the meantime, it may be possible to justify the small additional cost because of consumer willingness to support recycling efforts: packaging which is perceived to be environmentally sensitive can deliver an "added value" benefit, and create differentiation among competitors.

Biodegradable materials

Biodegradability has been proposed as one answer to the problem of the accumulation of ever-increasing quantities of long-lived materials such as plastics; it has also been suggested that biodegradable packaging could reduce the litter problem. But materials which biodegrade relatively easily – like paper – can give only limited protection to a product, and are therefore often coated with substances to make them resistant to decomposition. However, assumptions about the speed of degradation have recently been challenged, with the discovery in US landfill sites of almost perfectly

Above
Bales of crushed soft drinks containers made from PET are now collected and stored for recycling in many countries.

Right
Leading UK retailer Sainsbury's is committed to minimising the resources used for packaging its own brand products. One example of this is the development of new packaging for its garlic bread. A new single polypropylene and polyester plastic sleeve replaces a cardboard sleeve and plastic firm. Annual saving of 175 tonnes of board, and over 1 tonne of solvent-based glue, have been achieved. The packaging occupies less shelf space, and more items can be distributed per lorry load. Sales increased after the introduction of the new pack.

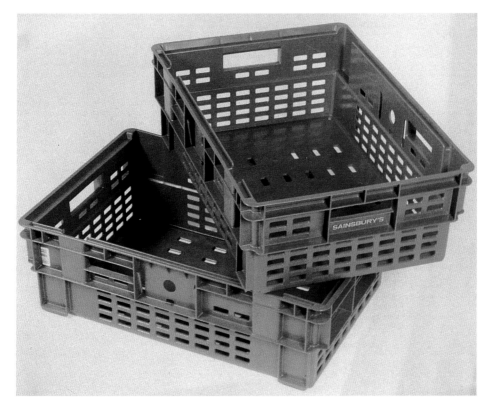

Left
For some goods Sainsbury's have been using returnable plastic crates in the distribution chain for over 25 years. They developed a strategy to extend this system into areas where single-trip cardboard packaging continued to be used, and to introduce a standard design. The universal crate is made from polypropylene and is designed to incorporate recycled material. One of the objectives was to reduce the volume of cardboard used in distribution packaging; the company has already saved 10,000 tonnes each year since the system's introduction and expects to double this by 1999. Each crate can be used in a stacked or nested position providing two internal working capacities as well as an opportunity for faster chilling of packed stock, with associated saving in energy.

preserved newspapers and even food: without exposure to air and water, biodegradability takes a very long time. Photodegradability – destruction through exposure to sunlight – has been explored as an option for plastic garbage bags, and for packaging which might end up as litter. But, clearly, precautions have to be taken to prevent the material from degrading prematurely.

A wide range of biodegradable plastics has been developed and promoted as an environmentally sensitive packaging solution. Most of the plastics, however, are biodestructible, rather than biodegradable. They are made by mixing special additives – usually cornstarch – with plastic polymers. This means that, although they do disintegrate over time, they do not break down completely, but instead leave tiny particles of polymer which may persist in the soil, possibly producing chemicals which may contaminate the soil or groundwater.

Left
"Bio Packs", produced by the Bio Pack company in Germany, are paper pouches filled with straw or other fibres. They give a flexible, absorbent, non-dusty packing material, which can be easily shaped around fragile objects. They are easy to re-use and clean to store, but if discarded they will decompose on a compost heap. They make a good alternative to polystyrene.

Biodegradable plastic is also less durable than conventional plastic, has less potential for re-use, and must be kept out of any plastics recycling stream because it has a destabilising effect. It is also more expensive to produce. For some uses, though, biodegradable plastic may be preferable to conventional plastic – if the plastic item will end up in the sewage system, for example.

A new generation of "bio-polymers", led by ICI's Biopol, could provide some solutions. These are produced from bacteria which manufacture natural polymers when grown on organic waste. These natural polymers can be removed and melted, moulded and recycled – just like oil-based plastic. Eventually, they decompose into carbon dioxide. High prices and limited versatility mean that applications in the short term will be restricted to speciality uses such as medical apparatus or high-value toiletries. Other attempts to produce 100 per cent degradable plastic involve increasing the starch content, and using vegetable oils as the base ingredient.

"Natural plastics" may in the long term provide a realistic alternative to oil-based plastics, allowing the many benefits of plastics technology to be exploited without the problems that currently exist. In the short term, however, most interest appears to lie in recycling as the most practical way of managing the waste problem.

Non-hazardous materials

Of course, packaging designers should try to avoid or minimise the use of any materials that are damaging to health or to the environment during production, use and eventual disposal. Additives such as cadmium have been found to pollute groundwater when packaging is degraded in landfill sites, and there are concerns about emissions or residues from some ingredients when they are incinerated. Some supermarkets are discouraging the use of PVC in packaging because of concern over the chemicals which arise during its manufacture

Below
Bionolle, by Showa Highpolymer, Japan, is a thermoplastic polyester which competes in processing performance with polyethylene. It is a biodegradable material promoted as having the potential to decompose rapidly in moist environments. Applications in Japan include compost bags.

Left
Toothpaste used to be
packed in metal tubes
which were packed in
board cartons to prevent
damage during transit.
Technical innovations
allowed the use of plas-
tic, and in this example
the top of the tube has
been made larger to
allow it to stand on its
head. The tubes are
displayed on shelves in
a notched plastic tray.

and disposal. The use of phthalates, which are
added to PVC to improve its flexibility, has
been criticised specifically because of the
chance that these may migrate into food
items from packaging materials. Hormone-
disrupting chemicals such as phthalates are
being linked with abnormalities in both
wildlife and human hormone systems, leading
to fertility problems. There are adequate
alternatives to almost every use of PVC
in packaging.

The fluctuating nature of concerns about
the hazards of materials will inevitably cause
problems for manufacturers and designers.
Clearly, avoidance of substances or processes
which may be more polluting or dangerous
than feasible alternatives should be the guiding principle, even though issues may not be
scientifically clear-cut. The "precautionary
principle" provides an approach which min-
imises exposure to risk.

Reducing the number
of containers

Reducing the number of containers used per
unit of product, or using bulk rather than
individual containers, helps to minimise the
amount of packaging used. Dispensing items
which are regularly purchased and easy to
store in larger sizes is one approach. Another
is to find a way of delivering the product in
bulk directly into the user's storage facility, an
approach now widely used in the transfer of
industrial ingredients such as cement or milk
powder, which could have applications for
consumer products through the growth of
home delivery systems

The ratio of product to packaging can
also be changed through the use of product
concentrates, which reduces the volume of
the product and therefore the amount of

Above

Radisson SAS Hotels redesigned their guest amenities with greater consideration for their environmental impact. All paper and carton packaging is made from recycled paper, and vegetable-based inks are used for printing logos on product labels. The packaging of the toiletries products is distinctive, and is in strong contrast to the elaborate plastic containers which have been favoured in the past for this application. The simplicity of the packaging is appropriate for these short-life products – although the logical development may be to avoid packaging altogether, or provide bulk containers.

packaging required. One obvious advantage for the manufacturer is that transport costs are reduced: diluting agents such as water are no longer contained in the product, but are added by the consumer at time of use. For consumers, the packs are easier to handle and store. Concentrated detergents use fewer materials, less packaging and less energy in production.

Secondary uses for packaging

In the interests of obtaining the greatest value out of the minimum resources, the possibilities of finding secondary uses for packs are being explored. Food packs that are resealable and dishwasher-proof are being proposed as re-usable food containers; a plastic soap package becomes a durable soap dish. However, this approach makes a significant contribution to overall waste reduction only if the pack fulfils a real need,

and makes it unnecessary to buy another product. Cluttering up the house with packs may simply delay the disposal issue, as there is obviously a limit to how many containers people actually need. But for one-off purchases this approach may be worthwhile. A beautifully made package may be retained for a long time, either as an integral and valued part of the product inside, or as an attractive decorative item in its own right.

Packaging and litter

Packaging represents only a proportion of litter, but its visual effect is disproportionate. Packs designed for visual impact in a store unfortunately continue to have visual impact while lying on a street or in a field. While litter is a social problem which can be countered only by a change in individual attitudes, packaging design can help to minimise the damage caused.

Left
Mobil Oil's "Drainmaster"
is designed to solve the
problem of what to do
with the used oil in a car.
The plastic container has
two screw caps. Once
the new oil has been
poured in, the used oil
can be poured from its
collection tray into the
larger, red, opening and
the bottle re-closed.
The used oil can then
be delivered safely to
an oil recycler.

Premium Motor Oil
Saves Gas

Mobil
super
10W-40

5QT   MOTOR OIL

Reducing the number of components in a pack can reduce the likelihood that small items, such as ring pulls, are dropped. Non-detachable tops means that the larger item is more likely to be disposed of correctly, or is easier to clear up if it is dropped.

Packaging litter can cause damage to wildlife. Plastic linking rings for multi-packs can prove hazardous to birds, for example, and plastic bags, if consumed by animals, can cause starvation by blocking the digestive system. Biodegradability and photodegradability have been proposed as ways of minimising these problems, providing that the materials are genuinely degradable. Photodegradability is most relevant to the litter problem, and may have some value, but is currently too expensive and impractical for most products. In the longer term, however, it may be possible to produce packaging material which can decompose quickly and safely, while still offering the product good protection when in use. It can be argued that making packaging more easily degradable will simply encourage litter, as items will be believed to disappear as if "by magic".

Eventually, the combination of packaging deposit schemes, improved litter bin availability and changes in public attitudes may reduce the litter problem. Until then, packaging designers may try incorporating bold symbols encouraging users to dispose of the pack carefully.

Detergent refills, Europe

Detergent manufacturers are now considering both their packaging and the form of the products themselves, in order to reduce materials and energy use. In Europe, Procter and Gamble have led the way. The fabric conditioner Lenor, for example, has usually been sold in large plastic bottles which are thrown away when empty. Now a concentrated product is available, allowing a significant reduction in the amount of packaging materials needed, savings in transport costs and a more efficient use of supermarket shelf space. The concentrated product is packed in refill packs, such as a flexible plastic pouch or a carton; different packs have been used in different countries to take account of consumer preferences.

The pouch refill was initially launched in Germany. It contains one litre of concentrated product which the user pours into a four-litre bottle and then dilutes with water. The pouch is made from low-density polyethylene film, with a gusset in the base, which provides the necessary product protection and mechanical strength. Overall, the pouch consumes around 80 per cent less packaging material per litre of product than the regular four-litre bottle; it is over three times more space-efficient in transport and warehousing, and the display tray can merchandise ten pouches in the same space as three bottles. There is also a significant reduction in the direct product cost. Consumers find the pouch easy to carry, store and dispose of, compared with the old rigid plastic bottles, although pouring the refill pack into the bottle for dilution can result in spillages.

The carton is easier to pour from, and can also be used as a measuring device for diluting the concentrate. It is compact, and easy to open and to store. It uses around 65 per cent less packaging material per litre than the regular Lenor bottle. Like the pouch, it also gives savings in transport and warehousing. A distribution vehicle can carry three times as much in the refill pack as in the regular bottle, with consequent fuel savings.

Below
Concentrated fabric softener in a sachet from Jeyes, UK. The contents are poured into a one-litre container, and diluted with water before use. The neck of the pack provides a convenient pouring spout.

Although the refill packs provide substantial advantages over one-use rigid plastic bottles, they themselves can only be used once, which might be regarded as wasteful. In some markets, we are likely to see a move towards returnable and re-usable bottles as the most environmentally sensitive option.

Below
Refill cartons are easy to pour into more durable plastic bottles, but they themselves are discarded after one use.

Left
These flexible pouches, filled with concentrate, consume 80 per cent less packaging material per litre of product than regular bottles.

The Body Shop refill policy, UK

The Body Shop is a franchised company with over four hundred outlets worldwide selling a wide range of toiletry products. The company adopts a non-exploitative approach to the environment, emphasising natural ingredients; simple, refillable packaging, and no testing of products on animals. Campaigning on environment issues is part of its ethos.

Minimal packaging includes cylindrical plastic bottles, with single walled caps, as standard. Plastic is used because it provides an effective barrier, and is robust, durable and light for distribution. It is also regarded as safer than glass, because of the potential danger if glass were to shatter into tiny particles.

But the virtues which make plastic so useful – its strength and durability – also create problems when it comes to disposal. The Body Shop considers that plastic packaging should be re-used wherever possible, and encourages its customers to bring bottles back for refilling by offering a small discount. Recycling is the next priority, with disposal considered as the last resort. Most products can be refilled, practically an unlimited number of times. The containers must be cleaned by the consumer before refilling, and hygiene standards require that they may be refilled only with the same product as before. This restriction is because of the permeable nature of plastic and the fact that only natural ingredients are used.

In 1990, the company launched an environmental campaign, "Once is Not Enough", to raise awareness of the need to reduce waste. The Refill Bar was the campaign's major focus, offering the best way to save resources.

Below
The number of different pack sizes is kept to a minimum, with customers encouraged to buy the larger sizes.

Left
This poster dramatises
the "re-use, recycle"
message, advocating
the extension of
packaging life.

To ease recycling. The Body Shop has minimised the number of different materials used for packaging, within the constraints of the need for compatibility between product and packaging. The clear bottles are made of PET (polyethylene terephthalate), and the opaque ones from HDPE (high-density polyethylene): both are recyclable materials. In future, the type of plastic will be identified on the pack to ease the sorting of waste, in anticipation of the development of recycling infrastructures. The Body Shop aims to recycle as much waste as possible, recovering materials such as cardboard and plastic film from the distribution system.

Left
Even the lorries used
to distribute The Body
Shop's products have a
communication role.

SC Johnson Pledge compressed-air aerosol

In 1975 S C Johnson became the first international company to discontinue the use of CFCs as propellants in its aerosol products worldwide, and they have led the race to introduce feasible alternative propellants. Aerosols, using propellants such as butane, have continued to be a packaging form favoured by consumers for their convenience and good functional performance; alternatives, such as pump sprays, have so far met with little success, despite their apparent lower environmental impact.

The main environmental concerns with CFC-free aerosols include VOC emissions, recyclability, flammability and the amount of packaging. The immediate challenge for S C Johnson was therefore to develop a form of aerosol with a much reduced environmental impact.

Below
Pledge has been awarded the Blue Angel label for its environmental performance.

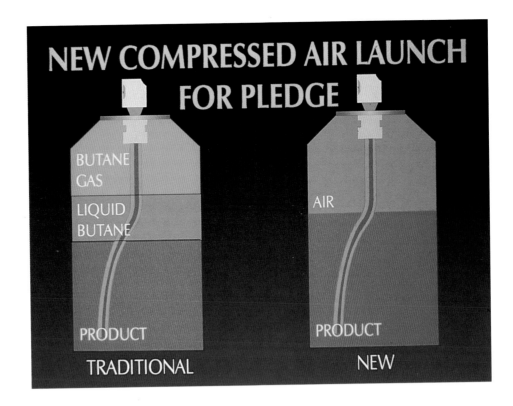

NEW COMPRESSED AIR LAUNCH FOR PLEDGE

BUTANE GAS

LIQUID BUTANE

AIR

PRODUCT

PRODUCT

TRADITIONAL

NEW

Above

Compressed air has replaced liquid butane and butane gas

Compressed air emerged as the most promising alternative to butane and furniture-care aerosols were identified as the first category for this new technology. Pledge, the market leader in Europe, was the first major brand to convert.

Using compressed air for Pledge has reduced VOC content by a third, and conserved over five million litres of butane a year.

The compressed-air spray performs as well as current aerosols with hydrocarbon propellants. Air is pumped into the can in a similar way to pumping up a bicycle tyre. When the cap is pushed down the pressure within the can forces the contents out as an atomised stream. A new, more complex, cap had to be designed, and the product itself had to be reformulated.

The compressed-air product gives a slightly different spray pattern, but the basic performance is unchanged, and consumers appear to be willing to accept the innovation. The company believes that consumers will not currently make significant compromises in terms of performance and price for products with environmental advantages; the design task is therefore to develop products which meet all the usual design criteria, but with a lower environmental impact. S C Johnson has adopted a Design for Environment approach to its product and packaging development process, to help achieve this goal.

The compressed-air aerosol may in the long term be an interim stage on the route to completely new types of aerosol with much reduced environmental impact.

cafédirect

cafédirect was the first product to be marketed by the Equal Exchange, Oxfam Trading, Traidcraft and Twin Trading consortium under the "direct" brand name. Their aim was to bring fair trade into the mainstream of retailing and consumer awareness. All cafédirect growers are always paid a good minimum price to cover the cost of production, however low the international coffee market falls. In addition, growers are guaranteed a 10 per cent premium above the market rate for investment in the local communities. The cafédirect products are high-quality products, which secured distribution through every major supermarket chain in the UK.

The packaging has been designed to tell a unique story to consumers, about a product traded in a way that ensures maximum benefit to the producer. The impact of the colourful striped identity stands out strongly in an area dominated by traditional coffee packaging standards. The design is attractive, sophisticated and eye-catching, demonstrating that the presentation of ethical products need not be dowdy and unappealing. The attractiveness of on-shelf presentation is a crucial part of the success of cafédirect, as it must fight to attract attention without the benefit of major advertising, in a market dominated by powerful established brands. The distinctive design, incorporating an important copy message, ensures a strong brand identity and the communication of the brand's main selling proposition.

Berol Karisam pencils, UK

Coloured pencils are usually packed in metal boxes, and colour identification is achieved through the use of a paint finish to the pencil which matches the colour of the lead. The Karisma brand of pencils, designed by UK consultancy Newell and Sorrell for Berol, broke with both these traditions.

The pencils are intended for use by illustrators, artists, designers and draughtsmen, and the design solution developed for the product and packaging keeps their interests very much to the fore: attention to detail, fine performance, and pleasure in use.

The intention of product and packaging was to give significant consideration to environment performance. The pencils remain unpainted, thus avoiding the use of an unnecessary secondary material and allowing the colour of the wood to be seen. The colour of the leads is revealed by cutting off the ends with an unusual champfered effect.

The unique "arts and crafts" look of the pencils had to be reflected in an appropriate packaging presentation, using simple craft materials. The card boxes are wrapped in textured, recycled paper; different coloured papers are used to denote pencil types. Recycled paper gives the pack a hand-crafted feel, an interesting texture and soft, unusual colours. Small points of detail on the design include hallmarks on the pencils, to denote quality, and brown paper document ties.

Above
Chamfered pencil ends make a beautiful detail, while providing the necessary colour identification

Left
Thread document ties form the closures to the box, giving an attractive appearance and preventing the need for any extra material such as plastic

This approach is labour-intensive, but the use of unusual packaging materials and a very simple but aesthetically attractive presentation of the product give an end result which is unique and valuable – an item to be enjoyed and treasured.

6 Printing and graphic design

The environment debate surrounding the use of paper and print has tended to focus on the use of recycled paper – the apparently simple, environment-conscious material choice. But there are several other significant areas of environment concern, right through the whole product life. Energy use, pollution, waste and land use have to be considered in the growing of raw materials, then there are the pulping and milling processes, the use and printing of the paper, and its eventual disposal.

Finding one's way through the complex maze of recycled papers is far from easy, because of the range of different grades and descriptions used. However, this area is one where designers should have considerable scope for including environment criteria in material selection and printing, and where the stimulus for innovative design is great.

Raw material cultivation and extraction

Ninety per cent of the world's paper supply comes from wood, and paper products use about 10 per cent of the world's consumption of wood. Although trees are a renewable resource, and more trees are probably planted by the paper industry than are cut down, many forests could not be described as sustainably managed. There are several concerns about how trees are currently grown and felled.

- The intensive farming of single species, such as conifers in Scotland and eucalyptus in Portugal, can disrupt local ecologies and cause soil degradation.
- Some "old-growth" forests are felled for paper requirements, destroying habitats that have taken hundreds of years to evolve.

- Tropical rainforest has been cleared to make way for eucalyptus plantations.
- The "clearcutting" method of logging involves cutting down all trees in an area, even though not all will be used.
- Pesticides used in forestry can lead to the pollution of waterways and damage to wildlife.

Responsibly managed forests, with appropriate trees grown in the right areas, are an important renewable resource, but the supply cannot be increased indefinitely.

Paper can be made from many other raw materials – the essential ingredient is cellulose, which is found in all plants.

- Leaf fibres – esparto, sisal and marilla.
- Seed fibres – cotton.
- Grass fibres – straw, maize stalks, cogan, bamboo and bagasse from sugar cane.
- Bast fibres – from the stems of flax, hemp and jute.

Until this century, materials such as straw, flax and rags were widely used, and there is growing interest again in these alternatives. Cotton fibres are separated from the seed when harvested, before the production of cottonseed oil: they contain a very pure form of

The French Paper Company in Michigan, USA, have developed a range of recycled papers called Speckletone, in reference to their distinctive texture and dappled appearance. The promotional material advertising their product and showing what can be achieved with it was designed by Duffy Design Group. Instead of making a standard-format brochure, they opted for a more durable book, attractive enough to be kept and valued. It combines various illustration styles, photography, die-cutting and thermography to create contrasting and imaginative effects. The highly textured paper creates a feeling as well as an image, and becomes an integral element of the design: inks combine to build up colour, while the unprinted areas are transformed from negative spaces into a positive visual element. The books have become collectors' pieces, ensuring a high profile for the company wherever Speckletone is sold.

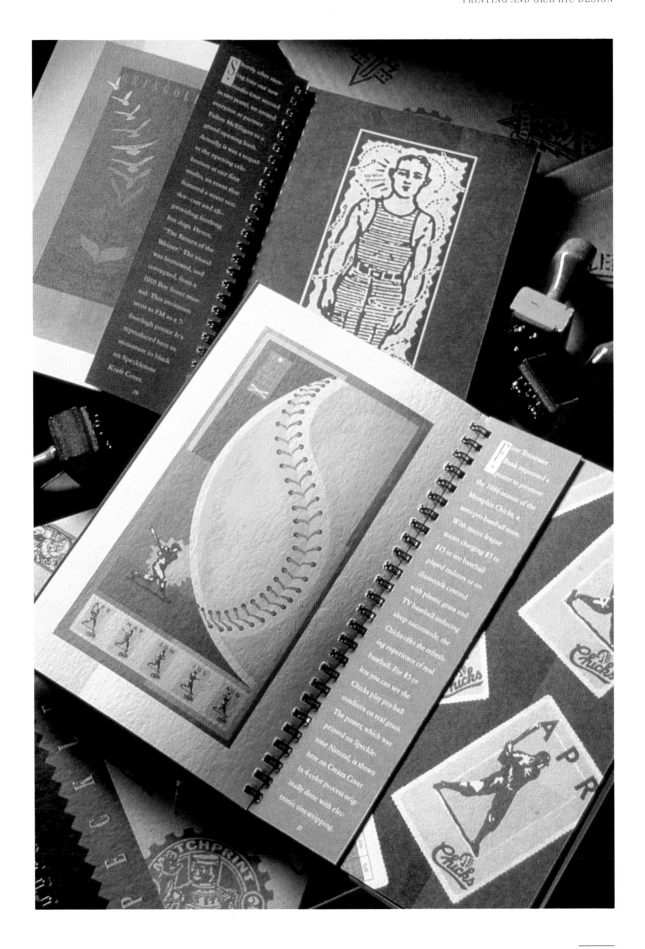

Above & right
Tayburn McIllroy Coates designed this brochure for waste management and recycling company J W Hannay & Co. The objective was to convince office managers – Hannay's potential customers – that waste management is an important issue, and that waste has value. All the images were assembled using real pieces of rubbish and recycled items. Strong graphic images and bold colours challenge preconceptions that environmental subjects have to be presented in shades of green or brown.

cellulose, and can produce high-quality papers, often with special strength or other characteristics. Of course, the growing of cotton is not without environmental problems, because of the widespread use of pesticides (see Chapter Seven, "Textile design").

The waste stubble from straw production, which in many countries would otherwise be burned, can be used to make straw paper, another high-quality product offering stiffness and opacity. There is even increasing interest in the production of paper from fruit and vegetable waste – such as banana skins!

Papers can also be made from cellulose-based man-made regenerated fibre, such as acetate. This gives an expensive, but highly durable product, suitable for applications such as banknotes.

At the moment, wood pulp appears to be the most economical raw material on an industrial scale, and the environment impact of tree cultivation can be controlled by careful husbandry. Other materials – especially those that use products which would otherwise go to waste – offer an interesting wealth of choice for the designer, and are well worth considering for special applications which can justify the cost (most are more expensive than wood-based papers).

The processes involved in paper production are much the same, whatever the basic ingredient.

Timber can be turned into pulp by two different processes. In the mechanical process, the tree is simply crushed to a pulp, using almost all of the tree. About half of the resultant material is fibres, with much of the rest being lignin, a stiffening material which binds the fibres together in the tree. The presence of lignin, which is light-sensitive, means that the resultant paper turns brown in sunlight, and it is therefore used for short-life products such as newspapers and for brown cardboard boxes. Mechanical crushing is a highly energy-intensive operation.

The alternative process is chemical pulping, which involves treating wood chips with chemicals to remove the resins. The lignin is separated off and used as fuel. About 50 per cent of the total tree therefore becomes pulp.

Milling

During the paper-making process, from pulping through to bleaching and converting, a wide variety of chemicals is used. Effluent from paper-making processes has created serious adverse environmental impacts in many parts of the world. The use of chlorine during the bleaching process has been particularly criticised, and there is a growing consensus that emissions of organic chlorine compounds have to be reduced significantly and phased out wherever possible. Chlorine compounds are toxic to aquatic organisms, and are known to affect fertility.

Many pulp producers have already switched to new bleaching methods. The main method currently is to use oxygen and hydrogen peroxide in place of chlorine. A new process uses ozone and peroxide. The wide variety of non-chlorine-bleached papers available should make it unnecessary to continue to use chlorine-bleached paper, as the quality of brightness achieved by alternative methods is excellent.

When choosing non-chlorine papers, it is important to appreciate the difference between ECF (Elemental Chlorine-Free) and TCF (Total Chlorine-Free). ECF pulp uses chlorine dioxide rather than chlorine. This gives lower emissions, particularly if modern production methods are used. However, in TCF, no chlorine-based chemicals are used at all. Wherever possible, TCF should be specified.

Paper production is very energy-intensive, and large quantities of water can be used. Many mills are now using closed-loop systems to recycle as much water as possible, and minimise effluent.

Virgin or recycled?

The recycling process is very similar to the paper-making process, although waste paper usually has to be cleaned (de-inked) so that a good quality new paper can be achieved. The waste paper is mixed with large quantities of water, and any contaminants such as staples are filtered out. The ink is then removed either by washing and rinsing, or by detergents which absorb the inks during a flotation process.

Some virgin pulp is often added at this stage. Cellulose fibres cannot be recycled indefinitely, as they lose strength and length. Recycled fibres are shorter and therefore less strong that virgin fibres, but this may not be a problem for many applications.

It used to be hard to find recycled papers which offered performance characteristics comparable with virgin; now there is a vast choice, offering performance often indistinguishable from virgin. However, paper made using 100 per cent post-consumer waste does offer different characteristics, and these have to be considered as part of the design process.

The use of recycled paper has a number of environmental benefits:

- Overall, the use of recycled paper should save energy, because of the total amount of energy used during the pulp-making process. However, clearly the amount of energy involved in collecting waste paper must not outweigh this benefit.
- The amount of chemicals used in producing recycled paper should be less than for virgin paper.
- Using recycled paper can reduce the overall demand for trees produced for pulp, which might prevent the spread of intensive monoculture forestry into new, inappropriate areas.
- Much paper is now disposed of to landfill sites; with space running out and costs increasing, the re-use of waste materials makes sense.

There is much confusion about the definitions used in describing waste paper, with some

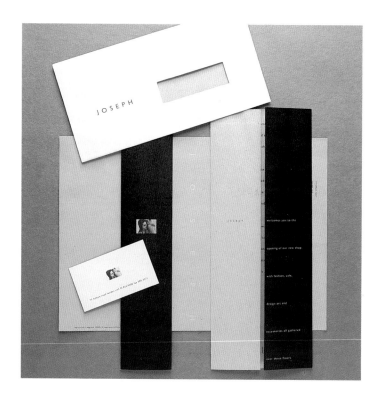

"recycled" claims being rather spurious. Genuine waste paper should be gathered from either

- Converters' and printers' waste, which may include unprinted waste, off-cuts, over-runs etc.

or

- Household or office waste, printed or unprinted.

Virgin paper which is wasted during the paper production process, often known as "mill broke", is not regarded as waste paper for the sake of most official definitions.

Most recycled papers are made from high-quality, pre-consumer waste, but an increasing number now incorporate a proportion of post-consumer waste. Lower-grade paper used for products such as toilet tissue or packaging can contain a much higher proportion of post-consumer waste.

Many new paper products contain non-paper ingredients, such as laminates, silicone coatings, metal films and non-water soluble adhesives which cause problems during the recycling process. Latex adhesives used on envelopes or linings cannot be incorporated into recycling processes. It is therefore important when specifying literature and packaging that the recyclability of the final product is considered too.

Above
Sugar paper was the choice for corporate literature designed for Joseph by N2 in London. It was selected for its texture, which gives a distinctive end result, rather than for any environmental considerations. The background is also sugar paper.

Right
Booklet designed in 1988 by Neville Brody and Jon Wozencroft to accompany a music album being distributed in the Soviet Union to launch the environmental organisation Greenpeace. The design had to take into consideration the limitations of Russian printing; the typeface, for example, had to be Helvetica. A non-chlorine bleached paper was selected, in line with other Greenpeace publications. Although originally intended to be printed in the USSR, the booklet was eventually printed in Britain. The album sold 2 million tapes in the USSR, and was then repackaged for other countries with different imagery in design to reflect different cultures. The background to the booklet is khadi paper, made from lokta (see pages 131-2).

Below & left
Printed proof sheets of postcards by Anderson Fraser, using images by contemporary designers and illustrators. The printing is on recycled paper, to show the high quality which can be achieved; each image will be mounted on recycled board.

Left
Chaps clothing, a new line in casual wear by Ralph Lauren, has both integrity and wit-qualities which must be conveyed in the product labelling and packaging. Recycled paper and corrugated card create an unusual and eyecatching identity. The design of the Scout relies heavily on negative space, exploiting the gritty texture of the recycled paper. Both paper and board were selected by the designers primarily for their aesthetic appeal, and offer a welcome contrast to the glossy material usually seen in the fashion world.

Designing and printing with recycled paper

Recycled paper and board have different technical and visual qualities from virgin material, and these must be understood by the designer right from the start of the design process. The choice of material will affect the performance and appearance of the design, and so the two ingredients must be considered together.

The wide range of recycled paper gives a choice of textures, colours and printing characteristics. Achieving an end result comparable to high-quality virgin paper is now quite possible with the highest grade of recycled paper, and it is now possible to produce fine four-colour printing on recycled paper to a very high standard. However, the use of lower-grade paper should be considered by the designer for the interesting effects which can be achieved.

In general, recycled papers are more absorbent, have a more uneven surface than virgin, and are less white. The higher dot gain resulting from the absorbency can give a soft-edged image with a sepia effect – like that seen in old photographs – and the printed image can seem duller, with colours lacking brilliance. If ink remains in the paper from its previous use, print may have a lack of "punch", but this can create an attractive effect.

Designer and printer have to be aware of print characteristics such as opacity, smoothness, absorbency, runnability and rigidity early on, and make sure the reproduction and printing processes are modified accordingly. Cylinder pressure may have to be adjusted, and print speed is likely to be lower; inks must be carefully selected as well.

This considered approach calls for a dialogue between designer and printer, and for time to be spent selecting the most appropriate combination of material and design style. The colour printing process must be undertaken methodically, with proofing done on the paper which will eventually be used.

Recycled papers can work particularly well as "negative space" surrounding printed matter, as the appearance of the paper alone can add interest and impact.

Designers can play an important role in changing public perceptions of quality. The view is still widely held that shiny white virgin paper, covered with varnish, epitomises quality, and many companies are reluctant to use recycled paper in their packaging, literature or corporate stationery for that reason. This means that paper is often over-specified – much higher grades are used than would actually be required in terms of functional performance. Concerns about the appearance of recycled paper can be addressed in two ways: by the use of higher-quality recycled paper which looks very similar to virgin paper, and by demonstrating, through imaginative design, how lower-quality paper can be aesthetically appealing as well as environmentally sound. Unnecessary over-specification of materials quality may come to be seen as bad design in the future, indicative of a lack of understanding and imagination.

There may be applications for which recycled paper is simply not suitable. In these cases a non-chlorine-bleached virgin wood paper, or a paper made from an alternative such as straw, should be used instead.

Inks and solvents

During the printing process, solvents and dyes may cause the risk of damage to the environment or may be a health hazard to workers. Many types of solvent are used as bases for inks for gravure, flexographic and letterpress printing; their evaporation ensures that the ink dries quickly. But solvents can be dangerous to health if inhaled in too high a concentration, causing potential problems for print workers, and their emission into the atmosphere contributes to the build-up of unwanted gases.

The alternative is to use water-soluble inks. These are cleaner and vapourless, but tend to take longer to dry, which means that drying equipment has to be modified or the printing slowed down. Efforts are being made to develop new additives which will speed up the drying process, but these may affect the quality of the end result.

Vegetable oil-based inks are being introduced in some newspaper printing as an alternative to petroleum-based inks. The main motive for this is the better colour brightness and sharper dot achieved, and their improved rub resistance, which prevents print coming off on to the hands. At the moment, vegetable oil-based inks tend to be used as an additive rather than on their own, but there may be increasing acceptance of them as complete alternatives to solvent-based inks.

The use of heavy metal-based pigments in inks, such as cadmium and lead, has been criticised because of their pollutant effect in effluent, and alternatives are being sought.

However, it is difficult to match their unique colour and opacity properties.

The environment-conscious option in printing appears to lie with water-based and vegetable oil-based inks, and the designer should request these wherever possible. However, new equipment may be required to handle them, and many printers are therefore likely to use solvent-based inks for some time yet. If solvents cannot be avoided, care should be taken to ensure that the chemicals are disposed of carefully, and emissions reduced to a minimum by using solvent burners. Designers should request information from printers about their ingredients and processes and about how they handle chemical disposal, as part of the procedure of selecting a supplier.

Resource consumption

Resource minimisation is always the aim of environment-conscious designers, and there are a variety of ways in which the quantity of paper used can be reduced.

Efficient use of space
In some applications, designers can condense information into a reduced format, through the imaginative use of typeface and layout, thus saving paper. When this is done for very large production runs, the savings can be very considerable – in paper, energy and waste. The saving in paper achieved by the redesign of British Telecom's telephone directories is significant, considering that 24 million books are produced each year, consuming 80,000 trees (see pages 128-9).

Product life
The potential life span of a product should be taken into consideration at the stage of design and material choice. Timetables, direct mail, even paperback novels have a very short life, and can therefore be made from poorer quality paper than, say, encyclopaedias, which have to be very durable. The design of paper products for instant disposability might be questioned. Direct mail consumes paper resources, but only a tiny proportion of mailings are ever read or acted upon. Perhaps the answer lies in much better designed, more original offerings which might not go unread, or alternatively in the use of other forms of communication which are better targeted.

Sometimes, pieces of literature are designed to be rapidly superseded by others: a company brochure, for example, may be

replaced every few months. There may be opportunities to replace a succession of clearly "disposable" brochures with one that is designed to last. If the information is not to be quickly superseded, and a long functional life span is possible, a more durable concept could reduce the need for replacement brochures or multiple copies. Duffy Design in the USA have produced a book for Dicksons instead of a standard-format brochure. It is highly functional in demonstrating the work of the company, but also attractive and durable, making sure that customers value it and keep it. Its distinctiveness also ensures that the company stands out strongly among competitors.

Alternatives to paper
While the rapid development of information technology has not yet led to a paperless

Above
Poster for a packaging design exhibition in Tokyo, designed by Kijuro Yahagi using straw as an alternative to paper. When combined with a small sheet of paper printed with the exhibition details, it produces an original and attractive effect. This choice of material was commercially acceptable for an edition of 1,000 posters. Yahagi won the Warsaw Graphic Design prize in 1990.

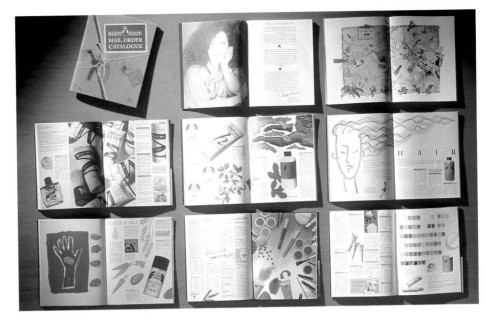

Right
London-based design consultancy Newell and Sorrell and printers Anderson Fraser made recycled paper a special component of the design of the 1989 Body Shop mail order catalogue. Eight different colours, four different weights of stock and five different textures were used. Close collaboration produced successful results despite the use of design features normally avoided with recycled paper, such as small type size, images across gutters and complicated tint-laying. The printing procedures were carefully adjusted to minimise the problems of printing on rougher, more absorbent paper. A range of 72 cosmetics colours had to be shown, with very subtle differences between colours: after tests, recycled paper proved more accurate than virgin, retaining softness while giving excellent colour reproduction.

existence, many types of communication will take place in the future through media such as the Internet, rather than through conventional publishing. CD-ROMs provide an opportunity to offer a vast amount of information in a format which suffers little physical degradation. There may be environmental benefits in opting for electronic communication; e-mail systems allow for quick and efficient distribution of information, but any environmental benefit may be lost if recipients simply print out messages before reading them. There is still a great deal to learn about how to design for electronic media, to ensure

communication is effective and attractive, and highly accessible.

The design decision
There are some general guidelines for the environment-conscious literature designer.

- Wherever possible, use recycled paper, selecting the highest percentage of secondary fibre consistent with functional and aesthetic requirements.
- Consider the paper type at the earliest stage of design development, to ensure that the design and paper are sympathetic.
- Assess whether the quantity of paper required can be minimised through layout and typography.
- Avoid papers which have been chlorine bleached; try unbleached paper, or paper bleached with hydrogen peroxide instead.
- Try water-soluble or vegetable oil-based inks as an alternative to solvent-based inks.
- Ask suppliers how they deal with effluent from the various chemical processes used throughout the paper-making and printing cycle.
- Remember that paper made out of alternative materials can sometimes be an interesting and attractive alternative to wood-derived paper.

Right
Exhibition catalogue for the Venice Biennale of 1990, designed by Kijuro Yahagi. For the covers, he scorched the pattern straight on to the paper, without the use of ink, reflecting a technique used by one of the artists in the exhibition. They were scorched by hand, giving each one an individual pattern.

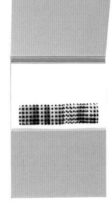

The Body Shop annual report 1988, UK

In keeping with the company's commitment to good environment performance, The Body Shop's 1988 annual report was designed to be printed on environmentally considered papers. Designers Neville Brody and Jon Wozencroft were given a free hand, and developed a theme of contrasting papers, textures and photographic techniques through the use of non-bleached and recycled papers. Four contrasting types of paper were selected after an extensive search; such papers had not previously been used for important company documents.

The cover is made from white-backed chipboard, which is usually restricted to packaging boxes for items like shoes. The two layers, of recycled and virgin materials, offer two completely different printing surfaces. The recycled side, on the outside, gives a minimal, grainy look, contrasting with the virgin side, which folds out to provide a surface for bold, sharp photographic imagery.

Inside the book sugar paper, in several colours with an absorbent surface, is used to create subtle, sensual imagery from photography. One hundred per cent recycled brown wrapping paper offers two surfaces – one matt and one gloss – while matt, non-chlorine-bleached paper provides more contrast of texture and colour.

The report is an early example of the use of environmentally conscious paper to create a high-profile, prestigious company report.

Above
The front cover is imaginatively layered, with recycled paper on the outside and virgin paper on the inside to give a smooth surface for a sharp image. This contrasts with the softer image on the right hand page, which is printed on a more absorbent surface.

It successfully challenges the traditional approach which assumes that quality must be conveyed through high gloss and brilliant white paper. The inherent properties of recycled paper have been exploited to the full to give a wide range of interesting and innovative effects.

Left
Brown paper provides a distinctive background with its laid lines. All of these pictures of the catalogue have been photographed on a background of Kraft brown wrapping paper.

Right
Sugar paper gives a rich, soft image.

British Telecom phonebooks, UK

British Telecom manufactures 24 million telephone directories each year, consuming around 80,000 trees. Laid end to end, the print run would stretch from London to Singapore. Any saving in the size of the directories would thus produce a significant saving in resources. British Telecom, working with designers Colin Banks and John Miles, carried out a research programme to see if, by redesigning the typeface and layout of the directories, they could reduce their size.

Because each entry must take at least one line, the major way of saving space is to reduce the space taken by each letter and the spaces between words. This produced a saving of 8 per cent, and at the same time gave a more readable result.

The change from three to four columns a page was made possible by the space economy of the type, and by dropping the repeat surname and the exchange codes. Scanning columns of names is now quicker, as the differences between them, rather than the similarities, are most apparent.

Directories are printed at very high speed, so they risk being underinked. With smaller type, under-inking could lead to a readability problem. A typeface was selected which had a strong, distinct letter form.

Savings of paper in excess of 10 per cent have been achieved, and market research has shown that 80 per cent of users prefer the new format. This is the kind of practical contribution that good graphic design can make to improving environment impact, reducing costs and increasing user satisfaction. The redesign won the Green Product Award, a UK prize sponsored by the petrol company Shell.

Above
The redesigned phonebook provided a good opportunity for corporate image-building, with this advertisement aimed at environment-conscious consumers.

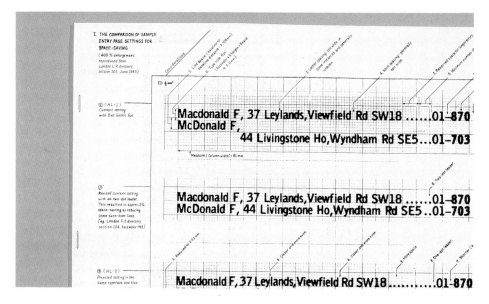

Below
A comparison of different designs, showing how reduced letter- and word-spacing and condensed type contribute to a 10 per cent space saving.

PRINTING AND GRAPHIC DESIGN

Left
Each letter was carefully redesigned to save space, while retaining clarity.

Below
The new layout (top) fits four instead of three columns across a page, and the names and numbers are more readable.

---

547   Hodges D — Where no exchange is shown it is BIRMINGHAM (021–) — **Hodgkiss J   547**

HODGES D, 49 Helmswood Dv 37 .... 788 1149
D, 352 Rednal Rd 38 .... 458 7594
D.A, 31/2 Masefield Sq 31 .... 475 5835
D.B, 31/2 Masefield Sq 31 .... 475 5835
D.C, 102 Shenstone Valley Rd,Halesowen .422 8213
D.G, 83 Arkley Rd 28 .... 745 1956
D.H, 9 Petersbourne Ct,Petersfield Rd 28 .777 5434
D.J.H, 31 Preston Rd 26 .... 706 3404
D.L, 10 Beacon Rd,Sutton Coldfield 355 5113
D.L, 6 Beechwood Clo,Shirley .... Earlswd 2986
D.R, 31 Richmond Croft 42 .... 358 1553
D.W, 38 Grassmoor Rd 38 .... 458 3622
E, 2 Bescot Clo 42 .... 357 3596
E, 6 Harold Rd,Smethwick 420 1115
E.A, 330 Alwold Rd 29 .... 426 1594
E.A, 28 Boscombe Rd 11 .... 708 1463
E.A, 128 Coombes La 31 .... 476 0252
E.A, 7 Old Mill Clo,Shirley 430 7003
E.L, 211 Beaumont Rd 30 .... 458 7509
F, 17 Crabmill Clo 38 .... 459 8176
F, 6 Moss Gro 14 .... 444 6637
F, 217 Ryde Pk Rd 45 .... 453 8334
F, 92 Southgate Rd 44 .... 360 2177
F, 15 Sutherland Clo 43 .... 360 7023
F.G, 24 Colindale Rd 44 .... 354 3093
F.M, 332 Lordswood Rd 17 .... 429 3799
F.S.W, 138 Clements Rd 25 .... 783 6412
G, 25 Avalon Clo 24 .... 373 7115
G, 150 Church Rd 26 .... 525 5230
G, 6 Mottram Clo,W Bromwich 525 5230
G, 55 Redacre Rd,Sutton Coldfield 354 2853
G.H, 82 Aubrey Rd 32 .... 429 2731
G.J, 47 Horse Shoes La 26 .... 743 8836
G.O, Ivy Dene,New Rd .... Henley-in-A 2557
G.W, 198 Baldwins La 28 .... 744 2376
H, 67 Worcester La,Four Oaks 308 6282
H.A, 66 Bishopton Rd,Smethwick 429 6229
H.C, 19 Redcroft Dv 24 .... 350 1848
H.E.D, 15 Harris Ct,Park Av 18 .... 523 6489
H.H, 6 Highbury Rd,Highbury Av,
　　　　　　　　　　　　Rowley Regis..559 3195
H.L, 10 Malcolm Rd,Shirley 744 6832
H.W, 21 Rowton Dv,Streetly 353 2351
I, 29 Short St,Halesowen 501 2379
I.M, 51 Mulwych Rd 33 .... 779 4659
J, 278 Cotterills La 8 .... 784 6663
J, 340 Cotterills La 8 .... 783 1563
J, 91 Electric Av 6 .... 326 8987
J, 85 Hampton La,Solihull 705 2343
J, 49 Holders Gdns 13 .... 449 8928
J, 93 Jacey Rd,Shirley 744 2416
J, 21 Pickwick Gro 13 .... 778 2391
J.B, 85 Forest Rd,Oldbury 422 3709
J.B, 306 Hagley Rd Wst,Oldbury 421 5665
J.E, 61 Belbroughton Rd,Halesowen 550 3609
J.E, 107 Loxley Av,Shirley 745 5775
J.J, 10 Whitesmith Croft 13 .... 444 3068
J.W, 28 Clent Vw Rd 32 .... 550 7763
K, 14 Middleton Rd,Streetly 353 8492
K.A, 127 Gibbons Rd,Sutton Coldfield 308 6899
K.L, 18 Leychester Clo 38 .... 475 4037
L.A, 56 Danford La,Solihull 705 6266
L.A, 35 Gainsborough Rd 42 .... 357 1574

HODGETTS A.N, 37 Haslucks Croft,Shirley .. 745 5361
A.R, 86 Seven Star Rd,Solihull 705 5739
A.S, 185 Redditch Rd 38 .... 458 3975
B, 90 Alexandra Rd,Halesowen 550 1471
B, 58 Charnwood Rd 42 .... 357 6477
B, 20 Downing Clo,Rowley Regis 561 2021
B, 63 Mackmillan Rd,Rowley Regis 559 5739
B, 134 Newlands Rd 30 .... 458 6012
B, 25 St. Michaels Cres,Oldbury 552 4430
B, 40 Sedgley Rd Wst,Tipton 557 1554
B.E, 108 Birch Rd,Oldbury 421 6824
B.G, 79 Selworthy Rd 36 .... 748 1840
B.J, 65 Cornfield Rd,Rowley Regis 559 9764
B.K, 60 Hillcrest Rd 43 .... 358 6563
B.L, 124 Kelymead Rd 33 .... 784 3652
Bryan M,
　　4 Mayfair Gdns,Park La East,Tipton..557 2277
C, 72 Chaffcombe Rd 26 .... 743 9585
C, 48 Ivyhouse Rd,Oldbury 552 4871
C, 24 Lea Green Av,Tipton 557 9277
C, 10 Tudor Rd,Oldbury 544 6606
C.M, 122 Blackberry La,Halesowen 550 6662
C.N, 18 Lilac Wy,Hurst Green 422 6646
C.T, 71 Chingford Rd 44 .... 384 2265
D, 57 Ascot Clo,Oldbury 552 7266
D, 31 Cattell Dv,Sutton Coldfield 378 3052
D, 70 Fenton Rd 27 .... 706 7059
D, 2 Gaydon Ct,Gaydon Rd,Solihull 742 9087
D, 43 Wentworth Ct,Kingsbury Rd 24 .... 350 8470
Dennis, 1 Burghley Dv,Millersdale,
　　　　　　　　　　W Bromwich..588 5279
D, 32 Nimmings Rd,Halesowen 561 2247
D, 184 Shenley La 29 .... 476 8943
D, 26 Martineau Tower,Uxbridge St 19 ..... 359 0456
D.J, 10 Plimsoll Gro 32 .... 421 5156
D.J, 11 Sedgley Gro 20 .... 551 5446
D.L, Plot 10 St. Johns Ct Calder Dv,
　　　　　　　　　　Sutton Coldfield..351 7843
D.M, 6 The Rise 42 .... 357 8404
D.T, 152 Hollydale Rd 24 .... 373 5262
D.T, 83 Jervoise Rd 29 .... 427 4447
E, 303 Birmingham Rd 43 .... 357 4448
E, 22 Henshaw Gro 25 .... 783 2933
E, 70 Old Oak Rd 38 .... 459 5919
E, 48 Rose Rd 17 .... 426 4655
E, 17 Troy Gro 14 .... 443 1187
E, 54 White Farm Rd,Sutton Coldfield 353 2662
E.A, 52 Eden Gro,W Bromwich 553 5015
F, 36 Honiton Cres 31 .... 476 0326
F, 33 Redhouse Pk Rd 43 .... 357 9947
F, 165 Stourbridge Rd,Halesowen 550 2974
F.A, 28 Haddon Rd 42 .... 357 9678
Frederick J,
　　85 George Frederick Rd,Streetly..353 1766
G, 37 Chelston Rd 31 .... 475 8225
G, 35 Kenrick Ho,Green St,W Bromwich ... 553 0641
G, 4 Harrowby Dv,Tipton 520 5298
G, 30 Hartshill Rd 27 .... 706 6293
G, 25 Hollydale Rd,Rowley Regis 559 5642
G, 98 St.Lukes Rd,Wednesbury 502 2299
G, 2 Totnes Gro 29 .... 472 3760
G.C, 31 The Lindens 32 .... 429 5459
G.E, 4 Garland Cres,Halesowen 422 7557

HODGETTS Michael, 106 Tyndale Cres 43 . 360 0350
M, 55 Whitgreave St,W Bromwich 520 1632
M, 110 Woodbury Rd,Halesowen 421 1932
M.A, 34 Bedford Rd,Sutton Coldfield 378 1359
M.G, 5 Milcote Rd 29 .... 476 9797
M.G, 87 Southam Rd 28 .... 777 6070
M.J, 75 Ardav Rd,W Bromwich 556 7738
M.J, 839 Washwood Heath Rd 8 .... 783 8647
M.& R, 21 Bodenham Rd 31 .... 475 4170
M.T, 21 Denegate Clo,Sutton Coldfield ... 351 5997
N, 45 Baxters Rd,Shirley 745 8436
N, 48 Beresford Cres,W Bromwich 525 5125
N, 35 Smithmore Cres,W Bromwich 588 3644
N.B, 57 Clyde Tower,Birchfield Rd 19 ...... 554 6622
N.D, 3 Aylesbury Clo,Hockley Hth .... Lapwth 3341
N.E, 34 Astley Av,Halesowen 422 2084
N.L, 29 Coney Gn Dv 31 .... 477 7304
O, 55 Chilcote Clo 28 .... 745 4864
O.J, 29 Sheepclose Dv 37 .... 770 5520
P, 90 Corisande Rd 29 .... 471 2559
P, 12 Potters La,Wednesbury 556 7286
P, 75 St. Giles Ct,Reservoir Rd,
　　　　　　　　　　Rowley Regis..556 5337
P.A, 108 Ralph Rd,Shirley 744 1501
P.J, 50 Beechwood Rd 14 .... 444 5422
P.N, 75 Lyndon Rd 45 .... 453 4935
P.W, 10 Maud Rd,W Bromwich 553 1269
P.W, 29 Pendragon Rd 42 .... 356 7085
R.A, 568 Bordesley Gn 9 .... 771 2310
Ronand, 22 Leslie Dv,Tipton 556 8355
R, 59 Rebecca Dv 29 .... 472 6808
R, 46 Wasdale Rd 31 .... 477 5498
R, 56 Wellhead La 42 .... 356 0551
R.A, 31 Bark Piece 32 .... 421 2282
R.J, 252 Birdbrook Rd 44 .... 360 5290
R.M, 13 Kesteven Rd,W Bromwich 588 4724
R.T, 18 Greenway Gdns 38 .... 459 0784
R.T, 61 Listowel Rd 14 .... 444 2626
R.W, 53 Meadowbrook Rd,Halesowen 550 6742
S, 180 Curbar Rd 42 .... 357 5253
S, 84 Irwin Av 45 .... 460 1672
S, 17 Penn Rd,Rowley Regis 561 5838
S, 18 Rowley Vw,W Bromwich 553 0716
S, 3 The Dowries 45 .... 453 4871
S.A.E, 14 Eastham Rd 13 .... 443 3286
S.E, 92 Gillscroft Rd 33 .... 784 9889
S.G, 45 Meadow Brook Rd 31 .... 475 8268
S.G, 112 Quarry Rd 29 .... 476 4926
S.J, 47 Aldersmead Rd 31 .... 476 7237
S.J, 29 Chesterfield Clo 31 .... 475 7245
S.J, 99 Elmay Rd 26 .... 743 2353
S.J, 193 Overdale Rd 32 .... 427 1722
S.R, 40 Kingswood Rd 31 .... 476 0870
S.T, 34 Belmont Clo,Tipton 520 7821
T, 58 Lindridge Rd 23 .... 382 2053
T.W, 25 Common La 26 .... 743 5889
V.G, 9 Holly Rd,Oldbury 422 8088
V.J, 55 Green Park Rd 31 .... 475 5545
W, 6 Brogden Clo,W Bromwich 588 5055
W, 22 Pitfields Rd,Oldbury 421 5264
W, 43 Richards Clo,Tipton 554 4006
W, Old Park Fm,Whitehall La 29 .... 475 3655
W, 7 Winsford Clo,Halesowen 550 7966

HODGKINS K, 33 Betsham Clo 44 .... 382 8014
K, 53 Gilbert Rd,Smethwick 565 2640
K.E, 18 Thompson Ho,Ockerhill Rd,Tipton .. 556 1987
K.F, 7 Park St,Wednesbury 556 6887
K.J, 223 Bassett Rd,Wednesbury 502 1921
L, 3 Cross St,Rowley Regis 559 6216
L, 215 Meadow Av,W Bromwich 588 5908
L, 37 Springfield Cres,Solihull 743 5636
L, 11 Wolseley Rd,Hill Top 557 4602
L.D, 12 Beverley Rd 45 .... 453 2892
L.G, 77 Beaumont Rd,Halesowen 561 3535
L.G, 18 Cook Clo,Solihull .... Knowle 79061
L.T, 10 Lorne St,Tipton 520 5559
M, 9 Bournes Hl,Halesowen 550 9907
M, 1 Reservoir Passage,Wednesbury 556 8639
M, 117 Rough Rd 44 .... 355 2076
M.A, 6 Pound Rd,Wednesbury 502 4130
M.J, 55 Dower Rd 45 .... 453 8944
M.J, 110 Masons Wy,Solihull 707 3005
N, 15 Hagley Rd,Hayley Gn 550 7889
N.G, 28 Lutley Av,Halesowen 550 5688
O, 1 Gretton Rd 23 .... 384 3932
P.A, 16 Blackrock Rd 23 .... 373 5391
P.J, 21 Duncumbe Rd,Sutton Coldfield 378 4687
P.J, 15 Hawthorn Croft,Oldbury 422 5324
R, 10 Gillingham Clo,Wednesbury 556 1602
Roger, 34 Northcote Rd 33 .... 784 5718
R, 58 Perrywood Rd 42 .... 358 5634
R.A, 568 Bordesley Gn 9 .... 771 2310
R.E, 9 Gosmoor Ho,Yew Tree La 26 .... 784 3963
R.J, 2 Ross Hieghts,Rowley Regis 559 5408
S.J, 9 Polden Clo,Halesowen 550 2192
T, 28 Hillview Rd 45 .... 453 4352
Thomas, 20 Pleasant St,W Bromwich 556 7698
T, 189 Station Rd,Cradley Hth 559 2840
T.H, 27 Greenacre Rd,Tipton 556 7643
V.D, 39 Little Aston La,Ltl Aston 353 2079
W, 379 Lode La,Solihull 743 4570
W, 8 Mynors Cres 47 .... Wythall 824979
W.A, 19 Jervoise Rd 29 .... 426 4543
W.C, 15 Farwood Rd 31 .... 476 3094
W.J, 51 Causeway Rd,Rowley Regis 561 2762
W.J, 46 Hawthorn Rd,Wednesbury 556 2404
HODGKINSON A,
　　29 Johnson Rd,Wednesbury..502 4373
A.C, 25 Peakhouse Rd 43 .... 357 2743
A.G, 151 Green La 36 .... 748 6853
B, 28 Rosafield Av,Halesowen 422 3024
C.R –
1 Cedar Av 36 .... 747 6709
C.W, 53 Falstaff Rd,Shirley 745 6200
D, 90 Waseley Rd 45 .... 453 4448
D.L, 24 Merton Clo,Oldbury 552 6719
D.P, 44 Kirby Rd 18 .... 523 7676
D.T, 28 Steel Rd 31 .... 475 5422
D.W, 12 Charlemont Cres,W Bromwich 588 5931
E, 78 Bear Hl 48 .... 445 2702
E, 28 Hampshire Rd,W Bromwich 556 3633
G.A, 22 Hilliards Croft 42 .... 358 6078
G.K, 164 Berkeley Rd 25 .... 784 3998
G.L, 22 Wakeford Rd 31 .... 477 8906
H.C, 28 Fifth Av 9 .... 772 1073
H.J, 31 Courtway Av 14 .... 430 8835

---

16   Appleby L — PLYMOUTH ASSESSMENT — **Armstrong A   16**

Appleby L, 25 Goswela Gdns,Goosewell ... Plymouth 41152
Appleby L.M, 15 Century Ct ...... Newquay 871385
Appleby M, 21 Dovedale Rd,Beacon Pk .... Plymouth 569713
Appleby Martin,
　　Summerleas,Yealm Rd,Newton Ferrers .Plymouth 872050
Appleby Paul O, 1 Rowters Cotts,Trematon .. Saltash 3567
Appleby R.J, 73 Beatrice Av,Keyham .... Newquay 569283
Appleby R.J,
　　Suhaili,Chelean Cott,Frogpool,Chacewater .. Truro 863088
Appleby R.M, 6 Maple Gro,Mutley .... Plymouth 664356
Appleby T.A, 15 Hurdwick Rd ...... Tavistock 66508
Appleby W.A.J, 38 Lyte La,W Charleton ...... Frogmore 509
Appleby Westward Ltd –
　　Wreho, Callington Rd ...... Saltash 3849
　　Do. ...... Saltash 3859
　　Moorlands La,Saltash Indust Est ...... Saltash 7358

APPLEBY WESTWARD Ltd,
FOOD DISTRIBUTORS –
　　Callington Road ...... Saltash 3171
　　Wreho. ...... Saltash 3849
　　Do. ...... Saltash 3859
　　Moorland Lane,Saltash Indust Est ...... Saltash 5131
　　Do. ...... Saltash 7358
Appleby W.G, Chamilmar,Alexandra Rd,St. Ives . Penzance 79493
Appleby W.M, 11 Spurway Rd,Lake La ...... Liskeard 43615
Appleford P.A,
　　4 Parkside,Barons Pyke,Ivybridge .. Plymouth 896014
Applegarth D.A, 154 Tailyour Rd,Crownhill ... Plymouth 789939
Applegate C, Derowennek,Shute Rd,S Milton .. Kingsbridge 560387
Applegate D, 3 Gwel-an-Mor,Boscoppa ...... St. Austell 65846
Applegate V.C.D, 7 Longwood Clo,Ivybridge .. Plymouth 892251
Applegath P.T, 9 Seaview Ter,St. Blazey ...... Par 5830
Applejacks,Rstnt, 19 Old Bridge St ...... Truro 73800
Appleton A, 59 Polgrean Pl,St. Blazey ...... Par 4702
Appleton C, 23 Crellowfields ...... Stithians 860417
Appleton & Cragg,Fishing Tackle Mfrs,
　　1,Egloshayle Rd .. Wadebridge 3321
Appleton D, 15 Higherwell Pk ...... Mevagissey 843605
Appleton E,
　　Caravan,Efford Fort,Military Rd,Efford .. Plymouth 672696
Appleton H.J,
　　Meadow Vw,St. Pirans Hl,Perranwell Station .. Truro 864888
Appleton J.A, 26 Wythburn Gdns,Callington ... Liskeard 43624
Appleton John M,
　　52 Reddington Rd,Higher Compton .. Plymouth 772032
Appleton J.W, 45 Well Way,Porth ...... Newquay 874491
Appleton K.D, 1 Fairview Trevenson Rd .. Wadebridge 4182

ARC SOUTHERN –
　　Premix Concrete & Mortars,
　　Cornwall Unit Off ...... Plymouth 267213
　　Falmouth,Chywoone Quarry ...... Stithians 860555
　　Gunnislake,Hingston Down Quarry ...... Tavistock 832271
　　Launceston,Pennygillian Indust Est ...... Launceston 3919
　　Menheniot, Clicker Tor Quarry ...... Liskeard 42166
　　Penzance,Castle-an-Dinas Quarry ...... Penzance 62377
　　Plymouth, Sutton Rd ...... Plymouth 267211
　　St. Austell, Carncross Wks ...... Par 2727
　　Quarries & Sand Pits,
　　　Bodelva Sand Pit ...... Par 2603
　　　Do. ...... Par 2727
　　　Gwithian Sand Pit ...... Hayle 753307
　　　Hingston Down Quarry,Gunnislake ...... Tavistock 832271
Arcade Cameras,Photog Rtl,
　　19 Helston Arc,Coinagehall St .. Helston 563738
Arcade Delicatessen,6a Alverton St ...... Penzance 62800
Arcade Fabrics, 11,The Arc Fore St ...... Bodmin 77614
Arcade Jeweller,Retail Jwlr, 25,
　　St. Austell Shopping Arc Old Vicarage Pl .. St. Austell 67846
Arcadia, 32 Eastlake Wlk,Drake Circus ...... Plymouth 220184
Arcadia Shoes, 10 Market Jew St ...... Plymouth 223394
Arcadia-Cobron Ltd,
　　Wallingford Ho,Wallingford Rd .. Kingsbridge 2288
Arch K.F, 7 Carnsew Clo,Mabe Burnthouse ... Falmouth 73634
Arch Restaurant, Fore St ...... Looe 2876
Archard Peter E, 55 Sea Rd,Carlyon Bay ...... Par 2463
Archard P.J, 10 Whiteford Rd,Mannamead .. Plymouth 661888
Archard S, 3 Glen Vw ...... St. Austell 67732
Archbishop Benson C.of E. Primary Sch, Bodmin Rd .. Bodmin 3707
Archdale C, 8 Redruth Rd ...... Helston 562097
Archdale N.S, 33 Wright Clo,Devonport Towers . Plymouth 560467
Archdale D.T,Frmr, Roseworthy,Barton ...... Camborne 713140
Archdale P, 2 Pine Vw,Gunnislake ...... Tavistock 833654
Archdeacon J, 29a Higher Market St,Penryn .. Falmouth 76691
Archer A, 105 Victory St,Keyham ...... Plymouth 551303
Archer A.G, Clarence Cott ...... Penzance 61000
Archer A.H, Jacwyn,Tregonetha ...... St.Columb 880772
Archer A.J, 113 Thurlestone Wlk,Leigham ... Plymouth 704539
Archer A.M, 9 Bosorne St,St. Just ...... Penzance 788185
Archer A.W, 14/2 Goldenbank ...... Falmouth 311520
Archer C, Daisycot,Harrowbarrow ...... Liskeard 50046
Archer C, 9 St. Dunstans Ter ...... Plymouth 229274
Archer C.A, 6 Wythburn Gdns,Estover ...... Plymouth 781583
Archer C.J, 12 High St,Delabole ...... Camelford 212394
Archer C.K, 29 Meadow Dv,Biscovey ...... Par 4198
Archer C.W, 235 Linketty La,Crownhill ...... Plymouth 705236

Ardell A.R, 10 Bungalow,Claylands,St. Breward .. Bodmin 850822
Ardell G, Milltown ...... Cardinham 298
ARDEN HOUSE,China,Pottery,Gifts,
　　55a West End .. Redruth 216224
Arden L, 33 Yelland La,Brook Rd,Ivybridge ... Plymouth 894894
Arden R.G, 7 Morrab Ter ...... Penzance 62818
Ardington D.V, 14 Ridge Pk Rd,Plympton .... Plymouth 342197
Ardington M, 31 Wavish Pk,Torpoint ...... Plymouth 814021
Ardis J, 30 Waycott Wlk,Southway ...... Plymouth 783729
Ardy A.A, 13 St. Pirans Rd ...... Newquay 876423
Area Music Tutor Central Cornwall, Daniell Rd .. Truro 73634
Aremia M.E, 3a Salt Mill ...... Saltash 3225
Aremia S.N, 69 Kenmare Dv,Plympton ...... Plymouth 341692
Aremia V.M, 27 Lyndrick Rd,Hartley ...... Plymouth 771164
ARENA ARCHITECTURAL SERVICES,
　　Property Arena,Charles X .Plymouth 662328
Arena Beds, 2 Coombe Park La,West Pk ...... Plymouth 369363
Arena Carpets Ltd, Property Arena,Hampton St .. Plymouth 223277
ARENA EXHIBITIONS,
　　Property Arena,Charles X .Plymouth 662095
ARENA PRINT, Property Arena,Charles X .. Plymouth 662315
Arend R.W, 17 Garrison Lane,St. Marys ...... Scillonia 22164
Argall B, 1 Chynance Alexandra Rd ...... Penzance 64814
Argall E.J, 26 Trelawney Av,Treserby ...... Redruth 213227
Argall R.W, 10 Lemon Rw ...... Truro 41331
Argall W.C, 12a Benson Gdns,Moresk ...... Truro 72812
Argall W.C, 50 West End ...... Redruth 217181
Argall W.D, 7 The Parade ...... Truro 71383
Argent H, 8 Pound St ...... Liskeard 48020
Argent H.R, 7 The Parade ...... Plymouth 661999
Argent R.E, 5 Amados Clo,Plympton ...... Plymouth 337973
Argent W.D.J, The Dolphins,Clonway ...... Yelverton 852455
Argles Capt C.R.L,RN, Enderby,Crapstone .. Yelverton 852812
Argos Distributors Ltd, 12 Royal Pde ...... Plymouth 221842
Argos Fire, 11 North Hl ...... Plymouth 661999
Argos Fire, Carrick Lodge,The Belyars,St. Ives ... Penzance 797590
Argrave P, 50 Penlee Pk,Torpoint ...... Plymouth 814619
Argue C.F, Myrtle Cottage,Riverside Rd West,
　　　　　　Newton Ferrers .. Plymouth 872327
Argyle Hotel –
　　3 Sutherland Rd,Mutley,Management .. Plymouth 266854
　　Residents ...... Plymouth 670595
Argyrou B, 38 Mount Gould Rd ...... Plymouth 269470
Argyrou S, 6 Lipson Rd,Lipson ...... Plymouth 261535
Aries Taxis, 52 Leader Rd ...... Newquay 875562
Aris P, 60 Spencer Gdns ...... Saltash 4497
Aristocats, Bretonside ...... Plymouth 220690
ARISTON DOMESTIC APPLIANCES,
　　Unit 1 Broadwyn Trading Est,Cradley Heath ..021–559 5068

129

Handmade papers, India, Nepal and the UK

Left
Handmade khadi cotton rag paper from South India.

Right
Produced by Maureen Richardson on a craft basis, these papers illustrate the contrasting textures that can be achieved with recycled and plant paper. Pictured clockwise from the top left corner: recycled printers' waste with straw; pure rush; recycled printers' waste with coloured thread; pure straw and manilla; recycled printers' waste with onion.

A wide variety of hand-crafted papers, made from recycled or plant materials, are now available for designers to use. These papers provide interesting opportunities for literature and packaging design, where small runs are required and a unique effect is desirable. Although many handmade papers are not appropriate for modern, high-speed printing presses, they can give excellent results if printed carefully.

Handmade papers are produced throughout the Third World, where in many places this traditional industry is being revived. The Body Shop, based in the UK, is sponsoring a paper-making operation near Katmandu in the Himalayas.

The papers are formed sheet by sheet, on a woven cloth or a covered rectangular frame. In both India and Nepal the sheet is formed by pouring pulp into the mould. Water helps the pulp to spread in an even film over the surface of the mould, and drains out when the mould is lifted. In Northern India, papermakers use a "chapri" – a paper mould made of grass stems strung together, which gives the papers their characteristic "laid" pattern. In Nepal, papers are made in a Japanese way on a "su" mould. In both Nepal and Bhutan, the paper is sun-dried on the mould and then peeled off when dry, whereas in India the sheet of wet paper is laid on woollen felt and pressed, then hung to dry. Many of these papers use only waste products for raw material, although some incorporate plant fibres.

Maureen Richardson, based in England, produces a selection of papers made from waste paper and plants; straw, wool and flax are used to give texture and colour. In India, the basic raw material for contemporary handmade paper is "khadi" – cotton in the form of rags and waste material from tailors; the long fibres give the paper great strength. Other materials can be added to give colour and texture – recycled jute and hemp sacking to give gunny paper, banana leaf waste to give banana paper, and waste sugar cane fibre to give bagasse. Mara Amats produces papers wholly made from grasses and banana plants. Other materials used include rice straw and rice husk, dried strands of algae, tea dust and wool.

Left
A selection of papers illustrating the opacity of these unusual materials. Pictured clockwise from the top left on a background of tsasho paper made from lokta bark are: pure flax, made by Maureen Richardson in the UK; tissue from the kozo plant bark from Japan; tissue from recycled lokta from Nepal.

Many of these papers provide good material for packaging, because of their stiffness and strength. The natural colours of, for example, the water hyacinth weed can provide strong visual impact.

In Nepal, paper is also made from the bark of the lokta tree. This can be stripped without killing the plant, and can be re-harvested within four years.

Above
Packaging material made from banana and paper made from water hyacinths in Nepal provide a creative opportunity for designers, as seen in these packs by The Body Shop for pot pourri, and in the gift-wrapped soap from The Conran Shop, decorated with a bodhi leaf.

CASE STUDY

Friends of the Earth acid rain poster

The advertising agency, McCann Erickson, created an effective environmental communications tool for Friends of the Earth. The outdoor poster, made from sheets of litmus paper, aimed to raise public awareness of the consequences of acid rain. The copy lines were spelt out in stuck-on plastic letters, which would be impervious to acid rain.

Careful selection of an appropriate site in which to exhibit the poster played an important role in ensuring its effectiveness in communication terms. Town air which is exposed to certain industrial emissions can be very alkaline, and might therefore have neutralised the acid rain in some built-up areas.

The budget allowed only a single poster site, but the communications opportunity was expanded by the creation of a film, showing time-lapse footage of the poster changing colour during the first fall of acid rain. This was shown in cinemas, and won the graphics prize in the 1994 BBC Design Awards, as well as a range of advertising awards.

7 Textile design

The textiles designer trying to be environment-conscious faces some confusing choices. Assessing the environment impact of textiles really requires a cradle-to-grave approach, in which all aspects of production, use and disposal are carefully considered. The materials themselves, and the processes used to produce them, are the major determinants of environment impact.

Right
Quilted blanket traditionally used by snake charmers in Northern India. Cotton household rags are collected by women who stitch them together and dye them with natural dyes such as indigo, tea and mangrove. The wavy embroidered patterns reflect the energy of the snake. For thread the women use commercially available mercerised cotton. This old technique is an example of the traditional recycling always practised by the poor; in this case, it creates an object of great beauty and value. The technique has been applied commercially by the General Trading Company.

At first glance, it might appear that sticking to natural fibres, and using vegetable dyes rather than chemicals, would ensure minimal environment impact. But even the production of natural fibres such as cotton can cause major environment damage. Pesticides and fertilisers are used in large quantities in cotton growing, and intensive cotton production can exhaust the fertility of the soil. It is much less energy-consuming, however, than the production of a synthetic fibre such as polyester.

Although a raw material may appear to be environmentally attractive, the processes used on it can be less benign. Fibres such as viscose, made from wood pulp-derived cellulose, come from a renewable source, and are biodegradable. But the process used to turn wood pulp into fabric involves the use of potentially harmful chemicals.

Textile production is split into different stages: fibre and yarn production, bleaching and dyeing, cloth assembly and finishing. The different raw materials take various routes to the bleaching and dyeing stage, after which the processes can be similar for different types of cloth.

Fibre and yarn production

Textiles are manufactured from three basic categories of raw material: natural fibres; regenerated fibres derived from natural sources, and man-made synthetic fibres derived from petro-chemicals. But although materials may be produced very differently, they all have some detrimental environment effects if produced on an industrial scale.

Natural fibres

Cotton, linen, wool and silk are the principal natural fibres used in textile production. Each one raises environmental concerns.

Cotton is grown with the aid of fertilisers, pesticides and fungicides, to boost yields and protect the plants from highly destructive insects and disease. It has been estimated that almost a quarter of the world's use of pesticides goes into the production of cotton. The shorter growing cycle of flax, used for linen, means that it needs much lower quantities of these items. Fertilisers and pesticides can seep into streams and rivers, causing a build-up of micro-organisms that deplete the water of oxygen and so starve out the plants and animals that live there. The water may also simply become too toxic for them to survive. Of course, the chemicals can eventually find their way into the drinking water supply of animals and people. In India, the pesticides used for cotton production, such as DDT, may well be banned in other countries.

Because some insects are becoming more resistant to general-purpose pesticides, alternatives are being developed. One interesting route is to use pheromones to control the breeding of pests and repel them. But such biological controls may be effective only for a specific species in a particular location, mak-.

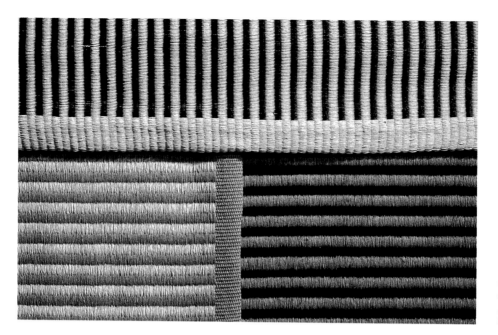

Left
Wood fibre is woven into a warp of strong cotton to produce "Papertex" carpets, which are hard-wearing and easy to clean. Finnish designer Ritva Puotila aims for simplicity and economy of materials, producing results which seem to draw inspiration from Japanese as well as Scandinavian traditions.

ing them very expensive to develop.

Cotton is an important cash crop for the Third World, and takes up 5 per cent of the world's productive land. Intensive production requires a great deal of water, and can make surrounding areas arid.

The production of wool also, perhaps surprisingly, involves the use of pesticides and fertilisers. They may be used on the plants that the animals eat, and to produce animal feed. Pesticides are also applied to wool during the sheep-dipping process, to prevent infestation by parasitic insects. Pesticide residues left on wool after the cleaning process are tiny, and not harmful to people; but the lanolin – the grease extracted from the wool – may be contaminated, and therefore unsuitable for use in toiletries and pharmaceuticals. The effluent from the cleaning process can be highly polluting and must therefore be strictly controlled.

Although sheep tend to graze on land which is not rich enough for other forms of agriculture, their presence can keep the soil poor and prevent the natural development of plant life.

Animal welfare may also be a concern in wool production. Sheep are often bred to carry unnaturally heavy coats of wool, which can cause them discomfort. During the shearing process they are routinely cut and distressed, and skin may be sliced off around the tail area to prevent infestation by maggots.

The production of silk might also appear cruel. Farmed silkworm moths are asphyxia-

Above
Shawls made in Nepal from the wool of the pashmina goat, woven with silk from China. Part of an aid programme, these products build on local skills, adapting them for more commercial use: shawls in the area have traditionally been made only with cotton. The darker shawl is dyed with a vegetable-based dye; the lighter one is unbleached and undyed. They are very soft, with a lovely sheen, and could potentially be produced in much larger quantities.

ted in their cocoons once they have spun their silk thread. However, wild silk, which accounts for some 15 per cent of silk production, allows the worm to escape, having spun its cocoon.

Fabric can also be produced from a wide variety of natural materials. The fibres from pineapple and banana leaves can be spun into thread, and turned into fabrics similar to linen and silk. This is a very time-consuming and skilled process, currently done by hand in countries like the Philippines.

Regenerated fibres

Regenerated fibres such as rayon, viscose and acetate are derived from cellulose, the basic building block of plants. This is extracted from wood pulp, from trees like the eucalyptus and spruce, which are fast-growing and cultivated for harvesting. Although wood is a renewable resource, care must be taken not to grow trees intensively in inappropriate

Above
Cotton yarn, coated with fibre from the Japanese banana plant "basho", is woven to produce a durable, linen-like fabric. Designed by Reiko Sudo and manufactured by the Nuno Corporation in Tokyo, it demonstrates the imaginative use of alternative materials for textiles. Environmental benefits depend, as in every case, on the chemicals and processes used during manufacturing.

Right
Cotton garments made in a Gambian village as part of an aid programme to create work for women. The cotton is home-produced and home-spun. It is quite untreated, and the designs show how well the features of uneven texture can be exploited to create a beautiful effect.

Right & far right
Acetate is made from cellulose derived from wood pulp, a renewable natural resource. Cool and comfortable to wear, it can be used to create many different effects of texture and colour. Georgina Godley's designs, entitled "Willow Tree" (right) and "Silver Birch Tree" (left) have a theatrical quality. Iridescent velvets, chevron pleats and slinky lengths of chain-mail demonstrate the versatility of this fabric, which has been promoted as a long-term alternative to silk.

areas, because of problems of soil degradation and erosion.

Once the cellulose has been extracted, it is mixed with chemicals such as carbon disulphide and sulphuric acid to form a spinning solution. The cellulose base of these fibres gives them an attractive natural origin, and they can offer an environmentally responsible alternative to natural fibres if they are processed with great care.

Synthetic fibres

Synthetic fibres include nylon, polyester and acrylic. They are predominantly oil-based, and can therefore be criticised for depleting a scarce, non-renewable resource. However, they account for only a tiny amount of oil (23,000 of the 57 million barrels used every day), and therefore do not represent a major drain.

Their manufacture is energy-intensive, however, and involves the use of a wide range of chemical processes which can, if not strictly controlled, produce emissions which are harmful to the atmosphere or water. They can take hundreds of years to biodegrade; research is being carried out with the aim of speeding this up. Because they are oil-derived, they could, at the end of their life, be used to produce fuel.

The design decision

Most environmentalists argue strongly in favour of the use of natural fibres on the grounds that they are renewable, long-lasting and non-allergenic. But even natural fibres can cause problems at the production stage, and the designer should seek out suppliers who are trying to produce in the least damaging way. "Organic" or "green" cotton, for example, is now emerging on a commercial scale (see pages 146-9).

For some uses, regenerated or synthetic fibres may be preferable. Regenerated fibres, in particular, offer a real alternative to the finest natural materials such as silk.

Viscose and acetate can be comfortable and versatile, and are favourites of leading fashion designers.

While it is often difficult to find reliable information on how these are produced, a good indicator is the manufacturer's overall reputation for environment performance. Is the company always hitting the headlines for discharging effluent into rivers, or is it a leading innovator in developing better products and processes? Courtauld's new fabric Tencel is a regenerated fibre for which the only major effluent is water (see pages 152-3), and many other manufacturers are trying to reduce the environment impact of their production process. Details of a company's and a product's environment performance should always be requested from suppliers, to enable a judgement to be made.

Textile manufacture

Many different substances may be used during the manufacture of yard and fabric. Bleaching, dyeing, mercerising, proofing and stabilising are just some of the processes a fabric may go through to give it the desired strength, appearance and texture. During these treatments, the most important environmental factor is the pollution that is possible if the correct controls are not used. Some of the substances used, like waxes and starches, may be relatively harmless and biodegradable except in high concentrations, but others may be toxic.

Pollution caused by the discharge of chemicals is one of the major "controllable" environment problems surrounding textile production, and in many countries tougher and tougher laws are being introduced to try to minimise it. More effective pollution-abatement equipment is expensive, however, and not all countries have the same standards. There is therefore a temptation to have fabric processed in countries where controls are lax and overall production costs are low. The pollution problem is then simply exported, often to Third World countries.

Sizing and bleaching

Before cotton is woven, starch or synthetic size is used to lubricate and strengthen the fibres during weaving. This is washed off when the cotton has been woven. Discharging large quantities of starch into rivers can stimulate the growth of oxygen-depleting micro-organisms, despite the fact that it is biodegradable; synthetic size needs to be carefully controlled. Very large quantities of water are used to clean and bleach silk; this both wastes and contaminates water.

Most natural, and some synthetic, fibres are bleached before being dyed. Bleaching with chlorine-based chemicals can cause the release of harmful organochlorides into rivers and seas; a much safer form of bleaching uses hydrogen peroxide, which does not result in toxic by-products.

Dyeing

Dyeing can be carried out at a number of stages in the production process from fibre to end product, and involves a wide variety of chemicals. Many dyes are not easily biodegradable, and are difficult to recover in effluent controls. They can pass through into rivers, where they can cause problems by preventing light reaching plant life.

Wool dyeing can involve the use of heavy metals, such as chromium, copper and zinc, which are water pollutants. New techniques are being developed by the International Wool Secretariat to prevent residual levels of metal in effluent.

Single-colour dyes can be recycled, whereas multi-colour printing produces a waste product of useless grey sludge.

Other chemicals may be used as part of the dyeing process. Solvents may be required, and the corrosive discharges from dye plants are neutralised with powerful acids. Some synthetic fibres, like polyamide, take dyes more readily than natural fibres, which results in less waste of the dye during the process.

Do natural plant dyes offer a realistic alternative? Their use avoids the problems of chemical effluents, but there are several drawbacks. Plant dye content is only around 5 per cent, so vast numbers of plants would have to be specially cultivated to supply the textile industry, and most of the plant would go to waste. Natural dyes do not match the performance of synthetic dyes in terms of colour-fastness and consistency, and cannot be used on some synthetic fabrics.

Attempts are now being made to produce "natural" dyes industrially through a fermentation process, with waste products being used as organic fertiliser.

Finishing treatments

After weaving or knitting, most natural fabrics are cleaned (or "scoured") a second time to shrink the fabric and fluff up the fibres. This process also produces potentially damaging effluent. Synthetic and regenerated fibres are set into place by heating under tension – a highly energy-intensive process.

Many fabrics are treated with special finishes to give them valuable properties, like waterproofing, crease-resistance or shrink-proofing. The use of formaldehyde, a carcinogen, has given rise to some concerns for human health, particularly that of workers involved in the production process. The pesticides used to moth-proof natural fibres may cause health problems as well as producing effluent which is toxic to aquatic life. Mercerisation, a process often used on cotton to give it a sheen, uses substances like liquid ammonia and caustic soda which must be carefully controlled. Synthetic fibres tend to need less finishing, as the fabric itself can be specially constructed to make it crease-resistant, for example.

The design decision

Unbleached, undyed, untreated fabric can of course be used. Cream, unbleached cotton is already used for clothes and furnishings, but the opportunities in aesthetic terms are limited. Natural dyes can give attractive and interesting effects, although absolute precision should not be expected in terms of colour matching batches.

The mechanical design of the yarn and the way the fabric is woven can actually reduce the need for chemical finishing treatments. An interesting example is "green cotton", in which the yarn in the cotton jersey is given a special twist: the resultant substance and springiness stops the material from spiralling and twisting. Close partnerships between scientists, textile designers and fashion designers may produce many interesting new approaches. Once again, good environmental solutions may lie in considering the early-stage, technical aspects of material production as critical components of the design process.

Where dyes and special treatments are needed, the designer may have a choice of supplier, and can therefore request information on the ingredients used in the dye, and on the pollution controls used in processing. Some substances are more hazardous than others: the metallic dyes used for navy, black and other dark colours are most likely to accumulate in the ground and leach into groundwater supplies.

Industrial production or craft?

Produced on an industrial scale, all textiles have pollutant effects. However, when produced on a small scale, environment impact is more controllable, and some environmentally sensitive

Above
A traditionally made rag rug, "Jeksen", marketed in large quantities by the Swedish-based furniture retailers Ikea. Traditionally, such rugs were made to recycle household rags, but they can equally well be made from manufacturers' off-cuts.

solutions become practicable. The use of natural plant-based dyes currently makes more sense as part of a small-scale, craft approach, where subtle differences between items enhance their individuality and appeal. Wool, if produced by small flocks of well cared for sheep, can retain its natural oils, which provide a degree of water-resistance and insulation.

The craft-based approach, while not likely to supply a major proportion of the world's demand, could play an important role in providing ideas about ingredients and processes that might then be adapted for larger-scale operations. For small quantities, craft production can be both more original and more economic, and there should be more opportunity to monitor environment performance.

Craft-scale textile production is widespread in small rural communities in Third World countries. Usually, traditional methods are used, with production predominantly hand-powered. Buying directly from workshops and cooperatives can help support local economies. However, production on an industrial scale in the Third World can be highly polluting, with little regulatory control. Higher prices and fairer world trade agreements might allow some improvement – but only if it is demanded by customers.

Use and disposal

Textiles usually have to be cleaned during the course of their life – in the case of clothes, perhaps hundreds of times. Dry cleaning currently uses chlorinated solvents such as per-chlorethylene, an ozone depleter. Alternatives are being developed, but at the moment fabrics which can be cleaned only through dry-cleaning should be avoided if possible.

Washing and drying, however, uses considerable energy and water. Man-made fabrics can claim to be energy-saving when they require low-temperature washing, and can be drip-dried. However, these savings have to be set against the energy consumed during their manufacture.

Textiles can be re-used or recycled, to prolong their useful life. Passing on unwanted clothing, carpets and household textiles to other people is obviously the first step. Designers can play a role, perhaps, in removing the social stigma of "second hand" by promoting the use of old or recycled materials.

Good-quality used cotton is often shredded to give a filling for furniture. Wool, a valuable material even when recycled, is used to produce felt, mattress stuffing and even suiting cloth. Plain coloured synthetics can be broken down into fibres and woven into new garments. Multi-coloured materials can be compacted and used as padding. A much higher quantity of all fabrics could be recycled, reducing the volume of new materials required.

Eventually, if they cannot be indefinitely recycled, materials are disposed of by incineration or landfill. Synthetics can produce significant amounts of energy, but can give off toxic gases. In landfill sites, biodegradability becomes an issue. Pure natural fibres can be composted, and the decomposition of organic material contributes to the methane gas given off by landfill sites, which can be harnessed as energy.

The design decision
Textile designers should bear in mind the durability and ease of care of the materials they produce. Consideration of the physical construction of the wool or yarn is important, as this can determine how long the fabric can retain its appearance and properties. Care instructions should consider energy use; for example, moderately dirty cottons can now be washed satisfactorily at temperatures as low as 40 degrees Celsius, using modern detergents, rather than using a traditional boil wash.

Designers could consider new uses for recycled fabric. The challenge lies in the development of new types of cloth that use this raw material. Can these be aesthetically attractive as well as being functional? Manufacturers must also consider what happens to waste product during the course of the production process. Can more waste be collected and re-used, as in the paper industry?

Fashion

Is there a conflict of interest? The fashion industry appears to thrive on waste and excess, with little correlation between wants and needs, and short product life cycles used to maintain consumption. The comfort and pleasure of the user in wearing clothes often appear to be neglected in favour of novelty and creating the right "look", with the results that too many clothes are not particularly human-friendly, let alone environment-friendly. With fashions changing so rapidly, designing long-lasting clothes might appear irrelevant – we should be aiming for flexibility and adaptability, so that clothes can be transformed to meet new themes. Reversible clothing could be one way of achieving flexibility. Another approach is to design "classic" well-made clothes that will continue to appear stylish whatever the passing fashion may be. Many people have already

decided to dress this way for economy as well as simplicity.

We also have to consider whether clothes always have to look brand new to be stylish. Many fabrics continue to look attractive when they have aged – even when they have been mended or altered. The attraction for the old and "interesting" is clearly seen in our fondness for antique rugs or curtains. Perhaps designers should consider how their products will age, and aim for materials which do not lose their colour and shape after the first wash.

Second-hand clothes
The continual throwing-out of wardrobes does provide a form of recycling, although most people are very reluctant to discard clothes, even when there is no realistic prospect of their being worn. Second-hand clothes can be of high fashion interest – as seen by the desire for worn jeans – but in general there is still a reluctance to accept them as a logical part of the normal wardrobe. Some fashion designers are beginning to consider recycled clothes as interesting materials, but so far there has been little serious attempt to design for recycled clothes.

Fur and leather
Demand for furs is falling as a result of successful campaigning by environmental and animal welfare groups, bringing to the public's attention the suffering endured by farmed as well as trapped animals. Some designers have moved from using real fur to fake fur. Some fake furs are obviously not intended to be realistic, but others aim to be indistinguishable from the real thing – an approach which will surely perpetuate the idea that furs are a suitable clothing material. Fake furs are produced from synthetic or regenerated fibres, with the environment issues mentioned above.

Designers can look for alternatives to leather products from both endangered and non-endangered species. A good example of this is fish leather, a by-product from food production which is an alternative to snakeskin.

Fashion trends
Green interests have been a recurring, if rather superficial, fashion theme during the 1990s. A few top designers are clearly trying to consider the environmental impact of the fabrics and processes they use, but on the whole the focus has been on the use of "earth-related" colours, or on minimalist styles. Some major manufacturers such as Levi Strauss and Esprit are

Right
"Peau de Mer" leather, made from the skins of fish caught for food, which would otherwise go to waste. The process was developed in Australia by Keith Taylor, and the products are marketed in North America where designers are looking for an ecologically acceptable alternative to leather from the skins of exotic animals. Cod, catfish and wolf fish — all caught in the North Atlantic — are used, with care being taken that the methods used do not contribute to over-fishing. The skin is removed when the fish are filleted, and tanned to make it soft and workable. Different species have different markings and textures: catfish is soft and suede-like, while cod is sleek and glazed, resembling lizardskin. Durable and colourfast, the leather cuts well and sews easily.

trying to lead the way in responsible sourcing and manufacturing practices, but there is still much to do to address the industry's environmental impact in resource consumption and pollution. As in other areas of environmental product design, however, appearance not backed up by reality will cause confusion and attract criticism. The "natural look", which aims to convince consumers that it is environmentally conscious but where none of the major issues relating to the production process have been considered, will have only a short-term appeal as consumer knowledge increases.

Overt "ethnic" looks, a recurring fashion theme, now appear more popular than ever. Katharine Hammet remarks: "Ethnic, ethnic everywhere. It's a rejection of Western values and the ugliness that surrounds us. People are bored with looking rich in Chanel, and want to be interesting and socially responsible."

Junichi Arai fabrics, Japan

The traditional jacquard weave incorporates the design into the weave, instead of later printing on a pattern. The Nuno Corporation in Tokyo use this technique extensively with undyed, unbleached materials to produce environmentally considered, innovative fabrics. These fabrics, all designed by Junichi Arai, are intended for mass production, and have distinctive features which make them appropriate for clothing or furniture.

"Korean Carrot" is made of undyed wool, using the jacquard technique of three-dimensional textures created by the felted finishing process. The "Basket Weave Pockets" design is a combination of unbleached and undyed fine cotton yarn and knitted tapes which give it an unusual and interesting texture: the pockets in the fabric are raised by using a double weave technique.

Acetate and rayon are mixed in "Zig Zag" to create a puckered texture. The acetate yarn shrinks during the finishing process, and this shrinking, combined with the tight twist of the yarn, produces the mesh pattern and the puckered effect. Again, no dyes are used.

Left
Puckered mesh
"Zig Zag".

Right
"Basket Weave Pockets".

Below
"Korean Carrot".

Novotex "Green Cotton"®, Denmark

Above & left
A wide range of colours and textures can be achieved with Green Cotton. The fabric is woven to have bounce and spring, and therefore does not require chemical treatment to give it body.

Novotex have produced a fabric which combines an environment-conscious manufacturing process with special shape-retention properties. "Green Cotton" is manufactured with the benefit of advanced technology from good quality, long-fibred and combed-cotton yarn. The fabric is designed to minimise the need to use chemical additives, reducing pollution throughout the dyeing and finishing processes by the use of sophisticated purification and monitoring systems.

Normally, knitted cotton fabrics are treated with chemicals, such as formaldehyde, which stabilise them and ensure that they do not shrink and crease. Novotex cotton is produced by solely mechanical treatments. The yarn is twisted to give the fabric extra springiness and substance: it is then pre-shrunk, to avoid the need to treat it with chemicals. Garments keep their shape and size even after repeated washing and drying.

Novotex emphasise the importance of looking at all of the environmental factors that play a role in each and every phase of the life cycle of cotton products – from cradle to the grave, "from seed to mould".

Green Cotton is manufactured exclusively from cotton hand-picked in South America. It has never been exposed to crop dusting with toxic chemicals, a process that accompanies mechanical harvesting. As a result, cleaner cotton is produced which does not need to be subjected to extensive chemical cleaning processes. Novotex are helping producers switch from polluting methods to grow organic cotton. The company became the first suppliers in the world to offer cotton that was certified as being organically grown.

Textile production processes traditionally create significant environmental impacts, in the form of waste water discharge, noxious odours, high energy consumption and high water consumption. Green Cotton is dyed in fully enclosed high-pressure jet machines. This reduces water consumption to a minimum and eliminates air pollution. The use of chemicals such as chlorine, benzidine-based dyes and formaldehyde has been associated with risk to employees and customers, and therefore

Left
The Novotex plant has been carefully designed to maximise worker safety and comfort.

these are avoided in the production of Green Cotton. Water-soluble dyes are used, and chlorine is avoided completely, all bleaching being done with hydrogen peroxide. Waste water is cleaned mechanically, chemically and biologically in a plant located at the dye works. The purification plant extracts the sludge, including surplus dyes and chemical residues, and exudes waste-water, providing a purity that exceeds official Danish standards.

In the factory, dust pollution is kept to a minimum, with constant ventilation and high humidity, to safeguard employee health. Noise from the knitting machines is reduced with the help of soundproofing and other sound-absorbing technology.

The Green Cotton label aims to eliminate consumer confusion over environmental information. Novotex have developed a model to help consumers assess and compare the environmental status of different products. Novotex have also developed their own life-cycle model to help them analyse and improve their products.

In 1994, Novotex received the EU Award for environmental management, the European Better Environmental Award for Industry. Green Cotton also received the North American Fashion and Ecology Award from the UN.

Above, right top and bottom
Green Cotton is used in a wide range of clothing, and has met with consumer approval because of its unusually silky texture, excellent washing properties and durability.

Above
Novotex has developed a
life-cycle model of Green
Cotton. This considers
eight main phases in the
life of cotton, from the
growing of raw cotton
through the manufactur-
ing processes to waste
disposal. All the activities
in the whole life cycle of
Green Cotton are con-
trolled to ensure that it is
produced in a way which
reduces its environmental
impact, when compared
with conventionally manu-
factured cotton products.

The Natural Dye
Company knitwear, UK

Right
Bales of wool are hung
up to dry after dyeing.

Natural dyes are frequently discussed as an alternative to synthetic dyes. But the large quantities of natural materials that would be required to supply the needs of industrial users mean that natural dyes are unlikely to be a realistic replacement for synthetic dyes; however, they are entirely appropriate for use in relatively small-scale craft industries.

Sarah Burnett, a British knitwear designer, produces elaborate multi-coloured garments with the use of natural dyes. Using tropical fruits, plants and nuts, she has created a wide range of colours. Indigenous materials she gathers herself provide subtle greens, yellows and browns, while the brighter colours are imported from South America, India and Mexico.

The yarns – such as wool, silk and chenille – are dyed in converted farm buildings. Each hand of yarn is washed to make the dye fast, and exact quantities are used to ensure that no dye is wasted.

Natural dyes can be subject to fading in the light. By combining two or more colours in each knit, any fading is subtle, and the overall result continues to be attractive and harmonious.

Although traditional techniques are used to produce the knits, the patterns can be sophisticated, often inspired by the surrounding countryside. Garments have a rather theatrical quality, and are unique pieces, owing to the nature of the dyeing process which ensures that no two pieces are ever exactly the same.

Left
A selection of jerseys,
demonstrating the rich-
ness and subtlety of
colour which can
be achieved using
natural dyes.

CASE STUDY

Courtauld's TENCEL, UK

TENCEL is a new regenerated cellulose fibre developed by Courtaulds, designed to be virtually free of the chemical additives which are widely used in the production of other cellulose fibres. Manufacture has been designed to produce no significant waste products, by using a closed loop process. Conventional viscose rayon is produced using chemicals which can be harmful to the environment if they are contained in effluent, as well as being potentially unpleasant for those involved in the production process. The resulting fibre can also contain small traces of chemicals which may limit its application.

TENCEL is produced by dissolving wood pulp in amine oxide, a chemical from the family used in the manufacture of shampoo. The mixture is passed through a continuous dissolving unit to produce a clear but viscous solution. This is filtered and spun into a dilute solution of amine oxide, which precipitates out the cellulose in filament form. The dilute amine oxide is purified and reconcentrated to remove the water, and then fed back into the process.

The fibre produced is considerably stronger than cotton or viscose, and approaches the strength of polyester; it is also easy to dye and print. One hundred per cent TENCEL fibres printed with reactive dyes or pigment require no caustic treatment, thus cutting out a potentially polluting process. TENCEL is suitable for woven, knitted and printed fabrics, home furnishings and speciality non-woven fabrics. Courtaulds intend to use its superior performance to extend the range of applications for cellulose fibres, and already have important niches in the soft denim market.

Left
TENCEL is easy to dye, and has a soft, luxurious feel.

Left
TENCEL offers a durable
and attractive material
suitable for high fashion
clothes.

8 The changing face of design

If we are to minimise the extent of environment problems design will have to change, because users and consumers of design — individuals and industry — will have to change. Legislation, changing customer priorities and industrial competition will make the pressure for change inevitable, irrespective of designers' personal concerns. The changes that will be necessary will not be minor adjustments or a thin veneer; the inclusion of environment criteria as an integral part of the design process will be one of the most important and far-reaching developments in the history of design. This will create new themes for design, as well as offering the designer a new, more central role.

The designer's task will become more difficult and more important than ever, demanding changes in attitude, education, approach and sophistication. The design skills required may change too, as many economies continue to shift from manufacturing to service-based industries.

The changing design process

Designers already have to consider a wide range of criteria as part of the design process: marketing, production, financial and technical considerations have to be included. Compared with these, environment considerations could be even more complex and hard to handle. There are very often no clear answers; information is hard to find; guidelines may not be available; so much original research and thinking may be necessary. What general changes might one expect to see in the design process, given the need to incorporate this new criterion?

Think environment up front
Increasingly, businesses and institutions are assessing their environment performance

comprehensively, through tools such as environmental auditing, recognising that good environment performance does not come simply from attempting to improve in one or two areas. The development of a product which is environmentally safer in use or disposal may well be desirable, but if its production consumes four times as much energy, the net result may be less beneficial.

Designers, equipped with a broad knowledge of environment issues and implications, should be aware of the context within which they are working, and understand the environment performance of the organisation with which they are working. A review of environmental auditing or assessment data may become an essential part of the background briefing of the designer, just as knowledge of the company's marketing strategy, or the institution's philosophy and objectives, are today.

Ask the right questions
The designer cannot rely on others being well informed. There are, of course, increasing numbers of experts on environment issues, and on the technical issues surrounding them

and their possible solutions. It is still the exception, however, for those likely to be commissioning design work to be very knowledgeable themselves on the issues which might appropriately be considered.

The designer must therefore expect to take considerable responsibility for asking the right questions, and raising the relevant issues. By demonstrating an awareness of potential problems, the designer is helping minimise risks to the success of the programme. The unfortunate discovery half-way through a programme of a major problem with the proposed raw material or production method can be avoided by a thorough consideration, before the start, of all the issues.

Above & right
The Philips-Alessi range of household appliances (toaster, citrus press, coffee maker and kettle) sets out to represent the ideal combination of form and function. The products aim to help "rehumanise" the kitchen, by encouraging human warmth, emotion and ritual, while providing high-tech convenience. The designs are highly original, the use of colour striking and the technical specifications semiprofessional. In contrast with most electrical goods, the products are designed to have a long life: they are intended to be reliable, and will remain aesthetically attractive even after years of use.

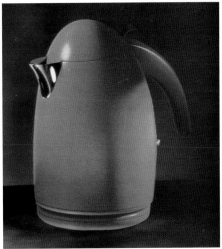

Seek information

It is still difficult to be aware of all the possible environment issue which surround design decisions. In order to keep pace with rapid developments in scientific understanding and the discovery of new causes for concern, the designer must stay in touch with the environmental agenda, by following media coverage, subscribing to environment organisations or demanding regular briefings from professional or trade associations. It is more difficult still to find detailed information on the environment performance of alternative materials or processes, or to identify sources of supply which are guaranteed to be environment-conscious.

Designers cannot be expected to have the time or specialist knowledge to be able to gather all the information they will need and, indeed, some information may take several years of research to emerge. Some designers may wish to spend an increasing proportion of their time devoted to background information collection and checking details; others will resist spending too much time away from the creative process. Designers can be instigators and commissioners of research, and can ensure that research is built in to the design process. There are already a number of environmental researchers working closely with designers, advising them on material specification, or reviewing work at concept stage to identify any potential problems. This may

Above & right Les Garennes, a housing development in St Quentin en Yvelines near Versailles, France, was used as one of the EC's Project Monitor case studies (for more details, see page 40). It illustrates that energy-saving design can be used effectively in domestic apartment blocks. Completed in 1985, it comprises 148 apartments in six blocks. Full-height "sunspaces" supply solar-heated air to the living rooms, thermostatically controlled by a fan. Roof-mounted active solar panels heat the water supply. All the windows are double-glazed for insulation. The buildings' dramatic appearance from the south side is due to the large glass and metal sunspaces, which provide extra living space as well as solar power. The average contribution of solar power to the heating requirements was 33 per cent, with a maximum of 41 per cent. Yet the solar design accounted for only 12 per cent of the total building cost. It is anticipated that it will have paid for itself in only twelve years.

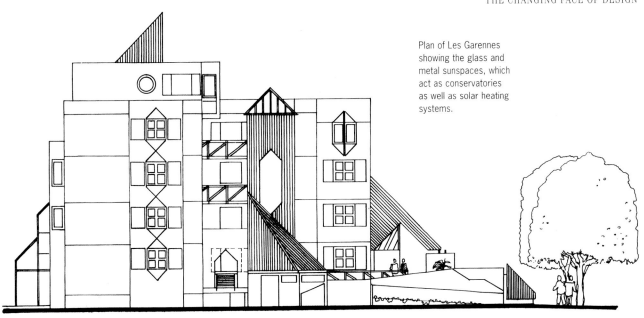

Plan of Les Garennes
showing the glass and
metal sunspaces, which
act as conservatories
as well as solar heating
systems.

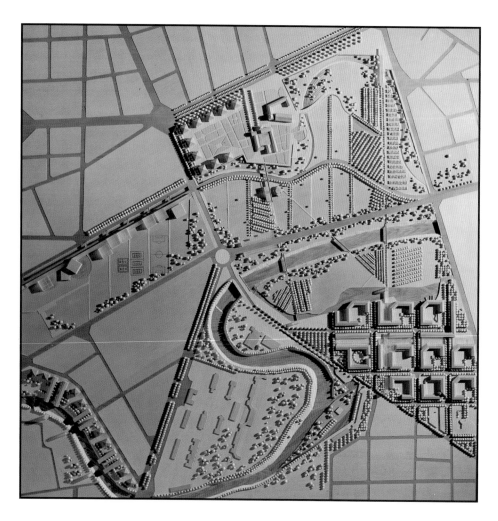

Below
Sun-activated lawn-mowers which browse over the lawn like sheep may become a common feature in the future.

become a common working arrangement. Environment specialists – who might even be designers who have chosen to focus on this area – could become an important part of the core design team.

Practical concept development
The separation of concept and execution will become increasingly difficult when environment considerations have to be at the forefront. Many environment issues will relate to aspects of execution – the materials used, the production process used, how a product will be disposed of, for example. These questions have to be addressed during the development of the design concept itself, not introduced as an afterthought once the basic concept has been agreed.

Closer liaison
Designers have never been able to work in isolation; they are necessarily team workers, if sometimes reluctantly. The need to consider

environment issues and executional details at an early stage in the design process will mean that close partnerships with other contributors to the programme – engineers, printers, construction companies, technologists – will be essential. The designer must establish a

Opposite & right
Model (left) and site plan
showing "La Città –
Rifugio della Natura", a
project designed for the
Italian city of Turin by
Barcelona architects
Martorell, Bohigas,
Mackay and
Puigdomenech. The aim
is to preserve traditional
patterns of the country-
side – but to do this
within the city, by
reclaiming land which is
no longer needed for
industrial purposes. The
land would then return to
its pre-industrial state,
highlighting the lost
structures of the tradi-
tional countryside before
it was built on. One function of the modern city is
to preserve history and
culture, so it is a logical
extension for it to pre-
serve a piece of agricul-
tural history.

capability that goes far beyond styling or pure visual appearance, and should not abdicate responsibility in technical areas. On environment issues – as on other issues such as cost and timing – the designer must be in a position to assess and judge the recommendations and output of a wide range of technical specialists. The fear that concentration on executional constraints inhibits creativity will have to be overcome.

Assessing the risk of failure

Environment problems, or risks to health and safety, are often hard to foresee. It will, however, become an increasingly important aspect of the designer's work to minimise the risks arising from the failure of a product or process.

Much of the focus in this area will be on the design of industrial facilities or building developments, where environment impact assessments must anticipate the consequences of modifications to the original design, or of human negligence. The eventual environment impact of a major construction, such as an industrial processing plant or a holiday village development, must be carefully assessed at the planning stage, to minimise the risk of long-term damage to the local ecology. Sophisticated electronic sensing devices may increasingly be used to detect the presence of undesirable gases, or of fire. Once again, the responsibility of the designer stretches further.

These are just some of the ways in which the design process may change to accommodate the new criterion of environment performance. Clearly, each design discipline will evolve differently, but in general terms we should see a broader interpretation of the design process, encompassing the cradle-to-grave aspects of the design and therefore necessarily covering many technical and executional aspects. Information gathering and interpretation will become even more important, and what the designer cannot cover may be sought from a new breed of specialist environment researchers.

Left
Extending the use of garments by designing for reversibility is a theme explored in this cotton jacquard material by Junichi Arai called "Magic Marker", from the Nuno Corporation in Japan. The four-layer weave structure allows a different pattern on each side of the cloth.

Technology – friend or foe?

There are many fears that rapid technological development has brought with it increasing environment problems. On the other hand, newer technologies often tend to be less polluting and dangerous than what they replace. While any new development obviously brings with it unknown problems – CFCs were embraced as a major advance when first introduced – there do seem to be many opportunities for using sophisticated technology to improve environment performance. Information technology could, if used properly, eliminate a significant amount of paper use; fibre optics offer an opportunity to save precious metal reserves; microelectronics make possible the miniaturisation of pieces of equipment, leading to possible resource savings, although to increased difficulties in recycling. The intelligent use of new technology should make it possible to derive more value from fewer resources: the use of photovoltaic technology could lead to massive savings in the use of fossil fuels; computer-based energy management and fuel control systems will become common in buildings and cars.

Designers may find themselves in the forefront of identifying problems which must be addressed by technology. Sometimes existing technologies may not be able to provide the solution, and the designer may have to stimulate and influence the development of a new technological approach. The role of the designer as the stimulus for, rather than the distant incorporator of, technological advance will again prove challenging and will require interests and skills which may go beyond those areas traditionally regarded as appropriate in design. Just as designers must monitor the environmental agenda carefully, so they must also follow technological developments, to be sure of incorporating the most environmentally advanced technology, or to identify gaps which need to be researched. Sometimes, however, very simple natural systems can offer

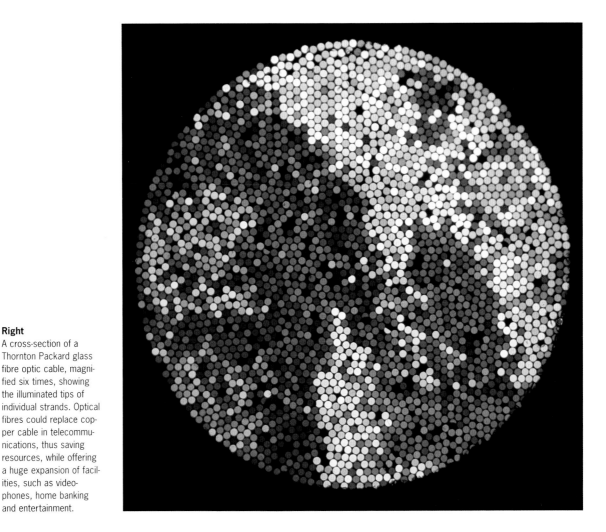

design solutions which are more effective, elegant and environmentally sound than complex
technology. The use of reed beds, for example,
as a means of filtering and purifying water,
can be a solution far superior to the incorporation of the usual forms of waste water treatment. Designers should be as ready to turn to
natural and biological designs for effective
solutions and inspiration as to "high-tech"
approaches.

Information design and communication
End users' demand for information about
products and behaviour will increase steadily
as people begin to make choices on the basis
of more complex criteria. Information about
the environment impact of a product – which
may have to encompass ingredients, manufacturing method, use and disposal instructions –
will be included on packaging, or in accompa-
nying leaflets. But in most product categories,
the information must be presented in a way
which is easy and quick to assimilate, and

incapable of misinterpretation. Consumers
wish to obtain an immediate impression of the
environment characteristics of their intended
purchase; they also require usage instructions
and disposal instructions which make the
right behaviour appear simple and desirable.

The development of information systems
which are at once comprehensive, easy to
absorb and motivating will give major scope
for graphic design. The growth of products
which are sold in many different countries will
pose the challenge of how complex information can be communicated by the use of visual
symbols. Official eco-labelling systems will be
one aspect of information provision, but these
will not cover all categories, and will necessarily be a summarised version of more detailed
information which may well have to be communicated in some other form elsewhere.

Information about the product or service
will become a part of the product offer that is
valued in its own right. It therefore may
assume a much higher profile than in the

Above
General Motors' "Sunraycer" car, competing in the 1987 Pentax World Solar Challenge, the first international race for solar-powered cars, run between Darwin and Adelaide, Australia. It was the winner, taking five and a half days to travel the 1,950 miles, at an average speed of 41.6 mph. It is powered by 7,200 photovoltaic cells, joined to form a hood over the top and back of the vehicle.

Left
The "Little Beaver" chair and stool, manufactured by Vitra International in Switzerland, is constructed out of packaging cardboard. Designer Frank O. Gehry believes that everyday items which are usually discarded can be recycled into serviceable objects.

Above
In this solar power station in the Mojave Desert in California, run by the Edison Electric Company, computer-controlled mirrors on the desert surface track the sun and reflect its radiation on to a 20-storey reflector tower. This concentrates the heat on to tubes containing synthetic oil which reaches a very high temperature. The heat is used to produce steam, which drives the turbines that generate the electricity.

past, when ingredients, technical specifications or usage instructions were consigned to tiny print on the back or base of the package or brochure. This may suggest, in some categories, less reliance on borrowed interest to give the product appeal, and more use of design themes which stem directly from the product itself.

Opportunities for information design may well expand far beyond the obvious area of product information provision. In many countries, government campaigns to encourage changes in public behaviour will be launched, perhaps in areas such as energy conservation and recycling. These will require co-ordinated communications programmes, supported by practical aspects of infrastructure development.

Growth in public transport systems will demand not only new ideas in vehicles and route development, but also excellent signage systems, new ways of delivering up-to-the-minute information to passengers, and the creation of station surroundings which are aesthetic and practical.

The increasing use of electronic media, such as the Internet, will create a demand for designers who can make on-screen communication accessible and attractive. Public

demand for better access to information from governments and companies, and the growing pressure on organisations to behave more transparently in order to win the trust of society will fuel an explosion of information available electronically. "Information overload" will be a major problem, however, and designers have an important role to play in ensuring that information is presented in ways which are easy to navigate and assimilate.

Future design themes and styles

The inclusion of environment criteria will influence design styles as well as function. New themes will emerge, some from designers who are inspired by the desire to contribute to a new environmental ethic, others from designers who simply wish to be at the leading edge of innovative design.

Many different themes are already emerging: an emphasis on quality and value in products or buildings designed for durability rather than disposability; a focus on social or spiritual development rather than on purely quantitative consumption goals; an increased role for the service elements of the total product offer, supporting the "dematerialisation" of some products into new services, based on

Above & left
The German retailers Tengelmann, wanting to improve the image of their own-brand choco-lates, focused on the plastic tray – could it be replaced with a more nat-ural alternative? In part-nership with the wafer manufacturer Loser, a wafer tray was devel-oped that tasted good. It does not taint the choco-lates, and contains any leakage should they break. This idea could be used for the millions of plastic trays used in chocolate boxes every year.

leasing or hiring items previously owned. The next major debate may well focus on what constitutes necessary or unnecessary consumption. Designing and selling products only to people who really need them would currently be regarded as a commercial disaster. However, we need to find ways to accommodate the theme of "less is more", in order to meet the challenges posed if we are to maintain our quality of life in developed countries while consuming less energy and other resources. Re-using and sharing products; developing "closed loop" manufacturing, usage and re-use systems which eliminate waste; using renewable, biodegradable materials; developing products and systems which are actually positively restorative in their environment impact, rather than simply less damaging – these are some of the themes which designers will be exploring.

Inevitably, if "eco-themes" become popular there will be attempts to use them purely as styling themes irrespective of the real performance of the product. Spurious green labels initially undermined "green product" marketing activities, and the bandwagoning of green design themes for products which are not in fact truly environment-conscious must be resisted. Environment-conscious design must not be seen as a styling exercise – indeed, it is not truly related to style at all. However, some obvious new styles may well emerge, based on a desire to embody in the look of a product the high importance given to environment considerations during its design and development.

- Natural, crafts heritage, sustainable: the use of natural materials, in an "untreated" form, particularly in the production of furniture, building materials and textiles.
- Utility, efficiency: the obvious use of recycled materials, emphasising sustainability, with a design style based on the requirements of function.

Right
A designer at the UK shoe manufacturers, Clarke, uses a light pen to work on computer-aided design and manufacturing techniques, which improve the speed and efficiency of the design process. High precision and a detailed information base ensure exact sizes for maximum user comfort. The designer can view the three-dimensional images on screen, eliminating the need for prototypes and materials wastage.

Right

A drawing made by a pupil at St Kilian's Deutsche Schule in Clonksea, Dublin, Eire, as part of a schools project run by The Body Shop. Children were taught to create new materials by weaving into sheets of paper items related to their environment. This painting of a bird in its nest uses leaves to add dimension and atmosphere to the basic paper which was made from lokta from Nepal (see pages 131-2). About 150 schools took part in the project, which is due to be repeated in the UK and in Hong Kong.

Below

Graphics to accompany a series of television programmes on environmental issues for children, designed by Gary Rowland Associates and printed on recycled paper. Children demonstrate a high level of environmental concern, and are keen to learn more. Much of the educational and promotional material produced for them demonstrates that it is possible to be environment-conscious without being dull or unattractive.

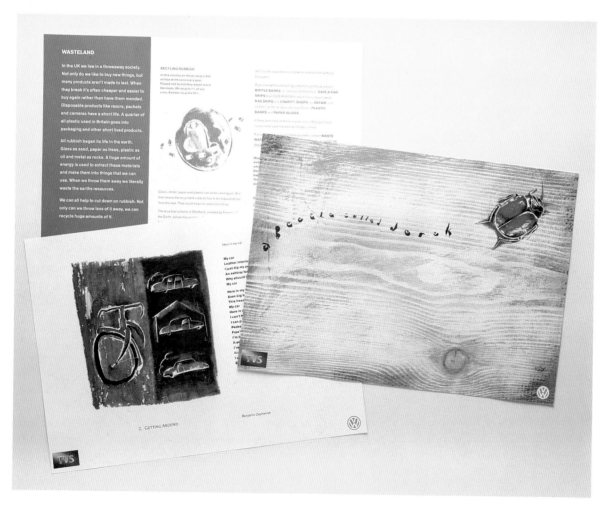

Above
Children's play structures
designed by Eiji Hiyama
of Papyrus, Tokyo, and
made from cardboard.
Simple houses and tow-
ers are joined together
with elastic bands;
stored flat, they can
easily be erected by the
children themselves.

- Minimalist: style emphasising economy in the use of materials; an absence of non-functional, purely decorative features; dramatic shapes to create interest and impact, or a return to classic simplicity.
- Multi-purpose adaptability: flexible design which can be changed to add interest, avoiding the need for replacement out of boredom; which can be updated, renovated or re-presented, with minimal additional use of materials, to prolong life; which uses "added intelligence", or dismantleable components.

Themes of nostalgia for a pre-industrial world may sit alongside deliberate use of "hi-tech" associations. Science may serve as a stimulus just as much as nature will, with the increasing acceptance of the need for advanced technology to play a role in solving problems, together with a simpler, more sustainable lifestyle.

What themes may become less commonly used in design? It seems certain that the excessive use of resource-consuming decoration, which does not enhance functionality, will become unpopular in many countries, although the importance of elaborate measures to enhance appearance in Japan may prove a countervailing pressure here.

Design which has an "inhuman" face, because it is remote, unintelligible, or difficult to access or use, will be at odds with environment-conscious design. Design must now aim to involve users, inform them, educate them and, often, introduce them to technology. Design must not place products on a pedestal and make them impenetrable; on the contrary, it must be highly sympathetic to user needs. A major challenge will be that of producing minimalist design which is warm and friendly,

rather than cold, over-sophisticated and obscure. Design which focuses solely on function, to the exclusion of any aesthetic satisfaction of the user, does not contribute as much as it could to the enhancement of the quality of life.

The social context of design

Environment is not simply a practical issue; it is also a moral one. The idea that, as part of their professional code of practice, designers should aim to minimise the environment impact of their work has been accepted in several institutions. Just as the medical profession observes the Hippocratic Oath, so designers have been urged to take responsibility for a "green ethic", because of the central role they play in influencing the environment performance of so many things.

Very many other moral issues are now emerging as possible influences on public purchasing and behaviour. The welfare of animals, fair trade with Third World countries, the treatment of minorities, military expenditure and many other issues are rapidly becoming part of the marketing agenda, as campaigning groups provide consumers with more information about the activities of companies and governments, and as companies begin to use very broad aspects of their corporate behaviour to establish a desirable image and achieve further differentiation in the market place.

It is beyond the scope of this book to begin to examine the role of the designer in addressing this wider sphere of ethical and social issues. But it is not unrealistic to expect that, irrespective of the designer's own moral code, ethical issues will become additional criteria in the design process, through the mechanism of consumer preference. Once again, the central, influential position of the designer provides a real opportunity to effect change.

The ability of designers to identify and solve problems through insight, and their mastery of a wide range of valuable skills equip them to make a significant contribution across a very wide area. Designers have always striven for a better way of doing things – now that better way can embrace environmental, ethical and social issues, too. Vast efforts have been expended in addressing problems which were not real problems – how to create a more chic or tasteful consumer durable, for example. The diversion of design skills into the many areas where real problems wait to be solved would provide challenging new outlets: appropriate housing and products for Third World countries, products for the handicapped or elderly, pollution-abatement equipment. These are types of design work that have been the "Cinderella" areas, unlikely to grab the glittering prizes or build reputations in the way that the styling of a new motor-cycle can. Perhaps this will now change, as social responsibility becomes a market-driven, user-driven benefit, in addition to a matter of personal feelings. Designing for the common good may come to be seen as a commercial necessity rather than an ideal.

Designers have often aspired to radicalism; many times that radicalism has been solely related to aesthetics, or has not created a net improvement in the utility or social impact of the item designed. Radical design now has new outlets, as many solutions to environment and social problems will be unexpected and unconventional. Only by re-thinking some basic assumptions about function, tastes and lifestyle will we be able to move any significant way towards a more sustainable way of living.

Training and education for design

Design and engineering courses are beginning to incorporate environmental issues into the syllabus, although environment is sometimes seen as an optional 'module' rather than as an essential underlying theme which should influence all aspects of the course. It is now essential for designers to understand the impact of design decisions on environmental performance, and thus environment must be part of the core curriculum.

There is an increasing body of good case-study material from which teachers can draw, but there remains a real opportunity for students to conduct original research and develop their own innovative solutions. No-one has a monopoly of wisdom or experience on this subject, so students and teachers will continue to learn together.

Designers wishing to take on the task of improving the environmental performance of current products will need a good understanding of environmental issues and impacts; this may require a higher degree of scientific and technical understanding than traditionally has been expected in many design disciplines. However, it will be increasingly important for those involved in design decisions to have an understanding of the underlying themes of sustainability, to operate within a global framework and to understand the connections between social, ethical, environmental and economic agendas. The re-designing of our society to minimise environmental problems will demand an integrated approach. Creativity, lateral thinking and breadth of vision will be needed as we attempt to cope with highly complex problems and the development of new infrastructures.

In order to anticipate problems and devise solutions, designers may draw on some of the subjects which are beginning to be regarded as legitimate aspects of the design curriculum: behavioural sciences, ecology, anthropology, life sciences and other areas. Breadth of formal education may be supplemented by an increased focus on travel and practical experience, reflecting the importance of learning from different cultures, and the need to master executional aspects of design.

The design discipline is a powerful vehicle through which the objectives of environmental education for personal and social responsibility can be met. Designers have an opportunity to exert considerable influence, and effect significant beneficial change.

Many people, particularly in influential positions in business and government, continue to underestimate the importance of design. Misguided by their perception that design is somehow superficial or optional, they fail to understand the potential role of design and designers in achieving the goals they consider important - whether these are innovation, industrial competitiveness or environmental improvement.

If designers can demonstrate that they will play an essential role in the long struggle towards a more sustainable way of life, the reputation of design and designers will surely be enhanced.

Right
The SL48 Solar Lantern, designed for BP Solar International by Moggridge Associates, converts sunlight into electricity using solar cells, providing a 40-watt equivalent light for up to four hours. It is lightweight and portable, designed to operate in remote areas in Africa, and requires virtually no maintenance.

Where to get information

Australia

EcoDesign Foundation, University of Sydney
PO Box 369 Rozelle, NSW 2039
Key Centre for Design, Royal Melbourne Institute
of Technology, GPO Box 24476V, Melbourne
Victoria 3001

Belgium

Commission of The European Communities
(Environment and Consumer Protection
Services), Rue de la Loi 200, 1049 Brussels
European Environmental Bureau, Rue de
Luxembourg 20, 1040 Brussels
Network for Environmental Transfer, 207 Ave.
Louise, BTE 10 B-1050 Brussels

France

Agence Nationale pour la Recupération et
l'Elimination des Déchets, "Les Transformeurs",
2 Square La Fayette, BP 406-49004 Angers
Organisation de Coopération et de Développement
Economique, 2 Rue André Pascal, 75775 Paris
Cedex 16
Programmes des Nations Unies pour
l'Environnement (PNUE) – Bureau Industrie
39-43 Quai André Citroën, 75739 Paris Cedex 15
World Packaging Organization, 42 Ave. de
Versailles, 75016 Paris

Germany

Bund für Umwelt und Naturschutz Deutschland,
Im Rheingarten 7, 5300 Bonn 3
Bundesminister für Umwelt, Naturschutz und
Reaktorsicherheit, Postfach 12 06 29,
Kennedyallee 5, 5300 Bonn 1
Institut für Baubiologie und Ökologie, Holzham 25,
8201 Neubeuern
Öko-Institut, Binsengrün 34a,
7800 Freiburg
Ökotest-Test Magazin, Postfach 11 14 52, 6000
Frankfurt 11
Umweltbundesamt, Bismarckplatz 1-3,
1000 Berlin 33

The Netherlands

The European Design Centre b.v., Schimmelt 32,
5611 ZX Eindhoven
Greenpeace International, Keizersgracht 176,
1016 Amsterdam
O2 Global Network, Graaf Florisstraat 118a,
3021 CN Rotterdam
UNEP Working Group on Sustainable Product
Development, UNEP-WG-SPD- International
Centre, 3rd Floor, J. H. van't Hoff Institute,
Building B, Nieuwe Achtergracht 166,
1018 Wv Amsterdam

Switzerland

International Environmental Bureau, 61 Route de
Chene, 1208 Geneva
OKO-TEX (Eco-Textiles), Gotthardstrasse 61,
Postfach 585, CH-8027 Zurich
Product Life-Cycle Institute, Chemin des
Bosquets 1, Ch-1297 Fonnex/VD
The Centre for Our Common Future, 52 Rue Des
Paquis, 1202 Geneva
World Business Council for Sustainable
Development, 160 Route de Florissant,
1231 Conches, Geneva
Worldwide Fund for Nature, 1196 Gland

UK

Association for The Conservation of Energy,
9 Sherlock Mews, London W1
Centre for Alternative Technology, Llwyngwen
Quarry, Machynlleth, Wales
Centre for Environmental Technology, Imperial
College of Science and Technology, 48 Princes
Gardens, London SW7 1LU
Chartered Society of Designers, 32-38 Saffron Hill,
London EC1N 8FH
Department of Mechanical Engineering, Design &
Manufacture, Manchester Metropolitan
University, Chester Street, Manchester, M1 5GD
The Design Council, Haymarket House,
Oxenden Street, London W1
Department of Trade & Industry, Environment
Unit, Ashdown House, 123 Victoria Street,
London SW1E 6RB
DTI Environment Enquiry Point Warren Spring
Laboratory, Gunnels Wood Road, Stevenage,
Hertfordshire SG1 2BX
Ecological Design Association, The British School,
Slad Road, Stroud, Gloucestershire GL5 1QW
The Environment Council, 21 Elizabeth St,
London SW1W 9RP
Environmental Production Information Centre,
228 London Road, Reading, Berkshire RG6 1AH
Friends of The Earth International,
26-28 Underwood Street, London N1 7JQ
Industry Council for Packaging and the
Environment, Tenterden House, 3 Tenterden
Street, London W1R 9AH
Intermediate Technology, Development Group,
Myson House, Railway Terrace, Rugby,
Warwickshire
National Environmental Technology Centre,
Culham, Abingdon, Oxfordshire, OX14 3DB
PIRA International, Randalls Road, Leatherhead,
Surrey KT22 7RU
Textile Environmental Network, Manchester
Metropolitan University, Cavendish Street,
Manchester, M15 6BG
The Centre for Sustainable Design, Faculty of
Design, The Surrey Institute of Art and Design,
Falkner Road, Farnham, Surrey GU9 7DS
The Open University, (Dr. S Potter), Walton Hall,
Milton Keynes, MK7 6AA
The Pulp and Paper Information Centre, 1
Rivenhall Road, Westlea, Swindon SN5 7BD

USA

American Paper Institute, 260 Madison Avenue,
New York, NY 10016
American Planning Association,
1776 Massachusetts Avenue NW, Suite 704,
Washington DC 20036
American Recycling Market, PO Box 577,
Ogdenssburg, NY 13669
Center for The Study of Responsive Law,
153 P Street NW, Washington DC 20005
Coalition on Design for the Environment,
The Design Management Institute, 107 South
Street, New York, NY 10022
Council for Economic Priorities, 30 Irving Place,
New York, NY 10003
Environmental Action Coalition, 625 Broadway,
New York, NY 10012
Environmental Defence Fund, 257 Park Avenue
South, New York, NY 10010
Environmental Protection Agency, Office of Public
Affairs, 401 M Street SW, Washington DC 20460
Friends of The Earth, 218 D Street,
Washington DC 20003
Graphic Arts Technical Foundation, 4615 Forbes
Avenue, Pittsburgh, PA 15213
Industrial Designers Society of America, 1142 E.
Walker Road, Great Falls, VA 22066
INFORM Inc, Sustainable Products and Practices
Department, 120 Wall Street, New York, NY
10005 4001
National Association of Printing Ink
Manufacturers, 47 Halstead Avenue, Harrison,
NY 10528
National Audubon Society, 950 Third Avenue,
New York, NY 10022
Rainforest Alliance, 270 Lafayette Street, Suite 512,
New York, NY 10012
Rocky Mountain Institute, 1739 Snowmass Creek
Road, Snowmass, Colorado 81654 9199
Sierra Club, 330 Pennsylvania Avenue NW,
Washington DC 20003
US Consumer Product Safety Commission, Office of
Public Affairs, Washington DC 20207
World Resources Institute, 1709 New York Avenue
NW, Suite 230, Washington DC 20006
Worldwatch Institute, 1776 Massachusetts Avenue
NW, Washington DC 20036

Picture credits

The author and publishers would like to thank
the following for providing the illustrations, or
permissions to use the illustrations, in this book.

A T & T/Lucent Technologies, New Jersey, USA
(p.85)
Alberts & Van Huut, Amsterdam (pp.9, 57, 58 top
and bottom, 59)
Mara Amats, London; photo: Shaun Roberts
(pp.131 top, 132 top, 135, 136 bottom,
137 bottom)
Anderson Fraser, UK, (p.121)
K.K. Arai Creation System, Tokyo (pp.137 top, 144,
145 top and bottom, 160)

Banks and Miles, London (pp.128 top and bottom,
129 top and bottom)
Javier Barba, Barcelona; photo: Lluís Casals
(pp.10, 11, 37 top, 39)
BayGen Ltd, London (p.35)
Bio Pack, Lippstadt, Germany (p.100)
Biss Lancaster plc, London (p.97)
BMW (GB) Limited, Bracknell, UK (p.77 top and
bottom)
The Body Shop, Littlehampton, UK (pp.108 top and
bottom, 109 top and bottom, 166 top); photo:
Shaun Roberts (pp. 131 bottom, 132 bottom)
British Gas, Natural Gas Vehicles, Staines, UK
(pp.88, 89)
Neville Brody and Jon Wozencroft; photo: Shaun
Roberts (pp.126, 127 top and bottom)
Sarah Burnett/The Natural Dye Company,
Stanbridge, UK (pp.150, 151)
Busse Design, Ulm (p.33 top)

Cafèdirect, London (pp.112, 113)
Calor Gas Refrigeration, Slough, UK (p.87)
Nev Churcher, Gosport, UK (pp.64, 65 top and
bottom)
Courtaulds Textiles, London (pp.152, 153) photo:
Hannah (pp.138,139)
Courtin Ltd, Bury St. Edmunds, UK (p.94)
Cousins Design, New York (p.22 top)

Duffy Design, Minneapolis, USA (p.117, 122)

ECD Partnership, London (pp.40, 43, 156, 157 top);
photo: A. Isola (p.42) ; photo: O. Sebart
(pp.156-7)
Electrolux, Luton, UK (p.70)
Environmental Picture Library; photo: Greg
Glendell (p.30 top)

Falkiners Fine Papers Ltd, London (pp.130
bottom, 131 top, 132 top)
Fern Green Partnership, London (p.44 bottom)
Friends of the Earth, London (p.27 top)

Greenpeace, London; 121 (left); photo: Menzel
(pp.13, 30 bottom)
Grolsch (UK) Ltd, Andover (p.33 bottom)
Gruppen for by-og landskabsplanlaegning a/s,
Kolding, Denmark (p.50)

Habitat Designs Ltd., London (p.28 left and right)
Thomas Herzog, Munich (p.51)
Eiji Hiyama/Papyrus, Tokyo (p.167)
Hoover European Appliance Group, Merthyr Tydfil,
UK (p.18 top)

ICI Biological Products Division, London (p.32 top)
Ikea, London (p.141)
Incpen, London (p.102)
Irma A/S, Copenhagen (p.16)

Jam, London (p.71)
Jeyes, UK (p.106)
S.C. Johnson, Frimley, UK (pp.110, 111)
Joseph, London (p.120)
Junghans Uhren GnbH, Schramberg (p.69)

Thierry Kazazian/O2, Paris (p.72)
Dorian Kurz, Stuttgart, Germany (p.73)

Lammbräu, Neumarkt/König Kommunikations,
Nürnberg (p.20 left)
Lintas: Hamburg GmbH, Hamburg (p. 20 right,
21 top)

The Geoff Marsh Partnership, Tonbridge, UK (pp.82,
83)
Martorell, Bohigas and Mackay, Barcelona; photo: CB,
Barcelona (p.41 top and bottom, 158 top, 159 top)
McCann-Erickson, London (p.133)
McKz Peau de Mer, Cleveland, USA (p.143)
Herman Miller Inc., Zeeland, USA (pp.80, 81)
Mobil Oil Corporation, USA (p.105)
Moggridge Associates, London (p.169)

Newell & Sorrell, London (pp.114 top and bottom,
115, 125 top)
Leif Nørgaard, Denmark (p.47)
Novotex, Ikast, Denmark (p.14, 147, 148, 149 top and
bottom); photo: Shaun Roberts (p.146 top and
bottom)
L'Oréal, Golden Ltd, Glamorgan, UK (p.17)
Osram Ltd., Wemble, UK (p.19 top)

Parachute/Parnass Pelly , Montreal (p.44 top)
The Parnham Trust, Beaminster, UK (p.45 top and
bottom)
Peake, Short and Partners, London (pp.52, 53 top
and bottom, 54 top and bottom, 55 top and
bottom)
Gustav Peichl, Vienna (pp.48, 49)
Michael Peters Limited, London (p.107 bottom)
Philips Corporate Design, Eindhoven, Netherlands
(p.155 top and bottom)
Procter & Gamble Ltd, Newcastle-upon-Tyne, UK
(pp.31, 107 top)

Ritva Puotila, Tampere, Finland; photo:Domus
(p.136 top)
Rank Xerox, Marlow, UK (p.71)
Reactivart, London (p.37 bottom)
Reed Corrugated Cases, Cowley, UK (p.92, 93)
Resource Revival, Portland, USA (p.22 bottom)

Gary Rowland Associates, London (p.27 bottom,
166 bottom)
Royal Melbourne Institute of Technology, (Key
Centre for Design), Melbourne, Australia (p.79,
158)

J. Sainsbury plc, London (p.99 top and bottom)
SAS, Stockholm (p.46)
Scandinavian Amenities A/S, Hilleroed, Denmark
(p.104)
Schüpbach of Switzerland, Stroud, UK (p.32
bottom)
Science Photo Library; photo: Alex Bartel (pp.7,
24-5); photo: Martin Dohrn (p.161); photo:
Peter Menzel (p.162 top); photo: Cowell
Georgia (p.163); photo: Jerry Mason/New
Scientist (p.165)
Siemens Domestic Applicances Ltd, Hayes, UK
(p.86)
Junko Shimada, Paris; photo: Stéphane Couturier
(p.36)
Showa Denko (Europe) GmbH, Düsseldorf,
Germany (p.101)
The Soil Association, Bristol, UK (p.119)
Stichting Milieukeur, The Hague,Netherlands (p.18
bottom)

TAG, Grenoble (p.26)
Tayburn McIlroy Coates, Edinburgh (p.118 top and
bottom)
Tengelmann Warenhandelsgesellschaft, Wiesbaden
(p.96, 164 top and bottom)
The Treske Shop, Thirsk, UK (p.76 top and
bottom)

University of Northumbria, UK (pp.66,67)

Vitra GbmH, Weil am Rhein (p.162 bottom)

Jijuro Yahagi, Tokyo (pp.91, 124,125)
Ken Yeang, Malaysia (pp.60, 61, 62, 63)
Yemm & Hart, Marquand, USA (pp.74, 75)

Zanussi, Newbury, UK (p.23)

Index